REIMAGINING THE SACRED

Richard Kearney Debates God

D1547761

INSURRECTIONS: CRITICAL STUDIES IN RELIGION,
POLITICS, AND CULTURE

INSURRECTIONS: CRITICAL STUDIES IN RELIGION, POLITICS, AND CULTURE

Slavoj Žižek, Clayton Crockett, Creston Davis, Jeffrey W. Robbins, Editors

The intersection of religion, politics, and culture is one of the most discussed areas in theory today. It also has the deepest and most wide-ranging impact on the world. Insurrections: Critical Studies in Religion, Politics, and Culture will bring the tools of philosophy and critical theory to the political implications of the religious turn. The series will address a range of religious traditions and political viewpoints in the United States, Europe, and other parts of the world. Without advocating any specific religious or theological stance, the series aims nonetheless to be faithful to the radical emancipatory potential of religion.

REIMAGINING THE SACRED

Richard Kearney Debates God

with James Wood, Catherine Keller, Charles Taylor,
Julia Kristeva, Gianni Vattimo, Simon Critchley,
Jean-Luc Marion, John Caputo, David Tracey,
Jens Zimmermann, and Merold Westphal

Edited by
Richard Kearney and Jens Zimmermann

Columbia University Press   New York

Columbia University Press
Publishers Since 1893
New York   Chichester, West Sussex
Copyright © 2016 Columbia University Press
All rights reserved

Library of Congress Cataloging-in-Publication Data

Reimagining the sacred : Richard Kearney debates God / edited by Jens Zimmermann and Richard Kearney.
    pages cm
    Includes index.
    ISBN 978-0-231-16102-2 (cloth : alk. paper) — ISBN 978-0-231-16103-9 (pbk. : alk. paper) — ISBN 978-0-231-54088-9 (ebook)
    1. God. 2. Death of God. 3. Religion and culture. 4. Kearney, Richard—Interviews. I. Zimmermann, Jens, 1965- editor.

BL473.R45   2015
211—dc23   2015008248

Columbia University Press books are printed on permanent and durable acid-free paper.
This book is printed on paper with recycled content.
Printed in the United States of America

c 10 9 8 7 6 5 4 3 2 1
p 10 9 8 7 6 5 4 3 2 1

Cover design by Elliott Strunk/Fifth Letter

References to Internet Web sites (URLs) were accurate at the time of writing. Neither the author nor Columbia University Press is responsible for URLs that may have expired or changed since the manuscript was prepared.

CONTENTS

PREFACE

The dialogues in this volume took place over a span of nearly four years and feature some of the leading thinkers of religion in our time. The idea for the book began in 2011, at a meeting of the American Academy of Religion in San Francisco, following a discussion of my recently published *Anatheism: Returning to God After God*. After a particularly animated session, my colleague Jens Zimmermann suggested extending the exchange into a volume on the theme of God after God. The aim of the volume would be to show how the anatheist question attracts the keen attention of many of the best minds of our generation, from philosophers such as Charles Taylor, Jean-Luc Marion, Gianni Vattimo, and Jack Caputo to theologians such as David Tracy and Catherine Keller and cultural theorists such as Julia Kristeva, Simon Critchley, and James Wood.

As it happened, I was offered several occasions to engage with these thinkers at different conferences, round tables, and colloquies—hence the variation of tone and voice from one exchange to the next. Some bear the mark of official academic seminars (panels held at Harvard with Caputo and at Boston College with Tracy, Westphal, Wood, and Zimmermann). Others resemble more informal and casual encounters—Vattimo in a Vilnius café, Keller in a Manhattan tearoom, Critchley in a New School office, Marion in a Paris bureau. And others again—Taylor and Kristeva—have the impromptu character of conversations over a kitchen table, followed by epistolary clarifications. I mention these different contexts simply to note, at the outset, the diversity and range of dialogi-cal styles owing to the specific circumstances of each meeting. But in all exchanges, I think it is fair to say, one senses a drama and urgency about certain timely and topical questions: What is still sacred after the death of God? What can we continue to call holy after the disappearance of the Alpha God of triumphal might and metaphysical certitude? Might anatheism open an alternate way of dialogue beyond the sterile polariza-tion of theism and atheism?

Each of my interlocutors rose to the challenge of debate, offering his or her own singular wisdom and perspective. Some migrate toward what I would call "atheist anatheism," others more toward "theist anatheism," while most cross over and back between the two in bold and adventurous journeying. For anatheism has many mansions, each with its antecham-bers, cellars, attics, and guesthouses. There is room for every traveler eager to engage the ultimate questions of meaning and value, immanence and transcendence, humanity and divinity.

It has been a real honor to host the ten guests in this volume, and I am immensely grateful for their generosity and seriousness of sojourn. I am also grateful to Jens Zimmermann for marshaling the various contribu-tions into their present shape, and we both extend our thanks to Wendy Lochner and Christine Dunbar of Columbia University Press for their stalwart and unstinting support for the project from beginning to end.

Finally, a special thanks to my Boston assistants, Murray Littlejohn, Matthew Clemente, and Sarah Horton, for their vigilant attention and enthusiasm, and to Sheila Gallagher for her cover image, *Pneuma Hostis*, which I believe vividly captures the anatheist wager that divinity dwells in the least and the last of things.

Richard Kearney, Boston College, December 2014

REIMAGINING THE SACRED

Richard Kearney Debates God

Introduction

JENS ZIMMERMANN

Richard Kearney is one of the most creative and insightful voices of the so-called theological turn in continental philosophy. His imaginative and constructive application of hermeneutic philosophy to postmodern debates about religion and culture characterizes Kearney's mature work, contained in the trilogy of publications titled Philosophy at the Limit: *On Stories, The God Who May Be*, and *Strangers, Gods and Monsters*. With these works, Kearney established himself as one of the greatest contemporary philosophical mediators of traditional concepts that define our humanity, such as narrative identity, practical wisdom, hospitality, and perceptions of God. Unlike many postmodern treatments of religion that jettison these important concepts along with their modernist distortions, Kearney makes the hermeneutic effort to recover such concepts in full acknowledgment of postmodern criticism. In *On Stories*, for example, he resists the postmodern trend toward throwing out metanarratives, because stories provide personal identity and history for our common humanity. Pointing out the healing value of stories for personal trauma, Kearney concludes with his characteristically mediating wisdom: to cope with personal suffering, our existence as historical, reflective beings requires that we refigure our lives through stories. We need the mediations of fiction because reliving the trauma as "naked reality" does nothing to work through the pain, and may lead to serious depression or even suicide.

In *The God Who May Be* and *Strangers, Gods and Monsters*, Kearney continues the hermeneutic task of recovering classic concepts for contemporary culture, particularly the idea of God. In these works, he explores the boundaries between philosophy and theology by charting a middle path between two extremes: the God of metaphysics, on the one hand, and the faceless transcendence of the postmodern sublime, on the other. While the God of ontotheological dogmatism induces intolerance and violence, the excarnate transcendence of postmodernity lacks the hermeneutical discernment that allows us to distinguish between the sacred stranger and the monstrous. Instead, Kearney's "diacritical hermeneutics" champions the God who may be, a God who cannot be objectified but whose presence shows up in the sacramentality of the flesh, whether in real life or in its imaginative refiguring by poets, artists, and writers. The radiance of this *posse* God is evident whenever and wherever the dignity of the human—especially that of the least favored among us—calls forth to be honored. The more recent book, *Anatheism: Returning to God After God*, is Kearney's clearest, beautifully eloquent proposal for the role of the sacred in human life and letters, which leaves behind the reductive options of secular and religious fundamentalisms.

The discussion of Kearney's concept of anatheism—the hermeneutic recovery of the divine after the death of the metaphysical God—is the central theme of the current volume. With the same conversational skills he demonstrated in *Debates in Continental Philosophy*, which is still the best single-volume collection of interviews with seminal thinkers in the continental tradition to date, Kearney once again engages important contemporary voices around the topic of religion, secularity, culture, and the nature of what it means to be human. These highly stimulating dialogues offer the reader three important benefits. First, the reader will come away from these conversations with an awareness of a consensus among prominent scholars from various disciplines that current reflections about religion take place in a post-Christian but also in a post-secular space. The "death of God" also entails the death of secularism. Second, in this space the role of imagination is paramount, thus highlighting those humanities (philosophy, theology, poetry, art, and literature) that have been marginalized under the objectifying regime of the scientific method. Anatheism, in other words, puts in a plea for the indispensable role of the humanities (and religion) in educating the imagination. Finally, this volume offers cutting-edge philosophy in conversational form, granting the reader easy access to important and often complex ideas. In order to provide readers still unfamiliar with anatheism with the necessary context for the following dialogues, the book opens with Kearney's own concise summary of his project (chapter 1).

In their responses to *Anatheism* and the ensuing conversations around Kearney's call to rediscover the sacred dimensions of ordinary life, the eleven interlocutors voice enthusiastic agreement but also important criticisms. Both reactions confirm that Kearney's project hits the central nerve of contemporary thinking about religion, and it will be helpful to identify briefly both criticism and affirmation.

The criticisms raised by atheists and theologians alike press for greater clarity about the attributes of an anatheist God. Kearney consciously positions himself between the two extremes of dogmatic metaphysical religion, on the one hand, and the utterly unobjectifiable, faceless deity of postmodernity, on the other. Thus, depending on his interlocutors, Kearney will naturally sound alternately more deconstructionist or more positively theological, and sometimes appears noncommittal to both sides, an impression deepened by his natural tendency to mediate between positions. Hence the question of James Wood, for example, in chapter 2: How substantial is this anatheist God? Has one not lost a Creator and Redeemer God? Is there still anyone to pray to? In chapter 10, David Tracy raises a similar concern from the side of theology: Does Kearney's beautifully executed but nonetheless one-sided reliance on the apophatic mystical tradition create a barrier to sustained dialogue with other forms of religion, including Christian, for whom the apophatic is a necessary complement to a fuller, more encompassing theology that allows for God's substantive presence in doctrine and liturgy? Even these critical voices make clear, however, that such probing questions do not gainsay Kearney's anatheist project but instead strengthen its important goal of dialoguing fruitfully about God. Kearney's exchange with Catherine Keller in chapter 3 concerning process theology, modern science, and the nature of evil is exemplary for such fruitful engagement.

The anatheist call to reengage with religion in a secular age is clearly recognized in the overwhelmingly affirmative response by Kearney's interlocutors. In chapter 4, for example, Charles Taylor acknowledges how Kearney's work helps him to envision a (post)-Christian humanism in which God is more important than the institutional policies of the church, and in which all human beings are embraced in a hermeneutic community that acknowledges the absence of knockdown arguments about what, exactly, religious transcendence looks like. Simon Critchley (chapter 7) likewise feels drawn to anatheism because it renounces epistemological certainty and emphasizes human fraternity. Jean-Luc Marion (chapter 8) underlines the timeliness of anatheism, as many have now realized that the problem with religion is not God but our understanding of God. Marion thus confirms the importance of Kearney's work in reframing the modern discussion of faith. Kearney has realized, as did Dietrich Bonhoeffer in his prison letters, that the traditional polemics about God's existence or nonexistence are two sides of the same metaphysical coin. What is really at stake in current discussions about religion and culture is not the battle between theism and atheism but our understanding of God in a less metaphysical way.

We have said already that the genius of anatheism consists in its hermeneutic effort to recover the sacred and sacramental dimension of our imagination through translating religious concepts into nonreligious language to find common points of contact with other religious and nonreligious thinkers. One of the most promising convergences emerging from the conversations in this volume is what one might call "anatheistic humanism." Kearney himself realizes that anatheism "reaches the edge of humanism," but he also believes, as does Charles Taylor, that secular humanism is not enough, because the other is like a sacrament for divine hospitality. The concept of an anatheistic or religious humanism could also serve Kearney very well as a deeper theological connection into the tradition of Christian humanism that begins with the church fathers and includes thinkers such as Bonhoeffer, Simone Weil, and modern writers such as Marilynne Robinson.[1]

The theme of humanism also emerges in Kearney's conversation with Julia Kristeva, who proposes a new "post-Christian humanism." This new humanism is inspired by the Christian understanding of love as embodied in the Incarnation and anatheistically translated into the recognition of the infinite, of transcendence as rooted in us. "It is," she explains, "a transcendence *incarnate* in my capacity as a human being to speak and love. . . . This capacity of speaking as loving experience is transcendence. And this, I believe, is very Christian. It is the Christian teaching of what God is."[2] For Kristeva, this capacity is what takes us beyond the purely biological and makes us truly human.

Kristeva's post-Christian humanism has at least one other proponent in Luc Ferry, who has suggested a post-Christian humanism based on a nonreligious use of the *imago Dei* in every human being.[3] This secularized idea of the divine image allows us to regard the human itself as sacred and thus worthy of love without any recourse to special divine revelation. According to Kristeva, the challenge faced by anatheist humanists is the preservation of this Christian idea of love in a globalized world, through intercultural dialogue. Without some such notion of loving transcendence or infinity, the true depth of our humanity will be lost to a superficial, consumerist culture.

Could a new humanism possibly emerge as the anatheistic rallying point for philosophers, theologians, psychoanalysts, writers, and poets? Could such an amplified humanism offer a space for reimagining the sacred, for creating the kind of anatheistic energy that pushes us past hardened doctrinal and disciplinary boundaries toward a vision of what it means to be human that is religious without being dogmatic? If so, Richard Kearney's anatheism and the discussions in this book are a very good place to start.

I

God After God

An Anatheist Attempt to Reimagine God

RICHARD KEARNEY

I hope it may be useful for the reader to preface this series of dialogues by offering a summary of what I mean by *anatheism* and the need to reimagine the sacred.

ANA: A QUESTION OF TIME

Ana- is a prefix defined in the *Shorter Oxford English Dictionary* as, "Up in space or time; back again, anew." So understood, the term supports the deeper and broader sense of "after" contained in the expression "God after God." The poet Gerard Manley Hopkins describes the moment of imaginative creation as "aftering, seconding, over and overing."[1] He speaks of poetic epiphany, accordingly, as a retrieval of past experience that moves forward, proffering new life to memory, giving a future to the past. What Hopkins means by this is that certain deep experiences can be followed by moments of disenchantment, after which we may return again to the primal experience in a new light, *over and over*. As a religious poet, Hopkins is speaking of a specifically sacred reimagining. But, though he was himself a Catholic, this notion of sacramental repetition is not confined to any particular religion. It refers to any poetic movement of returning to God *after* God—God *again*, after the loss of God. As in child's play, "gone, back again" (*fort/da*). We learn young that what disappears as literal comes back again as figural—that is, as sign and symbol, as a second presence in and through absence. And symbol here does not mean "untrue" or "unreal." The return of the lost one—in the case of religion, the lost God—may well be the return of a *more real* presence. It may in fact be a much more powerful and moving presence precisely because of its return through absence.

Thus, in the prefix *ana-* we find the idea of retrieving, revisiting, reiterating, repeating. But repeating *forward*, not *backward*. It is not about regressing nostalgically to some prelapsarian past. It is a question, rather, of coming back "afterwards" in order to move forward again (*reculer pour mieux sauter*). So it is in this sense that I use the term *anatheism* as a "returning to God after God": a critical hermeneutic retrieval of sacred things that have passed but still bear a radical remainder, an unrealized potentiality or promise to be more fully realized in the future. In this way, anatheism may be understood as "after-faith," which is more than a simple "after-thought" or "after-affect." After-faith is eschatological—something ultimate in the end that was in fact already there from the beginning. And that is why the *after* of *ana-* is also a *before*—a before that has been transposed into a second after.

Some people misread anatheism as a dialectical third term that supersedes theism and atheism. They construe it as a sort of Hegelian synthesis or final resolution. But I do not see it like that. It is important for me that anatheism contains a moment of atheism within itself—as it contains a moment of theism. Or should I say, anatheism precontains both, for it operates from a space and time *before* the dichotomy of atheism and theism, as well as *after*. The double *a* of *anatheism* holds out the promise but not the necessity of a second affirmation once the "death of God" has done its work. But it differs radically from Hegel's "negation of the negation" that sees the return as a synthesis or sublation (*Aufhebung*). My argument is that the moment of ana- is actually a risk and a wager—an existential drama that can go either way. It can also go wrong. It is up to us. It is a matter of discernment and decision on our part. The event does not take place behind our backs, irrespective of our agency, like theodicy or Hegel's dialectic of Absolute Spirit. There is no "ruse of reason." Anatheism is not some ineluctable dialectic leading to a final totality. It is not about uppercase Divinity, or Alpha God. *Au contraire!* Anatheism is about reimagining—and reliving—the sacred in the least of these. It is lowercase from beginning to end.

Anatheism concentrates, therefore, on unrealized or suspended possibilities, which are more powerfully reanimated if one also experiences a moment of a-theism—the "a-" here being a gesture of abstention, privation, withdrawal—a moment that is less a matter of epistemological theory, dogma, creed or proposition than a prereflective, lived experience of ordinary lostness and solitude, a mood of angst or abandon, an existential "dark night of the soul"—and who has never tasted such moments?[2] This privative moment—the first *a*—is indispensable to anatheism. But in *ana-* we have two *a*'s. And if the first *a* is the "a-" of a-theism, the second *a* is the "not of the not." The "a-a" of anatheism is a reopening to something new, after all.

So the ana- is not a guarantee of ineluctable progress or blind optimism. It is not only something that arises in the wake of religious collapse but also something that brings us back to the beginning, to a foretime before the division between theism and atheism. And in this respect, I think of Kierkegaard's affirmative reading of "repetition" as a reliving of the past, forward. This repetition of the former as latter, of the earlier as later, meant for Kierkegaard retrieving the event of faith not as a regression to some original position but as an originary disposition of openness toward the radical Other—what he calls a "leap of faith" in *Fear and Trembling*.[3] Abraham has to lose his son as a given in order to receive him back as a gift; he has to abandon Isaac as possession in order to welcome him back as promise. Isaac is not Abraham's (as extension, acquisition, projection) but another's, another, an Other (a return gift of what Kierkegaard calls the Absolute). In short, it is a matter of repeating forward rather than backward, a second retrieval of something after one has lost it. This goes beyond chronological time—that is, the notion of different moments succeeding each other in linear fashion from past to present to future—in favor of kairological time, a time out of time focusing on an epiphanic moment (*Augenblick*) of grace where eternity crosses the instant.[4] Thus *ana-* is a prefix that seeks to capture this enigma of past-as-future, before-as-after.[5]

To say this is not, however, to deny that ana- also involves historical time. Infinite time is in-finite; it traverses finite temporality and cannot exist without it. Anatheism, in its temporal aspect, does indeed coincide today with a concrete historical situation that comes after the death of God, culturally, socially, and intellectually. It is marked by the modern announcements of Nietzsche, Marx, and Freud; the atheist exposés of the Enlightenment; the French Revolution; the critique of religion as ideology; and so on. Anatheism expresses a typical modern anxiety in the face of what Max Weber terms the "disenchantment" of the world, the desacralizing of society, the general malaise of the abandonment of God, loss of faith.

In this sense anatheism is, in part, a historical–cultural phenomenon that engages with our contemporary secular humanist culture, but not in any teleological manner—the facile idea that we were ignorant and have now seen the light, that all faith was delusion but we have finally reached the "end" of religion and are free at last. In sum, it is not complicit with the current anti-God squad of Richard Dawkins, Christopher Hitchens, and Sam Harris, nor with Francis Fukuyama's neoliberal *hubris*. For me, to have lost the illusion of God (as sovereign superintendent of the universe) is to enjoy the possibility of opening oneself, once again, to the original and enduring promise of a sacred stranger, an absolute other who comes as gift, call, summons, as invitation to hospitality and justice. In short, anatheism is a radical opening to someone or something that was lost and forgotten by Western metaphysics—to cite Heidegger and Derrida—and needs to be recalled again.[6] And here we can translate from the historical formulation of the anatheist question—What comes after the disappearance of God?—to the more existential one: How might any contemporary self experience this in one's concrete, lived existence—that is, in one's personal, as opposed to impersonal, being?

This is why I constantly come back to "examples" and "testimonies" of the anatheist moment, to descriptions—scriptural, literary, testimonial—of lived abandonment, disillusionment, disorientation, followed by moments of turning around again—what Socrates called *periagoge*, what Augustine called *conversio*. The first negative moment of letting go is indispensable. It is key to a proper appreciation of anatheism. Without that, we have cheap grace—God as comforting illusion, quick fix, opium of the people. I often think here of the mystics' "dark night of the soul," of Dostoyevsky's sense of radical alienation, of Hopkins's dark sonnets ("I wake and feel the fell of dark, not day"), or of Christ's own abandonment by the Father on the cross.[7] These are all concrete moments of radical emptying that signal a return to the inaugural move of anatheism: the wager of yes or no to the stranger. This primal wager is first and foremost an existential wager—not a purely logical one à la Pascal, which is more a wager of knowledge than being, epistemological rather than ontological. And this anatheist wager—to turn hostility into hospitality—is, I contend, the inaugural moment of all great wisdom traditions. Admittedly, in *Anatheism* I tend to focus mainly on the Abrahamic tradition in which I grew up, trying to reimagine certain "primal scenes" of hostility-hospitality by revisiting the inaugural wagers of the scriptural narratives: Abraham and Sarah as they encounter the strangers in Mamre, Mary faced with the stranger called Gabriel, Muhammad faced with a voice in the cave. But this brings me already to my second question—regarding anatheism as an act of reimagining.[8]

REIMAGINING GOD: A QUESTION OF FICTION

Ana- is not just a question of returning in time but also of returning in space. It involves a *topos* as well as a *kairos*. It needs images. When it comes to reimagining the sacred, I travel the third of the three paths—philosophical, religious, and poetic—that I sketched out in my book *Anatheism*.[9]

I am interested in reimagining the sacred as a space of "negative capability." I take the term from the poet John Keats, who defined it as the ability to be in "uncertainties, mysteries, doubts, without any irritable reaching after fact and reason."[10] I see the poetic refiguring of the sacred as somehow occupying that open, empty space. This refiguring is by no means confined to Keats and Romanticism; it goes right back to the beginning of culture, as Aristotle acknowledged in *Poetics*, when he defined drama as a cathartic movement back and forth between pity and fear.

If pity (*eleos*) is the identification with the suffering characters on the stage, fear (*phobos*) is the withdrawal or withholding of participation. Belief becomes quasi-belief. Tragedy, as Nietzsche and others remind us, originally derived from Dionysiac sacrificial cults, but in the transposition from religious rite to dramatic representation a radical shift takes place. The work of *mythos–mimesis* (emplotment–redescription) intervenes to turn the literal into the figural. The term *tragedy* originally meant "goat's head," because the main protagonists wore masks that impersonated the

sacrificial animals, which themselves stood in for the *pharmakoi*, the sacrificial god-men (like Dionysus), who would have been celebrated in the
ancient cults.

In other words, the move to dramatic imitation opened up the fictional
space of "as if," where we suspend our belief in the gods and our disbelief
in fiction. Or, to quote Coleridge, we "willingly suspend our disbelief" in
the imaginary in order to act as if we believe in the fictional characters.[11]
This suspension of belief requires a simultaneous, and equally willing, disbelief in the religious—insofar as the latter implies truth claims. So as we
watch the great Greek tragedies unfold, there is already a realization that
the religious-cultic-sacrificial acts taking place on stage—the sacrifice of
Oedipus, Iphigenia, Antigone, and so on—are not making any claims to
"reality" as such. We respond to the play *as if* the gods and heroes were
present before us, but knowing full well they are not. The figural has
replaced the literal.

Now it is this detour through the kingdom of as-if—where all kinds
of possibilities can be explored in a "free variation of imagination"—that
allows for an anatheist disposition. We bracket our religious beliefs (provisionally at least) on entering the theater, in order to be able to believe
in the theatrical make-believe. This, as I read it, is an Aristotelian fore-
shadowing of Keats's negative capability (and, in a sense, of Husserl's
phenomenological *epoché*)—the agnostic liberty to explore all kinds
of different views and attitudes without the constraints of orthodoxy,
morality, or censorship.

But that is not the end of the affair for anatheism. Once we exit from
the theater, once we suspend this poetic detour in turn, we find ourselves
back in the real, lived world, with the option to believe in the gods again or
to not believe. But without such a negative capability—as a form of poetic
license—it is difficult to *freely* choose which, if any, religious truth claim
to embrace. Authentic faith commitments are, arguably, better fostered
by the hiatus of aesthetic atheism, which contains the anatheist option
within itself and reanimates a real sense of existential drama in the relationship between the divine and the human. Some kind of letting go of
one's received beliefs—even provisionally, momentarily, hypothetically—
is something that I consider central to the reimagining of the sacred, and
to the possibility of genuine faith, which, as Dostoyevsky reminds us,
comes forth from the "crucible of doubt."

So how might this hypothesis of suspended belief relate to more contemporary literature? In *Anatheism* I look at Joyce, Woolf, and Proust as three modernist writers who reimagine the sacred. In *Ulysses* we have Stephen replying to the question, "What is God?" with the response, "A shout in the street"[12] (a street noise retrieved in Molly's cry at the end of the book). *Theos* is echoed as *Eros*. But what does Joyce mean when he describes God as a shout in the street? What is the sense of the sacramental, the eucharistic, the sacred that Joyce is teasing out in that phrase and in the constant revisiting and rewriting of a grammar of transubstantiation throughout the book? There is a whole series of Eucharists—black masses, parodic masses, failed Communions—and then, finally, we have Molly's own retrieval of a "shout in the street": her climactic "yes," along with the remembered exchange of seed cake with Bloom as they kiss on Howth Head. Is this not a powerful example of what Joyce calls "epiphany"? The sacred at the very heart of the profane? The infinite in the infinitesimal? The sacramental in the quotidian?

In *Anatheism* I also try to show poetic epiphanies at work in Virginia Woolf's *To the Lighthouse*. My question is: What does Lily Briscoe mean when she talks about the "little daily miracles, illuminations, the matches struck unexpectedly in the dark"?[13] What's going on in the text? And what is Lily's relationship to Mrs. Ramsay, who prepares and performs a quasi-eucharistic feast in the first part of the book, which is then followed by the disenchanting interlude of death and war, before we return to Lily's final brushstroke, which completes her portrait of Mrs. Ramsay—"It is finished"—in the third part of the book?[14] Is Lily Briscoe not somehow retrieving the lost experience of the opening banquet *anatheistically*? Is it only when Lily has let go of the mystical Mrs. Ramsay—after her death and disappearance—that she can resurrect her in her portrait? What does "It is finished" signify? In what sense is it finished? What exactly does it mean for Lily to engage in that sacramental gesture of eucharistic memory?

And what, finally, does Proust mean by "*le petit miracle*" in *Remembrance of Things Past*? Here again we find recurring idioms of sacramental repetition, transubstantiation, and epiphany. We witness the return of "inexperienced experience" as a second experience, as ana-experience in an ana-time (*Le temps retrouvé*). I have in mind the various retrievals of forgotten moments when Marcel visits the Guermantes' salon at the end of the novel—the stumble on the cobblestones, the clinking of cut-lery, the reading of the George Sand story, and so on. What are these past moments that, *repeated*, return as epiphanies that open up a future—the meeting with Saint-Loup's daughter?

What does it mean for all three authors (Joyce, Woolf, and Proust)—who were avowedly atheist, agnostic, and apostate—to open up an imagi-nary space for rewriting the grammar of transubstantiation? I am inter-ested here in the relationship between imagination and faith—faith as wager, freedom, narrative, empathy. And this is more than a play of words. My wager is that the play of sacramental language in certain artists and writers opens up a sacramental space of experience: a textual world of epiphany. And as my philosophical mentor, Paul Ricoeur, taught me, if writing is the movement from action to text, reading is the movement from text back to action. We move in a hermeneutic arc from existential prefiguration to textual configuration back to existential refiguration—the reader's appropriation of the text in his or her life. In this odyssey from author through text to reader we may witness certain possibilities of transfiguration: the conversion from the powers that be to the *power to be anew*, or what I call an opening to the transformative call of the stranger.

Let me give one last example of reimagining the sacred. In the second chapter of *Anatheism* I revisit the primal scene of the Christian event—the annunciation. I do so not just theologically but poetically, because I believe that the annunciation, as we have received it over time and history, is in great part a scene of religious imagination, in the deepest sense of that term—a primal anatheist scenario that can be revisited in poetic imagin-ings, which may lead to a new faith. To be more precise, I am struck that the most effective ways of returning to this founding event of Christianity are through poets and painters rather than through preachers and theo-logians. The text of Luke is just a few lines, but we have countless poems about the annunciation throughout the centuries—and, more recently, extraordinary verses by the likes of Denise Levertov, Andrew Hudgins, Kascha Semonovitch, and others—which explore the original moment when Mary encounters the stranger in Nazareth and ponders whether she will say yes or no.[15] Just as Kierkegaard gets into the mind of Abraham in *Fear and Trembling* (a work of theopoetics, if ever there was one), and Kazantzakis gets into the mind of Christ in *The Last Temptation of Christ*, these poets succeed in getting into the imaginations of great holy figures.

(Note that we also find such poetics in non-Abrahamic traditions such as the enchanting Jataka narratives of the life of the Buddha in Ajanta and Ellora.) And to return to the annunciation, we may say that the various poetic retellings of this scene invite us to "anatheistically" retrieve Mary's moment of oscillation: her pondering of disbelief and belief as she responds to the summons of the stranger. Two thousand years after the event, we can still do so through imagination. In sum, in revisiting these images we relive the primal dramas as if we were there, as if we were encountering these sacred figures for the first time.

And as though poets weren't enough, we also have countless painters, from Botticelli and da Messina to Rembrandt, Rouault, and Sheila Gallagher.[16] What the artistic imagination is doing here is inviting us back to the inaugural moments of faith so that we may live them "again, anew"—in time (language) and in space (painting). Without such anatheist imaginings, all we have is dry dogma and abstract doctrine. But in thus anatheistically refiguring the moment of Mary's wager we discover that it, too, was an anatheist moment. Mary herself was engaged in an act of anatheist retrieval (back) and promise (forth). She, too, was caught in a hermeneutic circle of past and future, before and after God. Indeed, the fact that the maiden from Nazareth (whom I like to call "the Nazarena," for in the moment of wager she is no longer Mary and not yet Madonna) is almost always portrayed as reading at a lectern, indicates that she is recalling the narratives of her Abrahamic faith and the various wagers that her ancestors made when solicited by a divine summons—that is, by angels in disguise—from Abraham and Jacob to Tobias and Samuel.[17] The Nazarena is reliving the past as she makes her leap of faith into the future—freely choosing to believe that the impossible can be possible, that she can conceive a child, like Sarah before her, when visited by divine strangers.

This moment of free choice, recalling the past and anticipating the future, is a primordial instance of the ana-time of anatheism, for at this oscillating instant, when eternity hovers over the here and now, Mary is poised before the options of belief and disbelief. We are told in Luke that in this anatheist moment of freedom she "was troubled and pondered."[18] It is a hard one. A lot is going on in her head. The Greek verb for pondering is *dialogizomai*; she is dialoguing with the strange visitor, with herself, with all the voices in her mind saying, "Do it," "Don't do it." And from out of this welter of perspectives and possibilities, she chooses. Moreover, if she did not choose, or was not *free* to choose, from a space of negative capability, of imaginative empathy and openness to the stranger, the wager would have been false. The Incarnation would be an act of divine rape. Theism without anatheism is just that—a violation of human freedom and trust. But it is also important to recognize that this pondering, this after-ing, this drama of responding to the call, is *carnal*. It is a thinking again *in the flesh*—a hermeneutic act of wagering. Neither a reflex response to a stimulus nor a disembodied cogito with a clear and distinct idea, Mary is thinking through the body and embodying her text in action. That is why, in almost all the portraits, she has a book in one hand and a lily (represent-ing the senses) in the other. Mary's response to Gabriel is one of *savvy*—a felt knowledge, a thinking that is also a touching and tasting, *sapientia* as *sapere–savourer–savoir*.

Reimagining the sacred can thus revive faith, make it live again. Religious imagination can bring us back to the moment, and it brings the moment back into our lives again. We become dramatic contempo-raries of the wager. That's anatheism. If faith needs its prophets, it also needs its poets.[19]

THE SACRED: A QUESTION OF STRANGENESS

The sacred is somewhere between the spiritual and the religious. We often hear the phrase "spiritual but not religious." And we have all heard people say that a particular person, place, thing, or moment is "sacred" to them. The spiritual can include the sacred and the religious, but it can also operate independently of them. "Spirit" is a very capacious category that, at times, can mean anything and everything. But for the most part it means something, and indeed something important. We meet many in our secular age who are still hankering after "something"—they know not quite what—however that may be defined. This is often referred to as a "spiritual quest," and it can express itself in a great variety of ways, from an appreciation of the art of Botticelli, Bach, or Bob Dylan through theo-sophical New Age movements, astrological readings or, more recently, forms of transcendental meditation and yoga—a mix of Rumi and Ramakrishna. All these forms of spiritual journeying and self-discovery can occur without any commitment to a denominational religious faith, with its inherited rites, creeds, practices, and doctrines.

So, the spiritual can involve a seeking that does not necessarily involve religion, if by "religion" we understand a specific set of creedal truth claims, shared ritual traditions, and institutional behavior codes. The sacred, on the other hand, resides somewhere between the spiritual and the religious. It differs from the spiritual in that it is something you find rather than something you seek. It is "out there" somewhere, rather than "in here," so to speak. It is there before you are aware that it is there—before self-awareness, before consciousness, before epistemology. We do not cognize the sacred, we re-cognize it.

Let me offer some examples. We talk about things being sacred to us. Certain people, as mentioned, can be deemed sacred. (Think of Levinas's "epiphany of the face," in which another before me becomes utterly unique and irreplaceable). Times can also be sacred to us, signaling a specific *kairos* (before-time and after-time) that supersedes *chronos* (the linear, secular time of one moment after another). Whereas sacred time is one thing because (*dia*) of another, ordinary time is one thing succeeding (*meta*) another. Sacred time is about being *in* time; ordinary time is about being *on* time. The liturgical calendar—Advent, Christmas, Epiphany, Lent, Easter—offers traditional examples of holy times in Christian culture. And, in addition to people and times, places can be sacred too, as *khora*—a special space traditionally separated out from profane, one-dimensional space.[20]

In all three cases—person, time, and place—"the sacred" refers to something set apart, something strange and ineffable. Walter Benjamin referred to this extra dimension as "aura." In Latin, *sacer* has the same root as *secretus*, or "secret," which in turn is a translation from the Greek *mysterion*, meaning "blindfolded." So the sacred is something that surprises us, something that we haven't constructed or envisaged in advance, that blindsides us, as it were. It is, in Virginia Woolf's words, the "thing given not made."[21] In other words, the sacred, at its most basic, involves a deep sense that there is something "more," something radically Other, uncanny, transcendent, impossible for us to imagine until we reimagine it anew, until we make the impossible possible through a leap of faith. The sacred is the realization that there is something there that is more than "me"—or more than "us," understood as an immanent consensus of "we."

One could say much here about the notion of the *sacer* as something or someone numinous and ambivalent, inspiring "fear and trembling"

(Kierkegaard), "fascination and recoil" (Otto), "totem and taboo" (Freud), "blessing and curse" (Caillois). In short, the *persona sacra* is the stranger who surpasses the normal notions of law and logic, shattering our conventional horizons, perspectives, and presuppositions. It is the "other" in the other person who precedes and exceeds us—and thus, as Ricoeur says, *donne à penser*, gives rise to thought, provokes more reasoning, and amplifies our understanding. (I am no advocate of blind irrationalism and fideism.)

What I am trying to suggest with the notion of anatheism is that the sacred can be experienced in and through the secular. The hyphen between sacred and secular is crucial. So we might say that anatheism is an attempt to sacralize the secular and secularize the sacred. It is reimagining the sacred after the secular and through the secular. Bonhoeffer talks about being *with* God yet living *without* God. I call this double sense of "with and without" the movement of adieu. This two-fold movement involves both an atheist and a theist moment, and exceeds both. In its atheist guise, adieu is a departure, a leaving, a farewell to the old God of metaphysical power, the God we thought we knew and possessed, the omni-God of sovereignty and theodicy. Adieu, therefore, to the God that Nietzsche, Freud, and Marx declared dead. But in saying adieu to the omni-God, anatheism opens the option of a God still to come—or a God still to come back again. *Ana-* has two *a*'s: the double *a* of "ab" and "ad." The *ab deo* of departure from God opens the option of the *ad deum* of a return to God after God, a supplementary move of *aftering* and *overing*. But as soon as the before-and-after God becomes fixed or fixated, we need to deconstruct this latest fetish and "go after" God again. And so on without end.

In sum, the anatheist God is one of perpetual departing and arriving, conjoining negative capability with constant rebirthing of the divine in the ordinary. For me, this double sense of leaving and returning is at the heart of the sacred. And it may express itself either spiritually (as a general gracious openness to "something more") or religiously (involving creedal commitments and devotions). Anatheism has many mansions. One can be either an anatheist theist or an anatheist atheist, but whichever one chooses—belief or nonbelief—anatheism remains a wager.

Let me end this preliminary sketch of the anatheistic retrieval of the sacred with this description from *Anatheism* of the relationship between the secular and the sacred:

Anatheism is not an atheism that wishes to rid the world of God, rejecting the sacred in favor of the secular. Nor is it a theism that seeks to rid God of the world, rejecting the secular in favor of the sacred. Nor, finally, is it a pantheism (ancient or New Age) that collapses the secular and the sacred into one, denying any distinction between the transcendent and the immanent. Anatheism does not say the sacred *is* the secular; it says it is *in* the secular, *through* the secular, *toward* the secular. I would even go so far as to say the sacred is inseparable from the secular, while remaining distinct. Anatheism speaks of "interanimation" between the sacred and the secular but not of fusion or confusion. They are inextricably interconnected but never the *same* thing.[22]

The ana- of anatheism makes sure that the God who has already come is always still to come.

2

Imagination, Anatheism, and the Sacred

Dialogue with James Wood

James Wood is a well-known English literary critic, essayist, and novelist. His career as an increasingly influential writer includes positions as the *Guardian's* chief literary critic (1991–1994), senior editor of the *New Republic*, staff writer at the *New Yorker*, and professor at Harvard University. After publishing several volumes of essays, Wood has also written a theological novel, *The Book Against God* (2004). Not unlike his novel's main character, who struggles with his religious background, Wood, an atheist convert from evangelicalism, finds in literature a middle ground between belief and unbelief. Good literature, he argues in *The Broken Estate*, not only depicts the great complexity of belief but also provides a space where one can examine faith without total commitment. Great modern novels by Melville, Dostoyevsky, Tolstoy, Woolf, and Camus, for example, raise the crucial questions about faith and allow us to enter into the authors' beliefs without a total commitment. Wood calls this believing "not quite," or "as if," the "true secularism of fiction," and he prefers this hospitable space of freedom to the secular and religious fundamentalists, who want to clarify and simplify both religion and atheism through dogmatic claims.

This middle ground makes Wood, in Kearney's eyes, an "atheist anatheist," someone who seeks dialogue beyond dogmatism, but from the atheist side. Wood poses essentially four questions to Kearney: First, since Christianity itself contains a self-critical impulse against dogmatism, do we need anatheism? Second, do we need an anatheist God to live an ethics of hospitality? Third, does not anatheism jettison the personal God of the Christian tradition? Is there still a God to pray to? And finally, without this personal God, how does anatheism's eschatological impulse not succumb to an empty messianicity that could justify any crazy revolutionary cause?

The following conversation between Kearney and Wood took place at Boston College on November 18, 2010. The discussion was sponsored by the Institute for the Liberal Arts and was moderated by the artist and academic Sheila Gallagher.

> RICHARD KEARNEY (RK): It is a great pleasure to be here this evening with James Wood. A very good friend of mine in Dublin described James to me several years ago as the most articulate, challenging, and intelligent atheist writing in the contemporary God debate. And when, in preparing for our conversation, I read his wonderful books—*The Broken Estate* and *The Book Against God*—I found his arguments against belief so cogent that I thought of bowing out. But it was too late; the invitations had been issued and the venue booked. I realized I was just going to have to face the fire with this guy! So here we are.

James and I come from similar yet different backgrounds. Both of us hail from the British Isles—me from one island, he from another. I grew up Irish Catholic. He grew up English Protestant—which, for Irish Catholics, really means English atheist! We are both fascinated by the relationship between imagination and religion—something which has marked our respective and often overlapping national literatures—though we come to quite different conclusions about its fruits. And we have common teachers, students, and friends. Indeed, though I have not met James before tonight, I already consider him a friend. Or a *frère ennemi*, depending on how our exchange turns out! Indeed, I am reminded of how Douglas Hyde, Ireland's first president, described the relationship between the Irish and the English: "The English are the people we love to hate and never cease to imitate." This evening I hope to disprove Hyde on both counts.

Let me begin by saying that, for me, anatheism invites an open debate between various kinds of atheism and theism. I would even say that there can be anatheistic theists or anatheistic atheists, and that James and I probably find ourselves somewhere along that spectrum. And I suspect many of us in this room are often one or the other by turns. But whatever form it takes, anatheism is an existential wager: to leap or not to leap, to believe or not to believe. In fear and trembling. In uncertainty and mystery. As such, it invites new thinking about the relationship between the secular and the sacred. I hope that James and I may be able to tease out some of these thoughts. And perhaps, in particular, what forms the relationship between the sacred and secular might take in the domain of poetics, where James Wood lives and breathes and has his being.

> JAMES WOOD (JW): Thank you very much. I'm delighted to be
> here and very grateful to Richard for being such a delightful and
> eloquent partner in conversation. He told me just before we went
> on that he's been on the road a bit with his book *Anatheism*. He's
> been speaking with the philosopher Charles Taylor, the theolo-
> gian David Tracy, and will be in Paris shortly in conversation with
> Julia Kristeva and others. I have to say that I am distinctly the poor
> cousin when it comes to these massive names. Nor can I denounce
> Richard, as the archbishop of Dublin has done, from the pulpit.

When I was reading Richard's book, I was thinking that it's so right in so many ways, and yet I found myself asking, Why do I resist it? And one of the answers I came to was that I resist it because I am still the child of the particular theological limitations that shaped me. On the one hand, I had a rather Presbyterian mother, for whom any misbehavior was always called "unedifying"—that was the particular word. Even my first girlfriend was called unedifying. On the other hand, this Presbyterianism got mixed up in the early seventies, for my parents, with a particular kind of English evan-gelicalism. It was not quite identical to American evangelicalism, though it was taking some of its cues from it. It's an older kind of nineteenth- and even eighteenth-century tradition, perhaps. But it's not dissimilar in its emphases from American evangelicalism, with its heavy stress on the Gos-pel, for instance. That was the side of my childhood that had me singing things like "Your way, not my way, Yahweh," and other fine songs like that!

I broke away from this form of belief, but we are always shaped by our backgrounds. And I feel a certain narrowness, because *Anatheism* is so formidably ample, supple, and generous—generous to the secular, generous to the sacred, generous to the atheist, generous to the theist. And it contains many wonderful passages and revelations. There are two or three pages about Merleau-Ponty, for instance, which make a convincing case for Merleau-Ponty as a kind of Christian phenomenologist. And there are similarly wonderful chapters on Woolf and Proust. I also like its boldness. As some of you will know from reading contemporary theology or critical theory, there has been a certain "turn" toward God in the last twenty years, a recurrence of academic discussion about God, but very little practical discussion about God and ethics. And what is moving about this book is that Richard seems to decide, after a while, "Okay, enough of the high chat. Let's talk about some practical lives." And so he talks about people like Dorothy Day and Jean Vanier and people who have actually welcomed the stranger in. All that is very moving to me.

But I'm going to raise a few largish questions, not so much objections as shadow arguments, so that we can have a debate.

The first is this: Isn't it the case that the anatheistic position is already accommodated, already present, in some of the theological tradition— whether in the work of Meister Eckhart or Bonhoeffer, or even in those nineteenth-century theologians who were getting rid of biblical literalism and the divinity of Jesus but who wanted to keep the idea of Christianity alive, whether just as ethics, in George Eliot's sense, or as perhaps something a bit more divinely sanctioned than that, in the case of David Friedrich Strauss?

So I wonder if we need the term *anatheism* as urgently as Richard thinks we do. Following on from that, does Richard need God at all, or even an anatheistic God, in order to live the kind of ethical life that he so eloquently describes: turning to the stranger, welcoming the other, and so on? After all, Levinas, from whom he takes a fair amount, seems to have a more attenuated, possibly atheistical sense of God than Richard does. That is to say, there is a theologically affirmative mood in Richard's book which doesn't seem to be there in quite the same theologically positive way in Levinas, and certainly not in Derrida. And yet, those are two writers who are important to Richard, and in part because they are concerned with a real ethics, a real ethical politics. In some ways, Levinas and Derrida seem to have done without the anatheistic wager. This raises the question, then, of what Richard needs, theologically—and I think he does require something more, and it comes out in an interesting phrase when he is critiquing Derrida for having an empty messianism; he says that what Derrida does not see is "the face through the name of God." Now, I suppose that Richard could just mean, in an utterly secular way, the face, your face, my face, the face of the stranger. But there is an interesting ambiguity at that moment, because if one thinks of the veronica, for example, in the Christian tradition, one is thinking precisely of the face behind the shroud, which is nothing less than the face of Jesus, and thus the face of God.

Third, there would seem to be a tension—inevitable, and indeed acknowledged by Richard—between the nice, deconstructive openness of the idea of God as *event*, as surplus, as more, as opening the door and so on (where deliberately, and for obvious reasons, one is refusing to denote what God is, one is refusing in a way to give God attributes)—a tension between this necessary vagueness and the need to continue to use God or the idea of God as if we *can* indeed still pin attributes onto him. The need not only to keep God in the sentence but actually to say, "Well, my God does have certain attributes, my God is powerless, suffering, and suffers with us."

I'll give you a couple of examples from *Anatheism*: "The only God worthy of belief is a vulnerable and powerless one who suffers with us." Or "God is willing to lose his own being in order to give more being to his beloved creatures." If you heard that last sentence from an Anglican vicar in the pulpit of a little village church in Gloucestershire, you wouldn't blink. You'd say, "Yes, of course this is the God I worship and believe in, and the vicar has the right to project those attributes onto God, because these are the attributes from tradition, and this is the nice God I kneel down to and pray to." And though I don't believe in such God, or in any God, I don't have any problem, of course, with others believing in such a nice, weak God. It is just that I think there is some tension between that God and the more Derridean and deconstructive shelter of Richard's argument, in which he is in effect also saying, "Ah, but we can't talk about God, we cannot give God such attributes or indeed any attribute," because we want to free the *name* of God for what Caputo calls the *event* of God.

It is naming that is the problem, right? That is the idolatry. If God can be called all-suffering and weak and powerless, then perhaps God can also be called all-powerful and majestic? And if God can be called powerful and majestic, he can also be called "he," or can be said to be angry or jealous or disappointed. And if he can be called anything at all, then perhaps it is not madness for the evangelical believer to think that God should be consulted, and have an opinion about, whether that evangelical should take a new job in Colorado or about what he gets up to in the bedroom. The problem *begins* with attributes of *any kind*.

A fourth area of interest for me is the whole idea of the messianic. You can still hear in Richard's book the Christian ghost of the messianic, and indeed I think it's more strongly there still in Caputo's idea of the event. Richard writes very eloquently about God as an opening, as a surplus, as more, as something that could, as Walter Benjamin says, "explode the continuum of history." But the template is clearly messianic. Richard is acute at showing how, in Derrida, the messianic turns into messianicity; that is, into a form of simply playing up to the "idea" of the messianic without having to ever say what any particular messianism means.

Nevertheless, what if we think more Judaically of messianism as essentially the history of false messianism? Which it obviously is. That is to say, in Richard's book there is an optimism, a kind of hope that when he or Caputo says, "I pray nightly for the event; I pray for something, for truth to announce itself," that something might indeed happen. But what if the Messiah came and nothing happened? That's the atheistical—as opposed to anatheistical—lesson to draw from the false messiah that Jesus was. Jesus came, there was indeed an enormous event, and humankind did not change its ways. Nothing changed at all. It is true that since Christ appeared we have taken into ourselves the idea of redemption, but we have been awfully slow to actually redeem ourselves, if you look at human history.

Richard quotes Bonhoeffer as defining God as a God who wins power and space in the world by his weakness, which is of course an extraordinarily noble thing to say and to write, in prison. But one wonders if it can actually be true, given what happened to poor Bonhoeffer. Perhaps God (and Bonhoeffer) wins no power by his weakness. Perhaps he is just weak. This makes me think of those very eloquent words by the philosopher Emil Fackenheim, about the holocaust. He says Christianity had its *kairos* and failed. Christianity had its moment, in the thirties. It had its event, as it were. It was the moment when, if a million Christians had stood up and said, "We are Jews," then perhaps the Third Reich might have collapsed. But they didn't stand up. The event failed. The event turned out, in fact, not to be an optimistic or messianic event but to be something murderous and evil.

I want to ask Richard: What will happen if we open the door? I understand what he means when he is talking about hospitality and welcoming the stranger. But in sacred terms, is his idea of an anatheistic surplus (at one point he says, I think, that what God will do is give us more being, allow us to live more abundantly) actually different from the purely formal, empty messianicity that he criticizes in Derrida, where in effect one is saying, "Well, I don't really know what's going to happen, but I really like the idea of being messianic"? And, indeed, there is a fairly severe critique one could do, isn't there, of the whole philosophy and historiography of the event in French theory of the sixties and seventies, where actually what it looks like is a response to the failure of the event. Certain people in the midsixties believed that something was going to happen, believed that revolution was going to turn society upside down. That did not happen. And what you get then, in the next ten years, is a very sophisticated elaboration by various people, including Alain Badiou, of the idea of the event, where in effect people are saying, "I don't think anything is going to happen. We are probably going to have to resign ourselves to the emptiness of the event, but I don't want to give up on the idea of the event." I think it is worth asking Richard to distinguish his idea of the messianic from mere messianicity.

A final point. Richard writes, movingly, that nothing is lost in anatheism. He rightly then goes on to say, yes, certain people will feel there are things lost, but we can also see that there are gains, and if we are willing to convert the losses into gifts, then nothing is lost in anatheism. I do not necessarily disagree with that, because I do not believe in God. But if I believed in God, I might want to make a fairly strict accounting of what is lost in anatheism. As far as I can see, what is lost is both a Creator and a Redeemer. I do not see evidence of an anatheist understanding of God as the creator of the world, and I don't get a really strong sense, either, of the idea of an afterlife. For Richard, the kingdom of heaven appears to be the kingdom of here and now. (As Caputo says, not *where*, but *when*?) Given this, anatheism has largely got rid of the idea of a Redeemer, too. So a certain amount is indeed lost, is it not?

And this leads me to put my finger on a crucial absence in the book, which is that prayer is never mentioned, as far as I recall. There is of course a talk, a rhetoric—and a lyrical one, a beautiful one—about Eucharist, the sacred, the mystical. But there isn't talk in the book, as far as I can see, about prayer. And that would make sense, because there is no one to pray to. I'll leave it there for the moment.

RK: Thank you, James. I will try to respond to some of those very challenging thoughts—which you politely say are not objections. Only shadow arguments. Well, if these are shadows, what does darkness look like? So, let me try to recover some of that affirmative optimism you attribute to me. If I can.

I'll start with your question, Why anatheism and why now? Has it not all been said before by others, in different ways? What purpose does it serve to bring it up (again) now?

Well, first, I feel it is extremely important in terms of reopening a dialogue—the hermeneutic virtue par excellence, right? There's something going on at the moment, in this fierce debate between militant atheists and dogmatic theists. You, James, have written about this in the *New Yorker*—the "God in the Quad" piece—and elsewhere. In the left corner, we have the anti-God heavyweights practicing an exclusivist secular humanism—the view that once you get rid of all the idle talk about the spiritual, sacred, and religious you arrive at truth. It's a sort of eliminative materialism. Whittle everything away until you get back to the facts—namely, whatever empirical evidence tells you is true. That is it.

And then, in the right corner, we have the pugilists of dogmatic theism. You mentioned something of this when you spoke of evangelicalism. I certainly knew a fair bit about a Catholic version of this, growing up in Ireland in the fifties and sixties under some extremely reactionary Irish bishops. No time whatsoever for gays, contraception, divorce, abortion, not to mention good old honest dissent. And atheism dared not speak its name! Indeed, my little incident with the archbishop of Dublin (later cardinal), Desmond Connell, in 1984, which you just referred to, James, captures something of this. I had just published my first book, *Poétique du possible*, and was recently employed in the philosophy department of University College Dublin, chaired at the time by Connell. Having read the book, he called me to his office and said, "Richard, I feel like saying to you what Yahweh said to Adam after the Fall: 'Where are you?'"

I didn't know then—and I still don't know—but I do know that not knowing where you are is not necessarily a bad thing, especially if you are still trying to go somewhere. I am very suspicious of those who know exactly where they are, whether they be dogmatic theists or atheists. Which does not mean one shouldn't take a stand. One should. But I prefer someone who takes a stand knowing that there is still some element of doubt, uncertainty, and mystery (John Keats's three qualities of negative capability), some indeterminacy which makes the stand all the more courageous and difficult—and true. The person who is really interested in truth is always looking for *more* truth. That is my experience of authentic seekers. Or, to juggle with T. S. Eliot, "the way of possession is the way of dispossession." The bishop and I faced off at that moment. He was a gentleman, but a dogmatist to the core and, as it transpired, a hopeless cardinal. Philosophical truth for him was only available as a form of scholastic realism, hailing from triumphal medieval Christendom, and all the rest, from Kant and the Enlightenment forward, was quite simply error.

So I, like you, James, had my fair share of dogmatic theism growing up, and, worse still, this apologetics went hand in hand with a religious culture which fostered violence—in both Protestant and Catholic communities in Northern Ireland—even as it covered up abuse and discouraged real intellectual questioning. My favorite thinkers when I was at school were radical atheists—Camus, Sartre, Marx, Nietzsche. I loved "free thinking."

So maybe my personal experience growing up in a country torn by sectarian warfare and dominated by an ethos of intolerance for intellectual freedom marked me more than I realized. I wanted to resist. And so, when it came to the God question—which I do believe is a key concern for all civilizations, from the beginning of time to the present day—I felt a huge urgency to find an alternative to both unquestioning theism and arrogant atheism (in which camp, I hasten to add, I do not count your good self). So I must admit that anatheism, for me, was, from the beginning, a way of revolting against dogmatism of either stripe. I was horrified at the betrayal of Christianity by the official churches and wanted to reject it outright.

And yet I didn't want to throw everything out. I felt that, deep down, there was something irreducibly sacred and precious still there, something that might arise from the ashes after the collapse of the churches—one of my favorite Nietzsche quotes was, "When something is leaning, give it a push"—that it might still be possible to recover something from the ruins, some kind of god *after* God. There must be, I believed, another way of living with a "god" beyond the old Alpha God of oppression, paternalism, and false consolation. I was encouraged in this belief by my very liberal family, my enlightened Benedictine teachers, and later, by mentors in France like Levinas and Ricoeur, who spoke of a postreligious faith.

JW: And what about anatheism as rhetoric about prayer rather than prayer itself? Is anatheism concerned with something or someone beyond language? Is there more to the anatheist God than metaphors and metonymies?

RK: There is, but it is complex. In the beginning was the Word, after all. But it is not to be taken literally—which does not mean that it is not true. Truth goes beyond the literal to the figural, which does not mean the merely fictional but the figurational. The Word that was in the beginning as "creation" is a process of figuration—prefiguration, configuration, refiguration—as I tried to point out in my first book, *Poétique du possible*. In my own anatheist return to a god after God, I found myself replacing a literalist reading of a divine Creator and Redeemer with a figural-figurational one. By which, I repeat, I do not mean unreal or devoid of truth content. No, I simply refer to the hermeneutic awareness that all our names and attributes for what we call God are anthropomorphic—human interpretations and figurations. Wallace Stevens speaks of "supreme fictions"—supreme precisely because they matter so much. Anatheistically reimagined, the Creator can be seen, no longer in terms of a metaphysical first cause or creationist mechanic or magician, but simply as grace and gift: the awareness that there is a beginning before I begin, that something "sacred" gives itself to us out of the past and the future. The term *creator* is simply an anthropomorphic way of wagering—or trusting (*con-fidens*)—that there is a beginning before our beginning, a *fore*time. Just as "redeemer" is a way of saying there is an ending after our end, an *after*time. The prefix *ana-* can mean both "back" and "again," returning and aftering. This latter dimension of futurity is what you—citing Levinas, Derrida, and Caputo—call the "messianic."

The book of Genesis tells the story of human being coming from some Other that precedes and exceeds us, and this inaugural holy story speaks of this sacred genesis in terms of a *yotzer*, Hebrew for the one who creates, forms, shapes—and hence the related term *yetzer*, meaning "imagination" or "figuration." This divine configuring has nothing to do with the paper-knife manufacturer who fashions each creature after the manner of a blueprint or patent, as Sartre argues in *Existentialism and Humanism* (if

Sartre is right, then I'm an atheist). It is, rather, the idea of beginning as radical natality, a leap into the new, of more coming from less, of something coming out of nothing, *creatio ex nihilo*. In a word, the first act of the impossible becoming possible.

The same can be said of other names for God: father, mother, host, guest. It's all a matter of hermeneutics. The Johannine phrase "In the beginning was the Word" means in the beginning was hermeneutics. There is no way out of the hermeneutic circle, no way out of language. And why should there be? Words, names, and metaphors are all we have to express a deep sense—for many, myself included—that there is something irreducibly other in our experience, which calls, and that we receive this call from beyond ourselves even as we constantly reinterpret and recreate it for ourselves. So anatheism is really a vibrant conflict between names, an attempt to articulate and communicate—through word and action—what we mean when we say, "I hear a call from an Other; I receive a gift from an Other; I receive a power to make the impossible possible."

I call this hospitality to the stranger. And my wager is that this formulation or figuration of sacred experience is at the root of the great wisdom traditions *and*, I hasten to add, of many people's everyday faith experience. The former way of tradition works hermeneutically to provide us with narratives, myths, memories, and parables. The latter way of experience works phenomenologically to offer us ordinary, existential examples. And literature and art—what I call broadly poetics—often mix these two treasuries of testimony to provide us with vivid stories of the sacred. All the examples I cite in *Anatheism* are taken from these three narrative sources—sacred, existential, and poetic.

And that is why anatheism is never empty. It is not, as you imply, some abstract conceptual system, some purely formal deconstructive operation. In Derrida's terms, it is not merely messianicity but messianism—indeed, an interreligious play of messianisms, in the plural—with images and stories, with memories and aspirations, with faces and bodies. Lots of "body and blood," if you will. Which is why I so love when Hopkins says that God "plays in ten thousand places, / Lovely in limbs, and lovely in eyes not his / To the father through the features of men's faces." You won't find that in Derrida—though I owe a great debt to deconstruction.

So, to reply to your question, what interests me is not so much Derrida's "religion without religion" so much as religion *before* and *after* religion, the foring and aftering of ana-. Such a double step—preceding and exceeding religion—opens up the possibility of a return to God after the death of God, after the letting go of the omni-God that you knew in your evangelical upbringing in England and that I knew in the Catholic ecclesiasticism of Ireland.

Now you ask, James, what is so new about this? Have not Eckhart and Bonhoeffer and other religious reformers already done this? Why do it again? My answer is, yes, they have done it. Of course, you are absolutely right. And, as you note, I spend quite a lot of time in *Anatheism* revisiting the thoughts of many former "anatheists" who dared abandon God in order to return to God anew—not only Eckhart and Bonhoeffer but also a venerable list of brave heretics, mystics, and saints, from Teresa of Avila (who survived the Inquisition) and Marguerite Porete (who did not) to Teilhard de Chardin and Dorothy Day. All of these figures dissented from the dogmatic theism of their day and were, in different ways, rebuked for it. And, of course, all these "anatheists" (*avant la lettre*) saw themselves engaged in *imitatio Christi*. They let the idol of God go so that a living Advent could return. They died to their illusions of God, just as Jesus died to the sovereign Father on the cross ("My God, my God, why have you forsaken me?"—a double forsakenness of Father and Son), in order to return anatheistically to a God of renewed life and trust ("Unto thee I commend my spirit"). But the anatheist abandoning of oneself to the new God could only come after the atheist abandoning of the old God. Anatheism is the story of this double abandonment. It is a tale of sheer abandon.

> JW: But after the abandonment, you still seem to want to name and narrate something sacred that returns and remains?
>
> RK: I do. I personally choose to do that, but other anatheists might remain more apophatic or reticent about it. I like to fill in the spaces left open by the first adieu (the atheist moment, if you will, which we both share) with the names and narratives of saints' lives and sacred testimonies—including the stories of ordinary holy people down through the ages to the present day. In addition to those just mentioned above, or analyzed in more detail in *Anatheism*, let me say a few words here about another of my favorites, Saint Francis. Originally considered a heretic by his family and local church, he dared reimagine and reconsecrate the whole

meaning of Incarnation and Eucharist. He took the Euchurist and he said, Look, it should not be confined to two elements, bread and wine, but should be extended to the universe—and not just the human universe, but the animal and material universe, too. So everybody becomes, through this expanding, multiplying Eucharist, a Brother Sun and Sister Moon. Shared bread (a basic alimentary/elementary piece of matter) marks the exclusion of exclusion. The only ones henceforth deprived of earthly communion are those who exclude themselves.

Anatheism is the refusal of theodicy and the champion of free will. So here—and in many panentheists after Francis—one finds this gracious translation and transposition of the sacred from dogmatic exception to the potential inclusion of every living thing. The transcendent is invited to rejoin the immanent. It is not at war with the immanent, it is *in* the immanent. And God is no longer a God *beyond* us, as Merleau-Ponty notes, but a God *beneath* us!

JW: Could you come back for a moment to the question of God as Creator and Redeemer. Do you believe in any way in that kind of traditional God?

RK: For me, as mentioned, Creator and Redeemer are not literal roles, to be fetishized as a once-off omni-God; they are configurations in a larger narrative, a narrative of love and hospitality towards the stranger. Now I am not, I repeat, saying that is a purely *fictional* narrative. For some, it is—like Matthew Arnold or Strauss, perhaps even for Pater and Wilde, though I am not sure that Wilde's "faith of the faithless" is actually that faithless. Here we find the idea of the Bible as a great work of literature, a jewel in the Western canon for our aesthetic and ethical edification, an extraordinary product of human culture, to be revered as such. For me, it is of course that, but it is also more. It is a "sacred" text (though by no means the only one) which, unlike fiction, makes truth claims about the holy nature of a certain exceptional *caritas*—as impossible surplus over both moral justice and aesthetic beauty, while presupposing and embracing both. Such truth claims are not answered by fact but by faith. And faith is where the question of theism, atheism, and anatheism comes in. Theism, understood as a metaphysical proposition or proof of the existence of God, makes a dogma of faith. Atheism, if an absolute refusal of same, makes a dogma of nonfaith. Whereas anatheism, in contradistinction to both theism and atheism, disposes us to a creedal commitment while respecting the option of incredulity as a perpetual possibility.

This is what Dostoyevsky means, I think, when he says that true faith "comes forth from the crucible of doubt," or what Augustine intends when he prays, "I believe; Lord, help my unbelief." Genuine faith is never a once and for all; it is something that comes and goes and comes back again. Maybe, but not necessarily, and never certainly. Otherwise, it wouldn't be faith but knowledge. As Kierkegaard says about the leap of faith: you don't jump once and find yourself on *terra sacra* forever after. That is why even Christ, right up to the last minute on the cross, was able to doubt the Father, before he found a second faith. Christ is an exemplary anatheist, in dying and in rising again. Even in the narratives of the risen Christ we find the "Messiah" saying that he has not yet fully come: "I must go so that the Paraclete can come," "*Noli me tangere*, for I have not yet gone to the Father," and so on. In this sense, I repeat, anatheism exposes us to endless wagers of belief and nonbelief, divine presence and absence, immanence and transcendence, nearness and farness, fore and after.

JW: But why cannot it be one or the other?

RK: Because it is both/and. And to refuse such an anatheist tension is, in my view, to ignore the subtle knot between faith and nonfaith—the circularity and chiasmic reversibility between the two. Such a refusal is what I call dogma. It is settling for less than what the strange and the stranger demands.

So, if one does make a faith commitment—with the shadow of nonfaith, uncertainty, and mystery always in the background—one chooses to construe the stranger, who gives to you from beyond your own limits and possibilities, as a giver of gifts. And this giver can go, as mentioned, by many names: father, mother, creator, redeemer, lover, brother, sister, friend (not to mention more "proper" names, like Jesus, Shiva, Buddha,

Guanyin, Elohim). The experience of gift can come, potentially, in our encounter with any person or thing—it is a giving that goes all the way down, to the lowest of lowercases. No one is excluded from the horizon of the gift, unless one opts for hostility over hospitality. The gift of the stranger is something given to you. It is not something you make or make up. It is not something you project. It is not something you construct. So, I understand the primordial language of Genesis not as something to be taken literally—as creationism or some kind of omnipotent condescension, where a sovereign Alpha God superintends history from beginning to end. No, I read Genesis in the contrary sense, as what Rilke calls "the Open"—a sense of openness to something that comes from the Strange, the Other, the *mysterion*, the sacred.

And then "salvation" can, in turn, be read as an activity of endless healing (*salvare*), instantiated, for example, in multiple different stories of promise throughout the three Abrahamic testaments, stories of messianic hope for someone always still to come—Elijah, Christ returning, the Mahdi. (Not to mention similar promises of redemption in non-Abrahamic faiths. In all these cases, the only question to ask the Messiah is, "When will you come?"). And what is that messianic that is still to come? It is the promise that love is as strong as death, that Eros is as strong as Thanatos, that healing of our mortal woundedness (Greek *trauma*) is somehow possible. It is the oldest and newest story in the book, as Freud reminds us in the last paragraph of *Civilization and Its Discontents*, when he describes what's happening in Nazi Germany as a global battle between the ancient giants of Eros and Thanatos.

But it doesn't have to be a struggle between uppercase Giants. The promise of what Freud called Eros—the drive for love of life—is, for me, the messianic promise of saving the little things and little people (and we are all little, deep inside, which is our true greatness), as in healing reparation, caring for the wounded, and making broken things whole again. That is what Ricoeur, in *Freud and Philosophy*, calls the eschatological promise of the sacred. The sacred is the last thing—*eschaton*—which exceeds both the *arche* of the unconscious and the *telos* of history. And the last thing is the least thing, which is in fact the most important of all—the mustard seed that is the Kingdom, the widow's mite which is the gift of true salvation. The story of creation and redemption can thus be read as very lowercase, because creators and redeemers are everywhere, as are gifts and graces. They never need to be capitalized, in either sense of that loaded term. They can arrive or return at any moment. For every moment, as Walter Benjamin writes, is a portal through which the Messiah may enter.

> JW: This reference to Benjamin's messianism interests me. Could you say more about it? And, especially, how such an apparent mysticism limits or suppresses humanism?
>
> RK: I would try to put it something like this, at the risk of repeating myself: the sacred is the stranger at the door of every instant, the promise of something more, the surplus, the extra, the impossible beckoning the possible. And here, maybe, I reach the edge of humanism. And this, if I am not mistaken, is the ultimate question behind your questions, James, no? Why not just stick with humanism and accept the stranger as a human being *tout court*? What's God got to do with it? And in many respects, I think that is an entirely legitimate option.

Where I, for my part, am tempted, anatheistically, to keep open the question of God, however—and not just the "name" of God but the living, concrete face shining, speaking, summoning, calling through the name—is there, where something impossible becomes possible. Derrida and Caputo use similar language, but in the end they will not fill in the gaps; they will not connect the dots, name particular persons, times, and places; they will not paint pictures, tell stories, cite saints, invoke particular persons (real or imaginary). They will not sacramentalize the messianic. I will. That is what I try to show in *Anatheism*, for example, in retelling stories of Joyce's Molly, Woolf's Lily, Proust's Marcel. And in retelling the sacred hospitality of Mary and Sarah when confronted with strangers out of the blue. And other stories of ordinary holy beings in the most quotidian of lives.

> JW: The encounter with the strangers in Genesis is a primal story for you, isn't it? You open *Anatheism* with it, and keep returning to it.
>
> RK: Yes, it is a quintessentially anatheistic moment for me. Here we go (again). Abraham sees these strangers coming out of nowhere and is faced with the wager: Should I kill or embrace, withdraw or welcome? Hostility or hospitality? Thanatos or Eros? What

should I do? And he chooses, ultimately, to make the wager, to say, Yes, come in, sit down, and share bread. And in that opening to the stranger as a potential *guest* rather than *enemy*—they share a common root, *hostis*—a free choice is made. This is what loving your enemy means, ultimately. It is why Abraham, like Mary and Muhammad and countless others after him, "ponders and is troubled," experiences "fear and trembling" in this encounter with the sacred, with *das Heilige*, which Otto, following the medievals, tells us provokes a response at once *fascinans et tremendum*. And, before Abraham—the biblical prototype—has time to figure out intellectually what has hit him, he is already reading these strangers *with his body*. He reads the promise in their faces, carnally, the promise that he and Sarah will conceive a child, Isaac. And at that point, and that point only, the three become one, they are revealed as the divine. The impossible becomes possible: Sarah will be with child. Sarah laughs when she hears the promise. Why? Because it *is* impossible. It flies in the face of all that she knows, expects, anticipates, all that she is capable of (she is barren and old). Isaac, the name she gives her child, means "laughter" in Hebrew.

So I would say that the God of anatheism is a god of laughter. Not a deity of pompous piety and sanctimony. Holy people laugh. Unholy people complain, distrust, resent, fear. And I am not saying—God forbid—that atheists are unholy. The sacred is bigger than atheism or theism. That is why it belongs to anatheism.

What all these stories—great and small, biblical and literary, canonical and confessional, extraordinary and ordinary—illustrate is, I hope, a sense that there is *more* in the *less*. There is creation and redemption in a piece of bread. This I call the sacramental in the broad sense, not confined to Catholic or Orthodox or any single denominational rite, but extendable to include epiphanic transformations of little things into holy things in our most everyday experiences. This is why I keep coming back to the "*petits miracles*" of Proust, the "little daily miracles" of Lily Briscoe, the "cries in the street" of Joyce—all infinitesimal instants that transubstantiate seemingly inconsequential and inexperienced experiences from emptiness into fullness, disclosing an extra something, a surplus that makes the impossible possible.

JW: I notice that you have a propensity, throughout *Anatheism* and elsewhere, to move easily from textual questions to practical ones, from theory to therapeutic or social action. Anatheism is a two-step program that you sometimes compare to a twelve-step one.

RK: It is true, I like to move back and forth between text and action, and I often cite the example of AA. Here again we rediscover the double *a* of the ana-, the twin face of adieu. For the first basic move in overcoming "addiction" (what the Abrahamic tradition calls the compulsive character of "sin," what Buddhism calls the samsaric cycle of "attachment") is letting go, giving up, followed by healing. The first movement of adieu—to return to your question about the "content" of anatheism as it relates to Creator, Redeemer, and prayer—is a recognition that I am utterly helpless before my addiction. I am not, to use traditional lingo, the creator of the universe but a helpless creature, in need of help from another—a so-called redeemer.

So the first admission of any addict at an AA meeting is generally, "I cannot break this addiction. It is impossible." That is the initial acknowledgment. That is why you go to the meeting. And it is always preceded by the famous AA prayer—shareable by all faiths as well as by "the faith of the faithless" (to cite Oscar Wilde and Simon Critchley)—namely, "Please, Lord, give me the strength to change the things I can change, the humility to acknowledge the things I cannot change, and the wisdom to know the difference." And then, by handing one's powerlessness over to what AA calls a "higher power," however you define that higher power—redeemer, creator, father, mother, lover, stranger, sponsor—something impossible happens. One has suddenly supplemented the first adieu of letting go (surrender, abandoning of oneself) with the second adieu of "Unto you I commend my spirit" (another kind of surrender, of trust, of troth and betrothal). A match is struck in the dark, to recall Woolf's words. One opens oneself to something "given not made," to "It," however you define that It. (Woolf herself refers to the It in quasi-Buddhist, mystical terms.) But however you identify it, It works. The miracle happens. Healing takes place. Medical doctors and psychiatrists have written a lot of literature on this. They don't know why it works, but they are obliged to admit it works. To me, that is sacramental. And it is a powerful example of an anatheist hermeneutic wager invoking something *more*, that enables something considered previously impossible to happen, to take place in practice, in action, in life.

JW: Is "prayer" part of this?

RK: Absolutely. And that is why Thomas Merton has described AA as the most important spiritual movement of our time, on a par with the invention of Western mysticism by Dionysius, Gregory, and the desert fathers; or the establishment of monasticism by Benedict, Bernard, and Teresa; or of reformed Christianity by Quakers and Shakers. A few faithful sitting in a small room, breaking bread, and praying to change themselves and their world. So, in answer to your question, James, do I believe in prayer? The answer is yes.

JW: I am struck by the fact that your answers to my questions mainly take the form of examples, testimonies, images, stories. What makes you so confident in narrative as a way to the sacred?

RK: This brings me back, in a way, to your query about how I differ from Derridean deconstruction—or messianicity. There are many similarities, of course, but what I find most lacking in deconstruction is precisely narrative—the intuitive, incarnational filling out of the empty messianic structure of the event. I do not really want to talk about messianicity without messianism, as Derrida does. It does not really interest me as a quasi-transcendental structure of experience. It is too vacuous and vacant for me. So let me try to take on your suggestion that Christianity is a false messianism. I personally believe the Christian way is true—though by no means the only true messianism; for me, there is "messianizing" going on every day in everything and everyone, potentially.

You say Christ came, Christ went, and nothing changed. Therefore Christ was a false messiah. Quod erat demonstrandum. It is over. But is it over? Or are we still, as Gerard Manley Hopkins suggests, aftering and overing, still "abiding again in the glory of the particular"? As mentioned before, Jesus constantly said no to it being over. It is not yet. It is still to come. Let go of me so that the Paraclete can come, reembodied again and again in the "least of these" (*elachistos*, Matthew 25), in one more stranger *after* another—stranger after stranger, *hospes* after *hospes*, god after god. This means the messiah is potentially every single stranger whom you give water and food to, or who asks for it. It is that call that never ends and that is utterly concrete, singular, sensible, and irreplaceable, in each instance. We are seized by each messiah-stranger who knocks, and we respond to this seizure in one way or another—that's the wager of hospitality and hostility. After one stranger there is another stranger. Or as Dorothy Day says in her *House of Hospitality*, you never stop opening the door to somebody else who is going to arrive.

In that sense the messiah—and there are only lowercase messiahs in the plural, including Jesus, who renounced paternal sovereignty and omnipotence with the Father—is a perpetual beginning. Never an end. And that is why in the memorial acclamation of daily mass one commemorates Christ's act of kenosis and caritas *until* he comes ("When we eat this bread and drink this cup, we proclaim your death, Lord Jesus, until you come"). This is very close to the Jewish remembering of the suffering exiled servant and of endless radical hospitality to the stranger that one finds at Passover.

And at this point I think the difference between Christianity and Judaism almost withers away. We regain the temporality of anatheistic messianism that I started with. We keep the door open to the stranger that comes after this one, then this one, and so on, ad infinitum. It really is a waiting for Godot—with all the humor and humanity that Beckett musters for his characters, who await the child messenger day after day, never ceasing to believe, to have faith, that Godot *will* come one day. Even though, God knows, they have a million reasons to doubt it—the most obvious being the daily misery and suffering all around them.

So my final point is this: if we do not observe this special kind of anatheist vigilance, this basic mix of passion and patience (it is the same root, *patio–patire–passi–passum*) which defines genuine faith, we end up with the pathology of Religion—closure to the stranger in the name of some exclusivist, triumphal deity. Such pathology replaces a genuine religion of the sacred—that disposes and invites us to renewed trust in what is to come—with a false religion (and here you are absolutely right, James) that arrogates and imposes, that says the job is done. Even when little or nothing is yet done. That is why I do believe in the old adage, oft repeated by Ivan Illich, that "*corruptio optimi est pessima*," the corruption of the best is the worst. Injustice committed in the name of God is the greatest perversion of all. And if any religion—Christian or otherwise—says the messiah has come and there is nothing *more* to come, then that religion, in my view, deserves only one response: the salutary No of atheism.

So, as to finding myself this evening between you, James—my atheist friend—and many theist friends in the audience, between nonbelievers and believers, this is precisely the kind of anatheist drama I like. Why? Because many of us have both a theist and atheist inside us and never finally resolve the drama. In my experience, when you dig deep, there is a bit of a theist in most atheists and a bit of an atheist in most theists. That is anatheism, happily.

JW: I find myself in much agreement with what you just said, Richard, and I like the idea of the impossible becoming possible, as one definition of this surplus, this *more*, you talk about. I suppose this will seem a cheap shot, but may I be cheap for a minute?

RK: You may, indeed!

JW: It's cheapness in the service of richness! Could you, Richard Kearney, envisage praying for the impossible to become possible in your life, at a particular moment?

RK: All the time.

JW: Ah! You see, you scratch the surface and the atheist is just a theist underneath! I think you are also right about the fleshing of abstraction with narrative, the attention to "thisness." I was reading a bit of Caputo a couple of days ago, from his book *The Weakness of God*, and I copied out a sentence, which I think is an example of the problem we are talking about. The sentence talks about God's transcendence: "God's transcendence is a matter of the transcendence of the Event that transpires in the name of God." I would say that's a pretty long chain of intellectual (or indeed, grammatical) deferrals. And although, abstractly, you might say you do not have any quarrel with that, what's appealing about your work is that, essentially, you're filling in the gaps in all those deferrals. You are saying, "Okay, fine in theory, but here's the stranger at the door, here's the actual narrative."

One more thing occurs to me. As a child it used to drive me insane when my parents, particularly my mother, would always correct me whenever I said I had been "lucky." She'd always say, "You have been blessed." And, of course, as we have discussed earlier, there's a sort of evangelical absurdity whereby even good exam results became "a blessing." Whereas I am pretty sure I did the work myself, actually!

But, you know, as one gets older one understands the importance of creating a space precisely for gratitude, even if you do not know, even if you do not actually *believe* in the object of that gratitude. It is simply making a distinction, being able to put something in the linguistic register of gratitude or the moral or metaphysical register of gratitude, rather than simply, "Yeah, I was lucky and I did it all on my own." This is important, I think. On the other hand—and this comes back to our question, I suppose, of the sacred versus the secular—when we hear of a precocious young musician playing brilliantly on the piano or violin or something, and we say, "This child is really gifted," most of us, if we are not believers, use that word simply to mean that a sort of miraculous accident of genetics or whatever occurred, and so we are giving thanks for it. But in this case, the gratitude is distinctly not religious, right? We say the child is gifted, and that is that.

I suppose the question would be: If we make do with that, and rather definitely say, "No, I'm not sacralizing it. I have no need to. The child is gifted, and I give proper gratitude for that gift," is there a diminishment there? Is there something lacking that you would want to add? Is there a sacred, and not merely secular, surplus that you would want the language of anatheism to register?

> RK: It is an excellent point. I mean, the gift is there, either way, whether you call it sacred or not.
>
> JW: Right.
>
> RK: But I think I would want to hold to some possibility of sacred surplus. Yes. I think what religious wisdom traditions bring to us is a language, a grammar, a narrative, a memory—a messianic horizon of strangeness which enables us to attend more carefully to the giftedness of this gift. If you come blind to a gift, take it for granted as something exclusively human, in a strict anthropocentric way, and you just say the child is gifted, that is true up to a point. But I personally believe there *is* an extra dimension in

seeing this as not just coming from ourselves but also from something "more" than us, other than us. And this is so, even if the other is in us—I agree with the idea of being "oneself as another" (Ricoeur) or a "stranger to oneself" (Kristeva)—that is, even if that transcendent source or "higher power" (AA) is identified as immanent, beneath us rather than beyond us. Granted.

The great wisdom traditions tell us that the first creative acts come to us as a gift. All the great stories that begin "*In illo tempore*" start with stories of a gift—the gift of life (Genesis and cosmogony myths); the gift of the child (Isaac, Jesus); the gift of food and wine (Hermes and Philemon, Emmaus, the Taittiriya Upanishad); the gift of miracles (Cana, the Buddha and the puff of rice). The good begins in each instance with an act of hospitality between host and guest. But not just any hospitality. Impossible hospitality—made possible in some *petit miracle*. Hostility transformed into hospitality by an unexpected gift. Hence what I call "sacred hospitality."

JW: And does calling it "sacred" mean separating it from the secular?

RK: No, it doesn't. Because I believe that the sacred is in, for, and through the secular, though it is not "of" it. My quarrel is not with the secular but with what Charles Taylor calls a certain "exclusivist secularism" that would deny the possibility of sacred memories, traditions, and narratives. Such extreme or reductive secularism can lead to an impoverished culture. It is too controlling, calculative, categorical, unimaginative, no?

And one doesn't necessarily have to go all the way back to the Scriptures to find examples of sacred narratives of gift and grace. It is also amply available—to come back to my opening examples—in sacred poetics, in the sacramental imagination of countless artists and authors who have retrieved and reanimated primal scenes of the gratuitous gift. For a true gift is always without "why," isn't it? It escapes the circle of economy, the calculus of credit and debit, give and take.

Think of the extraordinary scene (am I being overoptimistic again, James?) in Victor Hugo's *Les Misérables*, when Bishop Myriel gives Jean Valjean—the criminal who arrives out of the night—his best food and silverware when he should, legally and rightfully, have sent him back to prison. Or the scene in the recent film *The Visitor*, where the vagrant stranger gives his cheerless host the gift of music.

And, speaking of music, since that was your example of the gifted kid: it always struck me as revealing that the etymology of "music," "muse," and "memory" (*mnemosyne*) is the same. The sense that your gift is not just a natural, genetically conditioned, homegrown talent (though of course it is that, too—I don't want to deny you did all that homework for your exams, James!) but somehow also comes *to* you, moves you, possesses you, takes you over. It is more than the Romantic notion of genius and inspiration. It is much older and deeper than that, and I don't think it has gone away. How many artists and poets—there is a long literature—have testified to this sense of something speaking, writing, painting, imagining itself through them?

Now, one might like to respond, in exclusive secularist humanist terms, that this is just one's unconscious, one's DNA, or some collective *pensée sauvage* (as Lévi-Strauss and the structuralists might say). But there is something more at work here, isn't there? Something that we might legitimately and colloquially call a sacred gift, without necessarily going all the way with your mother in calling it blessed. No?

JW: And you pray to this gift, for this gift? You give prayers of thanks?

RK: I do, though I don't talk about it in my writings. I pray in the dark and I pray in the day. My dark prayers are my secrets, my personal and private relationship to the one who heals and gives hope in moments of blackest desolation. My day prayers are more public, and I have less hesitation in speaking about them. One of the simplest is grace before meals. I find that form of prayer— common to most religions and even to many agnostics—is a way of standing back and saying a prayer that you didn't just invent out of your head, or that, if you did, some of the words still resonate with a shared tradition or narrative. And so you give thanks for the food. You don't need to belong to any specific religion to do that. You can be a humanist and do it, but then you are, I would suggest, a humanist with a difference—a humanist who is really, at least in part, an anatheist, an anatheist atheist. The fact that there is a prayer that can be shared with people, which enables you to receive the simplest of gifts (food) in a way that escapes economy—where otherwise you might just rush into your meal and consume it as a commodity you have purchased and now possess as "your" food—that taking of a moment to step back, that instant of distance, marks a deep sense of gratitude. And that is all that *eucharistos* means—thanks. It is about gratuity and grace. At some deep level, you are saying, I did not earn this food but am given it. And if one is really grateful, all the way down, one should, as they do in several cultures, also give thanks to the fish and animals and fruits of the fields one is eating. That may sound pathetically anachronistic in our consumer, capitalist culture—where, as Marx recognized, we hide the origins of productive labor behind the fetish (read: brand/status/trend/logo) of the commodity; use-value and surplus-value become mere exchange value. That was what Marx criticized in his brilliant reading of Shakespeare's *Coriolanus* in the essay "Money" in the Paris Manuscripts of 1884. How relevant it still is today! Grace before and after meals is not just a matter of politeness, of social graces, but of sacred grace. It is, once again, the before and after of ana-time which makes of the table an ana-space.

Now, I know there are many secular humanist equivalents of this, no doubt, like welcoming your guests to table, but I think even here we find traces of something more, of a surplus of gifting and gratuity (meaning literally free, not earned or expected, like Gide's *acte gratuit*)—a surplus that bears witness to something that precedes us and exceeds us. The surprise of what we call "luck" is perhaps not just fortuitous (a matter of chance) but gratuitous (a matter of grace). And perhaps there is a curious echo of this— I am taking this off the top of my head, I have not thought it through—in the notion of the tip at the end of a meal. It is strictly beyond the economy of consumption and production (price of the food, cooking, restaurant overheads), and even beyond the economy of service as something purely menial, laborious, and efficient. The tip is at the edge, or better, over the edge. That is why in French the *gratuité* is an extra, beyond *service compris*, something freely given for something freely received (the unexpected surprise of the giving). And this is why a really good waiter doesn't just "work" tables or "serve" tables but hosts them, graces them, gives beyond what is paid for in the context of consuming and remunerating. You give a tip in recognition of the incalculable little extra you have received.

(This is something largely lost in the American system, I think, where service is generally not included in most bills—am I right?—and one does not, in all duty and decency, have a free option to pay or not to pay the tip. It is expected, and the poor "servers" cannot survive without it. Here we have, in short, the option of grace reduced to the accounting of economy).

What applies to the gratuity of the giver/waiter may also be said to apply to the guest. I am thinking here, for example, of the gift of the uninvited guest in the poetry of Hafiz. The empty place at the table, witnessed in so many sacred hospitality customs, from Islamic feasts and Passover to the Rule of Saint Benedict and the Irish custom of Little Christmas— the Feast of the Epiphany, when strangers come from the East. It is the empty place for Elijah, for the Messiah, for the coming of the Kingdom on the Sabbath day. Even when secularized, this idea of the feast as gratuity, this sacramental element of the meal remaining a surplus, is, it seems, a continual and life-enhancing form of prayer. So that the most gracious way of responding to a good meal is, as the French say, to "*rester sur sa faim*"—remaining that little bit hungry right to the end, leaving that last morsel uneaten, that last drop of wine undrunk, that little gap of appetite unfilled—*until fullness comes*. This is more than a matter of genteel etiquette or epicurean finesse, isn't it? Mightn't it signal some extraordinary hint of grace in the most ordinary act of eating?

> JW: So, for you, it is a question of choosing grace over chance in the end?
>
> RK: Yes, seeing the world as gift is wagering on grace over chance— and there is, I am sure you'd agree, but a hairline difference between them. As in the old Jewish prayer that gives thanks each morning that one has survived the night to live another day. Or as when Dorothy Day opens the door to the stranger in the night. She doesn't know in advance whether the guy knocking at two o'clock in the morning is a child molester, alcoholic, homicidal psychopath, or some hapless victim of violence and hunger. She does not "know" the difference between Jack the Ripper and Jesus Christ. So it is always a risk and a wager. A matter of trust and faith. And to give it a further twist: supposing the guy

who comes in through the door is not a good person at all, but the host, in choosing grace over fear, and love over death, sees in this person the possibility of the impossible becoming possible—which is what Dorothy Day does every time she opens the door—then is there not something very radical about the action of grace that might—*mirabile dictu*—transform a killer into a giver? How many *petits miracles* happened when people who went into Day's hospitality houses came out different because of the unconditional love she showed towards them? And I think if you don't believe in at least the possibility (however ostensibly impossible) of love winning out over death, peace winning out over war, we are in ethical and political trouble for the rest of our days.

Let me end with a final example from my native Ireland. John Hume was a political prophet, deeply inspired by a spiritual vision. He was a seminarian in his youth, but decided for politics over the priesthood. He marched for peace, in the spirit of brave pilgrims before him—MLK, Gandhi—and ended up shaking hands with the devil. He talked to terrorists; he broke bread with the IRA. The impossible (for five hundred years of conflict) became possible at last. This was an act of political bravery. But it was also an act of self-sacrifice, faith, and pardon. The pact that resulted in 1998, as you know, was called, tellingly, the Good Friday Agreement. It was a constitutional, legal, sociopolitical treaty. But there was also something deeply paschal in terms of the resonances of the impossible becoming possible. There was something here, I believe, of a God of service, kenosis, and vocation. This is a sacred as well as a secular story. And it can be read as either, or both. When John Hume shook hands with the devil (leaders of the IRA), these terrorists became people of peace. As I read it, this act of radical hospitality—roundly denounced by the British and Irish establishments at the time—this risk of "chancing his arm," made a miraculous difference. The impossible became possible.

So, what I'm saying is that the sacred stories of hospitality which were so inspirational for Hume—from Christ and Isaiah to Gandhi and Martin Luther King—these sacred narratives of nonviolence brought about a little miracle which changed the climate of Northern Ireland. I began with Irish–British relations, and end with them. Let's shake on it, James! Though you are no devil!

3

Beyond the Impossible

Dialogue with Catherine Keller

Catherine Keller is professor of constructive theology at Drew University in Madison, New Jersey. She is a process theologian with wide-ranging theoretical interests, encompassing feminist theology, ecotheology, and poststructuralist and postcolonial theory. In her highly original and influential theological works—most notably *Face of the Deep, From a Broken Web*, and *On the Mystery*—she has sought to develop the relational potential of a theology of becoming. Her books reconfigure ancient symbols of divinity for the sake of a planetary conviviality—a life together, across vast webs of difference. Her latest book, *Cloud of the Impossible* (2014), explores the relation of mystical unknowing, material indeterminacy, and ontological interdependence.

Keller's work is exemplary in combining theology and science. She uses the findings of quantum physics to move theology from a modernist, static view of the universe to one in which all things are interconnected. Science thus allows theology to speak once again with integrity about a mysterious cosmos, a world of relation, interdependence, or the "entanglement" of all things. Keller thus shares with Kearney a deeply sacramental view of life, an embodiment of God in the material that Keller finds in quantum physics and Kearney in sacramental poetics.

Although they agree on most issues, Kearney challenges Keller to clarify her panentheism, for if God is in all things, and if nothing is outside of God, does not God then become responsible for evil? Kearney is not interested in classical theodicy, but he is concerned that panentheism downplays both human freedom and the uncompromising nature of divine love. Are there not actual evil acts, such as torture and rape, that are outside of God? This point remains a nuanced difference between Kearney's more Augustinian sense that evil is a deprivation of the good and Keller's insistence that "God has no boundaries outside of which begins the world, or even hell."

This conversation took place in a café in New York City in March 2014.

THE DARKNESS OF GOD

CATHERINE KELLER (CK): If I may jump out of character right into an overview: I see anatheism as operating on three main axes, each a kind of chiasmic interchange. First and most obviously, it oscillates between theism and atheism; second, it forms a crossover between Christianity and non-Christianity (which includes, for you, not just Judaism and Islam but also, vividly, Buddhism and Hinduism); and thirdly, there is a chiasmus between apophatic interiority and kataphatic outreach into action—toward ethical and political praxis. I am also drawn to these axes of relation, though in *Cloud of the Impossible* I deal more with the first and third. I am deeply sympathetic to the second, interreligious dimension but was not able to explore it in my recent work. But you have long traveled the path of religious pluralism.

RICHARD KEARNEY (RK): Your work develops the axis between apophasis and kataphasis in extraordinary ways. So let's dive straight into the "cloud of the impossible," and especially the core question, at least for me, of darkness and light. Every cloud has a dark and silver lining. You invoke oxymora like "luminous darkness" to express the inextricable link between the knowable and the unknowable, the opaque and the diaphanous. And I wonder how this particular chiasmus touches the question of the "dark side" of God. I am thinking of Bataille, but also of Jung's defense of a certain gnostic theodicy in the *Answer to Job*, or Schelling's dark God of becoming (*Abgrund*). Is the dark side of the cloud always part of God? Is it always divine? Or is there a certain dark capacity for evil, which should not be included in the divine? But left outside or aside? In short, darkness as evil: what do we do with that?

CK: Right, the dark as menace and destruction. Not the dark that frightens us because of our insecurity, fear, and vulnerability before mystery and enigma—but the darkness of evil acts.

RK: Torture, holocaust, rape.

CK: You deal with evil in *Anatheism* in your discussion of the question of "discernment": how can we tell the difference between the stranger as, one, malicious psychopath and, two, unknowable Other to be respected and hosted? You also touch on it in your very firm rejection of any theodicy. In my *Cloud* I pretty much presuppose the strong critique of theodicy, coming from my Whiteheadian background. It is almost a dogmatic assumption for me that God is *not* what makes what happens happen, but that it is we creatures who are actualizing the possible. So that evil in the world is not something that God is testing or teaching us with—willing or wanting or even "letting" happen. As if God could stop it (torture, the holocaust) but for higher paternal reasons permits it.

No. Evil, such as we know it, is a human activity. But it is the actualization of a certain *posse*, enfolded in the cloud. So the *possibility* of evil may be understood, perhaps, as divinely inscribed—as a sort of preawareness of the unpredictable diversity and inevitable conflicts between creatures. An evolving world invites greater and greater ranges of complexity, and so, at the same time, of capacity for good—or evil. Therefore God may, it seems to me, get the rap for our capacity for evil—not for any particular horror, but for the fact that there is evil in the world.

RK: God gets the rap rightly or wrongly?

CK: Rightly. God in this picture can be accused of having called forth a world in which the Fall is possible. Because if evil is not possible, love is not possible either, except as performed by marionettes. So that is a process theological riff, by way of a first response. God—*s'il y en a*—must be somehow responsible for the *terms* of the universe, in which a vast indeterminacy of complexity at the edge of chaos is encouraged and greater vibrancy may occur. There is a certain erotic risk in creation, as there is in each creative life—a risk of real harm to self and others. So, insofar as the cloud of the impossible carries the Cusan reference to a divine interior of the world, it is not the carrier of evil within us. Its darkness is of opacity, not evil; of an infinity of all things, indeed of each creature as a created god. But if we cannot simply know it, if the good remains cloudy even in its luminosity, it must also remain in some sense ethically ambiguous.

RK: If God is love, as Nicholas of Cusa believes—being a good reader of John's Gospel—and if "God is all he is able to be," as he claims in the *Trialogus de possest*, then surely this means: all that God is able to be is love, not nonlove—that is, evil. Surely to be nonlove would be precisely what God is not, what God is incapable of being. So if there is evil in the world it is *our* doing, something *we* do as creatures with freedom and choice. In this sense, I am with the Augustinian view that evil is *privatio boni*, and that the Good is Love. Evil is *not* a possibility of God but only of humans. Evil is both a human possibility or actuality, but never a divine possibility or actuality.

CK: I see what you mean. But I still cannot help allowing for some ambiguity in God. Evil is not a possibility for God, right. But even the kindest of Gods can't miss the possibility of evil entangled in advance in the good. The possibility, for example, that one's affection will lead to disastrous consequences, or the possibility that followers of Jesus will launch crusades and inquisitions. God is the possibility of love that lures more love. But this can engender anxiety, too, for as Whitehead's "Eros of the universe"—a universe where "life feeds on life"—it takes the risks of creativity. Or provokes them. It is also the God of the nonhuman universe, where predation and suffering run through the fabric of biology. Which is not to say that suffering is God's *will* for any creature, human or inhuman. But there is nonetheless an element of risk, insofar as divinity signifies the very *complicatio* of our complicated universe, which includes both the deeply nurturing and the deeply painful. The greater our decision-making capacity—and our chance to wreak havoc—the greater also the potential for embodying. There is, in the process picture (as I developed it in *On the Mystery*, for seminarians, mainly), that erotic side of love: divine desire calling forth all kinds of possibles. And then there is the agapeic love, which picks up the pieces, so to speak, which is perhaps more in tune with your own idea of the eschatological *posse*—the kingdom of justice and hospitality.

RK: I am with you up to a point. I resonate with your notion of the cloud of the impossible as an entanglement of divine Eros and agape; and I certainly agree that Eros is as central to the divine *posse* as agape. But I would not want to put Eros on the side of evil—even the risk of evil—if that is said to be an intrinsic dimension of the divine. Which does not mean I want dualism, God as transcendent Good out there in some pure metaphysical realm of light (e.g., Plato's Good beyond Being) and us humans here in some fallen world of darkness. I agree with your radical challenge of this whole transcendence versus immanence dichotomy, and I speak frequently in *Anatheism* of transcendence in immanence, God in the world, which is in a way the most fundamental kind of *coincidentia oppositorum*, isn't it? I would want to complicate any kind of metaphysical dualism—along with you and Cusa—between divine light and human darkness by saying that the divine–human chiasmus is both in the cosmos (as "chaosmos") and in each one of us creatures. The coincidence of opposites is in every relationship.

And here I rejoin your bracing notion of distributive difference—God is everywhere and in all things. Or, as Gerald Manley Hopkins puts it, "Christ plays in ten thousand places ... To the Father through the features of men's faces." I believe, as you do, that the divine is potentially incarnate in all things, explicating, implicating, complicating, duplicating, multiplicating all over the place, in everyone and everything. As the Brazilian sister Ivone Gebara (whom you often cite) also claims, with her appeal to a mixed Christian–indigenous incarnationalism.

But, in saying this, I would still want to hold that the divine that dwells in the human, finite, immanent world is nonetheless always love and not nonlove. Otherwise, there is no difference at all. So, while I agree that every creature is an ambivalent mix of human and divine, I still want to endorse the hermeneutic task of disambiguating certain situations into (a) love that brings life and (b) nonlove that brings cruelty, violence, and destruction. (Pain, death, and suffering are a very different matter, which can have both good and evil potentials.) In other words, I cannot accept that what I call God is *both* good and evil, love and nonlove. God, for me, is always good—both actually and potentially. And so, while I agree totally with your deconstructive push against the tyranny of certainty (epistemological and moral) and acknowledge the ambivalence of all relations, I still want to retain the capacity of "discerning between spirits," of being able to distinguish between Etty Hillesum (as loving) and Himmler (as nonloving) in a dramatic test case like the holocaust.

CK: I hope so! And I can see how this connects with what you say in *Anatheism* about what we should host and what we should not host, when we should open the door to the other and when we should not.

RK: Yes, and here I disagree with Derrida's claim, in his discussion of pure hospitality, that when we open the door we cannot make a distinction between a psychopath and a messiah who might enter. I grant, of course, that it is often an incredibly difficult call. I think of Dorothy Day saying that when she opened the door to someone at midnight in one of her downtown hospitality houses, she was often unsure whether it was Jesus or Jack the Ripper asking to get in. Or both!

So I do appreciate the ambiguities of such things. But I think that deconstruction goes too far sometimes in the apophatic direction, and I have problems with a certain wild reading of Derrida's "*tout autre est tout autre*." If this means God, as Absolute Other (*tout autre*), is *potentially* in all things, I agree. But if it means that God is *actually* in all things (including torture and rape), and that there is no difference at all between the divine other (as bringer of life and love) and any kind of other (as torturer, rapist, etcetera), I give pause. All "others" are *not* the same.

Which is not to say that, in theological terms, I oppose the idea of universal salvation, going back to Origen. Even Himmler and Hitler may be saved—to take extreme examples—but only as complex agents, insofar as there may be some glint of light mixed up in their appalling darkness. Maybe. Difficult as it is to imagine. But I would never go so far as to say that their evil acts are part of some secret plan of salvation. Here I remain utterly opposed to theodicy of any kind. I agree, rather, with Arendt's Augustinian option to separate the agent from the act. Namely, we can forgive agents (releasing them into the possibility of an alternative future, as Sonia forgives Raskolnikov), but we can never forgive their evil acts, as such (Raskolnikov's brutal murder of the Jewish lady). So if, at the limit, I might admit that there is no human agent that is irredeemable (in some respect—that is complicated and needs to be unraveled), I would have to insist that there are certain irredeemable acts. *Every* act is not divine.

> CK: Surely not. But no act is simply divine, I am saying. Divine action happens in synergy with the creativity of creatures. Every act might be an invitation to the divine, every relationship might invite us to love—as in the hard (almost impossible) imperative to love the enemy—but this does not mean I let the enemy kill my children. It might actually involve killing the enemy, because of deep apophatic entanglements and ambiguities in intensified encounters where we have both love and enmity; unless it passes over into indifference, which is another matter. Original sin means that to love is also to be mixed up in a chaos that involves hostility, pain, and darkness. We are all mixed up and mixed up in all. And at some time, the love of the enemy suggests that the infinite is here, as *non fini*, nonfinished redemption. There is always work to be done. So I think I, too, can be quite Augustinian here and say God is the love that is there, but it can be deformed into hideousness by us—into a misguided love of power and possession. Loving the enemy requires some sense of the divine love being actually everywhere, albeit hideously actualized at times.

> RK: I am with you, again, up to a point, and I want to come back to that point: the problem of distinguishing between agent and act. I agree, I repeat, that we should try to love the agent, no

matter how adversarial or repugnant. And, theologically, this has the support of the Gospel command to love one's enemy, and of the thirty-four injunctions in Deuteronomy to love the stranger—not just the neighbor, which is relatively easy, as they are closer and familiar to us. Yes. But to love the torturer—who is potentially pardonable as an agent, absolved and freed from his/ her act and turned toward the future—is clearly not to love, or even condone, the *act* of torture. There is no ambivalence in the gratuitous maiming of an innocent child. It is unequivocally evil. Granted, an agent may do evil while misguidedly seeking some good, as Aquinas notes. Think of today's political terrorists and jihadists. But whatever about the agent's mistaken intentions and aims, the *act* of evil is evil.

CK: We need to be able to say that, to call the deformation of good intentions deformation. And I agree that only psychopaths choose evil for evil's sake.

RK: So I would argue that there are events of sheer malice and destruction that have nothing to do with love, no matter how unknowable or opaque the cloud of motivation from which they emerge. There is a certain darkness, *privatio*, absence of love, which I am prepared to let disappear into the void. Which is maybe what the Psalms mean when they speak of evil as that which will not be remembered but rather will dissolve into nothing. Malicious darkness, it seems to me, is very different from the "luminous darkness" you write of in *Cloud*, no?

CK: Unlike that apophatic lineage of the brilliant darkness that comes to us from Gregory of Nyssa through Pseudo-Dionysius, you are speaking of a darkness in which there is no luminosity, no glow. No possible coincidentia between darkness and light. But there is still a spectrum of variations, from deeply implicated darkness-light to the darkness of unambiguous malignity, with no trace of light or love, except perhaps in the initial moment of actualization, where there once was some link, however tenuous, between divine call and human response. For there was always some mixture at the outset, even if, as we move into human decision, we may well suppress the divine element in the mixture and make love into hate.

RK: Would you go so far as to deny that there could be certain events of radical evil that are *outside* of God? I realize how risky and complicated this sounds. But let me be clear: I am not talking of natural life–death cycles here—"life feeding on life" or earthquakes or tsunamis, etcetera. I am speaking of the human freedom to choose nonlove over love, to take certain things outside of love (that is, God), to radically deny love and hospitality. Indeed, is this not an ineradicable part of human freedom? To be able to choose evil over good, to leave God behind, outside, unheeded. To reject the call.

Now this, it seems to me, is a difficult one for Whiteheadians and panentheists. And, don't get me wrong, I am not claiming there are any creatures ineligible for love or redemption—even the demons come in search of Jesus in the Gospels, again and again; indeed, they are often the first to recognize him! As in the story of the Gadarene demoniacs who are transferred into swine who rush into the sea (poor swine!) (Matthew 8). And I am mindful of the daring of Etty Hillesum declaring that "life is beautiful" even in the blackest hell. She is not in any way condoning genocidal butchery, or angelizing human agony, merely saying that existence can be beautiful in spite of the worst evil imaginable. Not, I repeat, *because* of evil (the temptation of theodicy) but *despite* it (the indomitable defiance of love in face of hate).

CK: She suggests that the universe in which horror can occur is nonetheless in some sense beautiful. There can be a defiant glow in the darkest darkness. I resonate with what you mean when you ask if there can be certain events outside of God, but I resist any dichotomy of inside and outside. More ambiguity! And to come back to the notion of infinity, I want to be able to say that this means, theologically, first of all, that all things are in God—yes, panentheism. God has no borders or boundaries, outside which begins the world, or even hell. "I descend into Sheol, and behold, you are there." You may call the evil act a godless event, but is the agent actually void of God? Is the "outer darkness" into which the damned are cast actually some hell outside of God, who is therefore finite; or perhaps the symbol of that which forfeits its participation in the world beyond itself—and therefore in the eschatological future?

So how about this: in *Anatheism* you take on the theodicy debate and rightly critique the notion of God as sovereign omnipotence. Amidst all the current discussions of political theology and Schmitt's model of sovereign power, this is key. You mention Greenberg, who was influenced by process theology, as was Rabbi Artson, who responds to the question of theodicy from the personal perspective of someone with an autistic child.

RK: As does Julia Kristeva, who proposes a Scotist—rather than Thomist—account of disability to affirm the positive singularity of "difference" rather than deficiency; she has just published a book with Jean Vanier on this, called *Leur regard perce nos ombres*.

CK: And one finds a similar repudiation of the God of Sovereignty and Power in Elie Wiesel. The post-holocaust Jewish refusal of traditional theodicy shares a logic with the process deconstruction of divine omnipotence—on behalf of divine goodness. Which priority, by the way, while apophatically smudging the binaries a bit, I do not dispute. So that one has to think differently of the relation between divinity and darkness. God may be present even in the torment, being tormented by the torment. Divinity is there in the disabled child—or Wiesel's tortured one. And in every cell and in every quantum. God in the world doesn't really have an out. And I would conjecture that God is not only in the suffering body of the tortured child but is also feeling torment at the deforming and disfiguring of love exercised by the torturer. Would not God feel the internal agony of the self-betrayal of love?

RK: You are going to the limit here—almost hyperbolically—of how present God is in *everything*. This is very challenging. God present not only in the sufferer but in the perpetrator; that is, suffering the disrelation of the doer of evil to the good itself. A sort of struggle with its own hateful twin, as a lost and violent part of itself. An alien or alienated side of the creature seeking to kill the creator, so to speak. A difficult thought. But I like the unconditional character of the love you are proposing—an utterly inclusive understanding of the divine. I would be inclined to phrase it thus, however: if there are indeed no creatures outside of divine creation, there are nonetheless certain human creations (evil acts and events) which refuse the call of divine creation— and so choose *not* to belong to God. And we could not in fact be free agents were we not able to so choose.

CK: Yes, exactly, a disrelation of creation within itself. A form of complicated self-contradiction. If God is in the creature, there can be no fundamental separation between the creature and the creaturely act. Of course, I take to heart Augustine's admonition to love humanity and not the sin (Gandhi translated it as "hate the sin and not the sinner"), but this can turn back into the old dualism of substance and acts, which obstructs any deep relationalism. One cannot separate the agent from its agency without reinstating the separative ego that is the problem to start with. This is a thorny business.

RK: Especially from an ethical and political angle, which we are both committed to. In *Cloud of the Impossible*, you speak frequently about bringing the cloud into relation with the crowd, and you raise questions of practice and performance, beyond mere theory. You acknowledge, for example, the liberationist aspects of John Cobb's theology of process and also engage with the narratives of Gandhi, Howard Thurman (Martin Luther King's mentor), Tolstoy, and recent black feminist theologies of gender, race, and class—albeit always introducing a certain apophatic critical reserve. I feel a great proximity with this liberationist view, but just a mite of hermeneutic tension regarding the different kinds of darkness, as noted. I suppose I would want to suggest that, eschatologically speaking, all that is just and good would be preserved, whereas what is radically evil would be forgotten, erased, voided from existence and memory.

CK: Into the outer darkness. Because it doesn't deserve to be remembered.

RK: Exactly. And I think this comes close to Whitehead's notion of divine memory. The interconnectivity of all that is good being preserved in the mind of God?

CK: Yes, "the consequent nature of God" composes itself of all that is redeemable, and it isn't just the memory but the becoming of God. I'll just suggest, to be perverse, that the good that manifests, for instance, as resistance to oppression would mean nothing in memorial abstraction from the evil struggled against. There comes that smudge of ambiguity, not immortalizing the evil but remembering the struggle. But really your stress on the sheer goodness is more like process theology than is my smudge.

So, to come back to our proximity, I noticed that in *Anatheism* you do mention panentheism in a positive way. And I did wonder about the relation of what you call "mystical panentheism" to anatheism, which I suspect may be closer to "process panentheism," in the ethical force of its affirmation of liberation and justice, though it does render Beauty irreducible to morality. There is not a huge emphasis on apophatic unknowability in Whitehead—though he understands all metaphysical first principles as "metaphors mutely appealing for an imaginative leap." But process theology has been creatively kataphatic. It put lots of positive alternative God talk to work against traditional theism and its patriarchies, its theodicies. I see my current work on the mystical as being, in that regard, in a bit of critical tension with both process and liberation theology.

RK: Yet you ultimately want to preserve a chiasmic connection between apophatic and liberation theologies.

CK: Oh yes, my apophatic approach is basically in sync with the insistent relationality of liberation and of process theology, but I affirm its *theos* more lightly, more darkly.

RK: So your concern is to deepen and complicate the kataphatic affirmations of liberty, justice, and equality (which you clearly espouse) by exposing them to the iconoclastic and entangling energies of the nimbus? You want apophasis to keep kataphasis in check. And so you are rightly wary, it seems to me, of any attempt to fetishize the Good—observing the cautionary maxim "Perfection is the enemy of the good."

CK: Yes, all the internal contestations, intersections, and multiplications of good movements complicate where good ends and evil begins, where justice and injustice converge and diverge. What I call the "apophatic supplement" is a way of keeping the religious commitment to ecosocial justice going, alive, open, because otherwise it can become noncredible to a critical mass of intellectuals and teachers, overly pastoral and instrumental, or mired in identitarian rivalries.

RK: So it is a question of apophatic reserve keeping God decent, so to speak; keeping the divine free from closures and dogmas.

CK: Yes. Well, lovable if not always decent! And this is where I return to the reading of the infinite as *in fini*—that is, nonfinished, ever unfolding, refusing premature ontologies, ideologies, certainties.

RK: This reminds me of Levinas's idea of the infinite as in-the-finite—God as trace and passage through the face of the human other. Though I think we would agree that he takes the Platonic route to vertical transcendence and height too quickly, pushing toward an extreme of absolute exteriority and separation.

CK: I first got the idea of *in fini* from Luce Irigaray, who was both close to and critical of Levinas. This also raises the question of the crucial movement from Platonism to the Neoplatonic infinite. Before this, the boundless, the *apeiron*, had been too akin to formlessness to be conceived as divine. Gregory of Nyssa wraps it into the dark cloud of God at Sinai; and the journey of the soul to the infinite becomes itself an infinite unfolding, the *epektasis*.

RK: It seems to me your *in fini* seeks to avoid two kinds of closure: on one hand, the apophasis of too much non-knowing, to the point of silence and paralysis; on the other, an equal if opposite extreme of kataphasis, risking too much affirmation and appropriation. I associate the former with dogmatic atheism and the latter with dogmatic theism. And so anatheism, as I understand it, is an attempt to invite a dialogical space between open theists and open atheists. And the conversations in which we are involved in this volume are, I would hope, also unfolding in such a space.

CK: I, too, see the anatheist option as a third space between polarized positions: on the one hand, "This is it!"; on the other hand, "It's all a mystery!" And I see it as in line with the Cusan legacy of *coincidentia oppositorum* as a way of co-implicating such extremes into a chiasmic fold.

GOD AS METAPHOR

RK: I would like to return to the question of metaphor. I think we both agree that theology involves a metaphorics of God, which is not just about *metaphors* of God but metaphors of *God*. It is both a subjective and objective genitive. In other words, it is not a matter of the divine dissolving into metaphor but of metaphor carrying us over (*meta-pherein*) to something else, something other, something beyond our present consciousness. Not, I suggest, to the beyond of some metaphysical Absolute that absolves itself from relation (Levinas), or which totally overwhelms and saturates us (Marion), but a carrying over that is a creative saying, unsaying, and resaying between an I and Thou (Buber). And, in this respect, I do like the way you invoke the later Derrida's attempt to reinscribe alterity within relationality, no matter how impossible, with the notion of the "possible beyond the impossible"—a notion drawn from Cusa and Silesius.

CK: And also very inspired by your own work on *posse* in *Poétique du possible* and *The God Who May Be*, as Derrida acknowledges in his "Perhaps" essay and elsewhere.

RK: I confess I was flattered by Derrida's references to my work, but I think you take the notion of the "perhaps" to new places in *Cloud*. As does our good friend Jack Caputo, in *The Insistence of God*. You take the *posse* into dynamic relation not only with the mystical but also with the manifolds of immanence, matter, and nature, including the debate with quantum physics. That is really a brave new world for the possible, and I admire your daring. Agamben makes a distinction between two kinds of contemporary philosophy—one of radical alterity (following Levinas and Derrida) and the other of radical immanence (following Deleuze and Foucault). I think you find a middle way. And it is one I share.

CK: Maybe in that shared medium we could also make a distinction between internal and external relatedness. What Deleuze takes from Whitehead is a notion of the mutual constitution of things. Relations are not set up between separate entities that preexist each other as distinct substances but come to be in the rhizomes and networks of interlinked events. Deleuze develops this idea particularly in *Le pli* (*The Fold*), his book on Leibniz, with a climactic chapter on Whitehead, arguing that with Whitehead we can get free of Leibniz's determinism while retaining the notion of microcosm—in the event of each creature. He uses Whitehead to prize Leibniz open.

RK: How influenced by Cusa was Deleuze?

CK: There are no major acknowledgments. Cusa was a Catholic cardinal, remember. And Deleuze is French!

RK: Though he does cite and celebrate another Christian philosopher, Duns Scotus, particularly in his *Logic of Difference*.

CK: Well, Scotus was just a simple Franciscan friar. Deleuze does mention Cusa more fully and warmly in his book on expressionism, where he offers a fascinating history of Neoplatonism. He draws his Cusa through his reading of Bruno's folds.

RK: Joyce also got his Cusa through Bruno, incidentally, and makes great play of the fact that one of Dublin's main bookshops was called Brown and Nolan, which chimes with "Bruno of Nola." Joyce cites Bruno as exponent of the whole interconnectivity of things—the "chaosmos of Alle," the "circumbendibus" of "intermisunderstanding minds." *Finnegans Wake* is brimming with *coincidentia oppositorum*—so central to Joyce's profane take on the *Divine Comedy*, what he called his "jocoserious" poetics. I try to talk a bit about this in my "Sacramental Imagination" chapter in *Anatheism*. And I am delighted to see you citing *Finnegans Wake* in an epigraph to your Cusa chapter.

CK: "I am not hereby giving my final endorsement to the learned ignorants of the Cusanus philosophism."

RK: I would enjoy cross-reading your *Cloud* with *Finnegans Wake*—there are so many reverberations. And I am also delighted to see you developing your theological poetics in your reading of Walt Whitman.

CK: Whitman is all folds! And of course there is the conflation of the cosmic self with the personal self—"I, Walt Whitman, a kosmos"—which many readers misread as narcissism. But then: "For every atom belonging to me as good belongs to you."

RK: American transcendentalism gone mad. But I am not being fair to Whitman. There is a genuine theopoetic mysticism at work, isn't there?

CK: Yes, the opposite of megalomania. It is mystical co-implication par excellence—"Whoever degrades another degrades me." So the power of the I as cosmos is simultaneously the entire cosmic order—atoms or other others—in a constant circulation. I confess I did not originally intend to have a chapter on Whitman, but it forced its way in, perhaps in a way similar to how Hopkins, Joyce, and Proust seem to compel themselves upon your anatheist theopoetics. I also needed some poetic relief from my Cusa–Deleuze–Whitehead portion. At the end I deal with theopoetics more directly, and find many resonances with your own approach—as you demonstrate how to philosophize while keeping poetry in play.

RK: I think the work of theopoetics has become more and more central for both of us.

CK: I have been intrigued by the ancient *theopoiesis*, which was contracted as *theoisis*, the making divine of the human, the becoming god, god making. Even Athanasius recognized the call to become divine: "God became human so that the human could become God." Theopoiesis as making-divine recognizes a certain cocreativity between the human and divine. But the term was too risky and was quickly laid aside, and perhaps has needed to await the poets to come back again—as in Whitman.

I was also recalling your treatment of the *dieu capable* as a mutual capacitating of the divine and human; *deus capax* as a God who capabilizes the human to become divine. This radical idea was already present in *The God Who May Be*, becoming more explicit in *Anatheism*. So my question to you here is this: How does one claim such theopoiesis of the self without immediately washing the self out? You avoid letting theopoetics become megalomania—a mystical narcissism of self-inflation—by quickly moving toward kenosis and self-emptying. But I think it is important not to move there *too* quickly. Is it not necessary to fully acknowledge a strong moment of capax, of *dunamis* of poetic selfhood—as human-divine selving—before abdicating any subject?

Perhaps it is an old feminist concern: having spent centuries trying to escape subservience, subordination, and self-sacrifice in order to be able to become empowered subjects—"our bodies, ourselves"—shall we immediately let it all go? Kenosis can fall differently on the ears of men and women, though there is a wonderful feminist rendition of kenosis by Anna Mercedes, as a self-giving that does not disempower or overpower, *Power For*. I wonder if the Church actually didn't become more arrogant—not less—when it jettisoned the notion of theopoiesis?

RK: Why more arrogant?

CK: Because historically the disappearance of theopoiesis corresponded to the rise of the Church Triumphant—the centralization of power coinciding with the disempowering of the capacity of each ordinary believer for divinity.

RK: Was it because ecclesiastical hierarchy opposed the liberation of everyone into their potential divinity and wanted to keep believers obedient, as in "The Grand Inquisitor"?

CK: Yes, theopoiesis has a dangerously democratic potential. It emancipates persons and threatens powers.

RK: I am reminded, to shift gears slightly, of how psychoanalysis speaks of the child having an initial primary narcissism that is healthy. Every little boy wants to be a king and every little girl a queen. And why not? This is good unless it goes unchecked by a later limitation, which for Freud and Lacan coincides with the No (*non/nom*) of the father; namely, the cut or limit of symbolic castration as one enters the social-symbolic order of language, moving beyond the fused imaginary (or at least enfolding it into a complex Borromean knot with the real and symbolic). Put in terms of the possible/impossible chiasmus we have been discussing, we might say that the *posse* possibilizes each child from the outset. Even Cusa speaks of the child saying "I can run," "I can eat," "I can play," and compares divine *posse* (the power to be able to be) to a child's shout in the street. An echo perhaps of Joyce's "What's God? A shout in the street"? And this initial childlike capacity also finds poetic voice in Nietzsche's child in *Thus Spoke Zarathustra*, and Beckett's little boy at the close of *Endgame*. It is a very prevalent theme in poetic and mystical writings. The child of rebirth who returns after loss and suffering, in a sort of ana- moment of "back, again, anew." So there is a first child of omnipossibility and a second child of what we might call "ultra-possibility" that comes back after the cut, the loss, the mourning of the lost object, the kenosis. And the second child of *posse* is, I would argue, the possible beyond the impossible, the child of Isaiah who plays with the cobra.

CK: Left to itself, the *posse* of self can go megalomaniac, but once in relation—mindfully—everything changes.

RK: Exactly. And relation is pivotal here. In terms of the becoming-divine movement of theoisis, I would insist that our capacity for divinity comes not from the ego but from the stranger. The stranger is the *deus capax* who calls on each one of us to become deus capax in turn for the next stranger. At least in that sacred moment of radical opening and hosting. We learn divinity from the other, not from ourselves, not alone but always in relation, in response to the *hospes* in front of us: the one who calls each of us to divinity by asking us to become the host to it as guest, to become a giver of gifts, of food and water. As with Abraham and the strangers under the Mamre tree—the inaugural epiphany of the Abrahamic tradition. Or as, again, with Matthew 25, where Christ returns five times as the stranger (*hospes*) who *asks* for food and water. In this passage, Christ is not first the one who gives food and water, as one might expect; he is the one who calls *us* to give food and water, and in so doing to become Christ as giver of life, as ongoing host. The messiah—who as Benjamin argues can enter the portal of each moment if we open to its knock—is every stranger who calls us to become givers of food and life. Hence the crucial messianic role played by Samaritan and Phoenician strangers in the Gospels. The Phoenician woman teaches Jesus to become divine (*theoisis*) by asking him for the crumbs he feeds to dogs but is, at first, refusing to her, an outsider. And when Jesus responds to her summons, he becomes divine (again). Thanks to the foreign woman, he rediscovers his messianic call. And the woman's child is healed. Just as the centurion's (another foreigner's) servant is healed.

The scenes of healing and rebirth are prefigured by the respective annunciation scenes—of Sarah at Mamre and Mary at Nazareth—where a child is conceived at the visitation of strangers, visitors who give life to an "impossible" child—namely, Isaac and Jesus. What is impossible (*adunaton*) to the human is possible (*dunaton*) to God, as the angel tells Mary in Luke—in the very same Greek words that had been used in the Septuagint (which Luke read) to describe Sarah's conception of Isaac! It is remarkable re-citation. In both these cases, the impossible becomes possible at the moment of responding to the stranger's call. Sarah and Mary are thus, I believe, exemplary figures of theopoiesis. As is Jesus himself, when he responds repeatedly to the calls of strangers, right up to his death, and once more, after his death, when he is reborn as a stranger on the road to Emmaus, and on the shores of Galilee, unrecognized by his disciples until he asks and gives food, until he breaks bread, until he touches and is touched as *hospes*.

> CK: I like that image of Jesus becoming divine in rising to the Phoenician woman's challenge: "Give me the crumbs you give the dogs."
>
> RK: Yes, it is deeply radical. She is the stranger who calls Jesus to divinity as he is tempted to remain closed in on his own group, huddled around a table, refusing to share food or healing, even what they give to the animals lying at their feet. And when Jesus does heed her call and learns from her—the divine care for the widow and stranger—the Phoenician woman's child is healed, reborn, the impossible becomes possible. Strict dichotomies of inside and outside, pure and impure, male and female, family and stranger, us and them, are dramatically transgressed. Exclusivism is blown apart. Christ, as messianic apprentice to the Phoenician stranger, becomes more divine as he explodes the shackles of Christocentric tribalism.
>
> CK: What is the significance of the child?
>
> RK: Jesus is, in a sense, reborn through the gift of healing, in bringing the Phoenician woman's child back to life. It is a second baptism of sorts: rebirth into second life, more life. And I strongly believe that, in addition to baptism by water, fire, and desire (recognized in the Catholic catechism), we should also recognize baptism by the stranger—in fact as the primary sacrament of baptism! Theopoiesis can thus be read as the other/stranger/guest making each one of us divine by enabling us to become givers of life rather than death, to become divine in the act of hospitality and

healing, leaving behind our tribal gods. (The Phoenician has to open herself to Jesus even as she invites Jesus to open himself to her. It works both ways). I repeat: Jesus grows in his divinity, and bids us do likewise, by learning from Samaritans and Syrians—in this instance, the Syrio-Phoenician woman, who represents the "other" of class, race, gender, and religion par excellence. She is treated (at first) as less than a dog! The startling thing is that it is the stranger who teaches the Messiah that he has forgotten his messianic mission; that is, his divine capacity for giving, feeding, hosting, birthing, healing strangers—for bringing new life, again and again. Ana-.

CK: Could you say something more about how this relates to Levinas's ethics of the stranger?

RK: I agree with Levinas's ethics when he speaks of the "humanism of the other." In other words, humanism is not only about my rights but also and primarily about the "other's" rights, even when we—quite correctly—universalize and equalize rights in a politics of justice (what Levinas calls the introduction of the "third," approximating, for example, the Enlightenment morality inscribed in the French Declaration of the Rights of Man). Ethics is first and foremost a matter of religious responsibility for the singular stranger, preceding a universal politics of fraternity and citizenship where we are all (rightly) one and the same. One recalls the maxim of Dostoyevsky's Father Zosima, often cited by Levinas: "Everybody is responsible for everybody else, but I am *more* responsible for everybody else than anybody else."

But where I leave Levinas and rejoin you is on the question of relation, so central to both our thinking. You call it entanglement, I call it hospitality; both are categories of chiasmic crossing. For Levinas, the ethical rapport with the Other is a "relation *without* relation"—an encounter without dialogue or reciprocity. It is a teaching from above rather than a touching from below. (I address this in *Carnal Hermeneutics*.) In Levinasian ethics we have a voice from a distance rather than a hand across a distance. This distinction is important, and I think both my carnal hermeneutics of mediation (*metaxu*) and your ontology of the fold challenge Levinas's asymmetry in this regard. And curiously we both use the metaphor of "membrane" for this primacy of chiasmic mediation—which is not a regress to Hegelian synthesis but a radical affirmation of connection.

> CK: Yes, in Levinas exteriority trumps relationality. Creation, understood as separation, disqualifies creation understood as co-implication. And I suggest in *Cloud* that Marion's Absolute is also too much of an ab-solution from relation and entanglement. It demands a one-way saturation by the Other, rather than a multilateral enfolding and unfolding. Pure surrender without agency.
>
> RK: I, too, have difficulty with extreme forms of "heterology"—whether it be Levinas, Marion, Derrida, or even our mutual friend Jack Caputo—where the *tout autre* (the Other beyond being) comes to us from outside as rupture, irruption, invasion, persecution, obsession, interlocution, trouble, even violence, though I think Jack (Caputo) seems to be softening the trauma of deconstructive violence in his renewed emphasis on hospitality and possibility in *The Insistence of God*. My question to my deconstructionist friends has always been this: How do we build a politics of practice from all this? How do we *do* the good, justice, hospitality? What is to be done? And here I think Cusa has stood as something of a salutary corrective for all of us—tying apophatic theology to a politics of community (in his case a radical ecumenism well before its time) in a genial "coincidence of opposites."
>
> CK: Cusa was a speculative mystic and a church leader. A rare combination, then or now. The negative theology becomes the key to the affirmation of diversity—if even a Catholic cardinal does not *know* God, the truth of every other religion cannot be ruled out.
>
> RK: Relational connection rather than absolute knowledge. I think we are in constant need of bridges, liaisons, crossovers. We need stories and histories—hermeneutic mediations that go all the way up to God (as Other par excellence) and all the way down to subatomic physics (as you suggest in *The Cloud*). Mediations between clouds and crowds. The problem with deconstruction is that it is a messianicity without Messiahs. It risks becoming

purely structural and formal, without recourse to biblical or Gospel narratives, Hassidic or kabbalistic tales (where is Buber, Scholem, Heschel?), without Sufi lore or mystical poetics. Not to mention, as we open the Abrahamic traditions to Eastern religions, the holy stories of the Buddha and the Gitas (the Bhagavad Gita, the Gita Govinda, etcetera). And, more recently, the testimonies of ordinary holy people in their struggle for love and justice. In *Anatheism* I invoke continuous narrative revelations going from Abraham and Moses to Jesus and the lives of the saints, upper and lowercase: Teresa, Eckhart, Francis, Etty Hillesum, Dorothy Day, Jean Vanier, and millions of unsung holy ones.

CK: The cloud has a great crowd of witnesses, *à l'infini*!

RK: Yes, witnesses without end. And that is my difficulty with deconstruction, at times. As a pure messianicity without singular witnesses, testimonies, icons, epiphanies, and liturgies, it risks becoming abstract and isolationist. Derrida's apophatic deconstruction cries out for the kinds of mediating entanglements and engagements you provide, with materiality, with physics, and various concrete historical examples—Elizabeth Johnson on Mother Sophia, Ivone Gebara on nature and liberation, Thurman's journey to Gandhi, Whitman's passions. You are constantly citing histories and historicities that bring the apophatic cloud into living connection with the earth.

CK: I am particularly glad that I enthroned Elizabeth Johnson in my first chapter, given the most recent inquisitorial assault from the Vatican's Congregation for the Doctrine of the Faith. Her ecofeminist theology has always drawn strength from the apophatic tradition. These stories do all illustrate an ongoing struggle of enfolding and unfolding, a messy messianic journey with lots of pastoral and human complications. The task is to find a balance between these liberationist engagements in the history and politics of the Church and the contemplative unknowing. And I am wondering if your own anatheist chaosmos doesn't epitomize a certain yin and yang between what you call an internal journey into the mystical and the movement out into right action and ethico-political commitment, a creative equilibrium between negative capability and positive capability.

You locate this interflow particularly—anatheistically—in the stranger. The stranger as manifestation of the apophatic other who always remains somewhat opaque and unknowable, no matter how much one engages in relation. Some nimbus of residual, irreducible mystery hangs about the stranger. And this chiasmus between mystery and ethics—the *vita contemplativa* and *vita activa*—seems powerful to me. It does come close to the structural chiasmus in *Cloud*, between apophatic reserve and affirmative relation. But a difference would be that I work with a language of ontological connectivity (right down to the quantum level of cells), whereas you come more from the language of otherness and strangeness (though I sense a softening of alterity in the transition from *The God Who May Be* to *Anatheism*). In *Anatheism*, the absolute gains a greater fluency and plasticity—and relationality. And nowhere more so than in your treatment of the sacramental ontology of "flesh"—especially in your reading of sacred embodiment in Merleau-Ponty and Kristeva—and in your favorite examples of "sacramental imagination": Joyce, Woolf, and Proust.

RK: Yes, I feel an increasing affinity with your ontological relationalism. In the conclusion to *The God Who May Be*, I tried to sketch out what I called an onto-eschatology of everyday epiphany. I wanted to break with the polarity between a messianic eschatology of the Other and an immanentist ontology of the Self, a dualism which often expressed itself in a ruinous dichotomy between text and flesh, between *l'écriture* and *la chair*. So my concern is to bring the Other always-to-come (*deus adventurus*) into liaison with a phenomenology of the here and now (*Hoc est enim corpus meum*). A realized eschatology, if you like, according to the ana-time of "back, again, anew." And that means bringing textuality back in touch with carnality—something I am pursuing in my current project of carnal hermeneutics.

In this regard, we might speak of a threefold ontology of relation. First, the "natural" attitude of relating to others in terms of a first naïveté (including prejudices, certainties, projections). Second, the "negative capability" of suspending and dissolving this natural appropriation of the other into a "cloud of unknowing" (Julian of Norwich, Cusa's *docta ignorantia*, Husserl's *epoché*, your own embrace of apophasis). Third, the ana-retrieval of relationship as a free enfolding-unfolding (Ricoeur's second naïveté, Buber's I–Thou, your notion of entanglement). It is at this third level, I reckon, that we can talk also of *posse* as a second possible beyond the impossible, a divine possibilizing beyond egological potency and power, a God beyond theodicy.

> CK: At this third level of relationality, coming is *becoming*, right? This is something forbidden by the anti-ontologists. They do not perceive the possibilities already here—they wait for some pure outside to break in. Coming versus becoming. As though, otherwise, we only repeat the same. But what if the possible beyond the impossible can only break open from within? Of course, that "within" is entangled in the whole fragile web of the world. Perhaps this is a more messy and redemptive view of the world itself. The other does not collapse into the same but comes differentiated into multiple folds, the stranger no longer an alien ego but another as self, another self.
>
> RK: Or, as Ricoeur puts it, "oneself as another." Yes. And also recovered in this new order of relational becoming is Eros—to come back to your opening point—as one can only desire what is other than yourself through a glass darkly, "*in aenigmate*" as Cusa says, never as pure mirror image or imago. The theopoetic relation with the divine stranger becomes theoerotic. In this manner, "becoming" keeps the gap in the relation, refusing fetishism and fixation. It allows the Other to be released from the box of alter ego (the first, "natural" attitude) into the guest—the traveler, visitor, refugee, émigré, nomad, *homo viator*. The Other as guest can be welcomed into one's host language and community, without ever being reduced to the same—for a guest who becomes identical with the host ceases to be a guest, and that is the end of hospitality. As Walter Benjamin observed, true hospitality respects an "untranslatable kernel" between host and guest.
>
> CK: And it lets us translate that untranslatability from external relations into a language of entangled difference. Then the gap, or

even the abyss, hosts the becoming—at least in the hospitality of the cloud.

Speaking of the need for mediations and relations, Hegel was one of the first to appreciate the "becoming" of God. That meaning of the *in fini*—the divine itself unfinished—is insinuated in the *explicatio* but never made explicit.

RK: We could probably speak here of an ana-Hegelian retrieval, which would include a reappreciation of God's becoming by such thinkers as Schelling, Boehme, and the Rhine mystics, going back to Cusa, Silesius, Hildegard, and Eckhart. The hermeneutic recovery of this mystical genealogy of the forgotten God could include a recovery of the body of God—the carnal aspect of mystical becoming, Eros as well as agape, as we witness it so powerfully in Teresa of Avila and the Beguines.

CK: Yes, desire and compassion both express that carnality, that incarnationality. The *complicatio* suggests also the folds of a female body. In *Cloud*, I echo Sallie McFague's ecofeminist body of God and Ivone Gebara's "sacred body," her incorporation of indigenous cosmology. Attention to quantum microbodies is also disclosive. As is, needless to say, Cusa's notion of the maximum incarnate in each minimal body. In the "Love" chapter of *Cloud*, I stress how Neoplatonic apophasis needs to be supplemented by a return to the materiality, the unbounded embodiment, of God.

RK: I think your engagement with physics is extremely salutary—and one neglected by so many of us working in the continental philosophy of religion. I recall Ricoeur saying, on his sixtieth birthday, in Naples, that one of the big tasks of phenomenology and hermeneutics (he might have added deconstruction) in the twenty-first century would be the dialogue with physics. But you are one of the first to seriously take up this challenge.

CK: Some kind of physics infects any process thinker (as the late Ricoeur well knew). While still at graduate school I read a book by David Bohm—until recently deemed a heretic among physicists—called *Wholeness and the Implicate Order*, which sprang to mind again when I started reading Cusa. Bohm had tried to make sense of the wave–particle relation in the quantum universe with the very metaphors of enfolding/unfolding, implicate/explicate order that I found in Cusa.

RK: Did Bohm know Cusa? Did he refer to him in his writing?

CK: Fleetingly, in an interview. The implicate order is the enfolding of the subtle energy of the waves forming the nonlocal relations of what is now called the quantum field or vacuum. The explicate is something like the Cartesian order of things, unfolded and distinct. Bohm was trying to bridge the gap between quantum physics and philosophical reflection. In the fifties he was a student of Oppenheimer and then a junior colleague of Einstein's. He refused to testify against Oppenheimer before the House Un-American Activities Committee, then was fired at Princeton and fled the country. The extraordinary coincidence of metaphors between Cusa and Bohm prompted me to delve into the affinity between the physics of nonlocality, or entanglement, and the apophatic relationalism I was theologically imagining.

From a divergent vector, Karen Barad's theorization of entanglement as ontological relationalism confirms this direction. (We recently had her to a conference at Drew on religion, science, and the new materialism.) Barad interprets Niels Bohr's quantum theory to stress what she calls the "intra-activity of becoming." For her, the mutual responsiveness of material beings goes all the way down to the quanta. And for her it is all about ethics. The becoming of the world, she claims, is a deeply ethical matter.

RK: At one point you mention the indigenous phrase "mind your relations." I gather it comes from Thomas King's novel *Green Grass, Running Water*. How does this notion of relationality tie in with the notions you draw from apophatic mysticism and physics?

CK: King's novel is a delightful satire on the effects of Christian supremacism on the world. It is witty and mythic in its retrieval of the delicately tuned relationality of the web of life. Such First Nations wisdom is not considered part of the dialogue of the great world religions and is often just dismissed as New Age fantasy.

RK: Which is terribly wrong, almost a second lobotomy—this time an intellectual exclusion, following the original genocide of the indigenous peoples. I was very struck when I read the phrase in your book, as I attended a native sweat lodge ceremony with my brother, Michael, in Santa Barbara recently, where the recurring invocation was "All my relations." This referred to a whole web of interconnected communities, from those actually present in the lodge (many bringing their pain and testimony, like an AA meeting), to one's own family relations and friends, and then to all the ancestors who preceded one and all those who would come after one in the future. "All my relations" is a widening circle of connectivity extending back and forward in time and space, going right back to the first living things, the original elements of earth (in the ceremony lava stones are placed at the center of the mud-and-hide cabin), fire (the stones are heated for days in wood fires), water (buckets poured over the red-hot stones in clouds of steam), and air (the inhaling of the vapors and expiring of breath/perspiring of sweat). It is an extraordinary liturgy of death and rebirth through the four elements, in four unfolding movements corresponding to the four directions of the sun. The age-old ceremony was conducted by native elders and open to people of all religions—Christian, Jewish, Buddhist—as well as atheist seekers. And it was free, like the four material elements themselves (our oldest relations), which it spiritually celebrated.

CK: Those lava stones sound like ancient bodies of the earth coming to life. We need to discover ways to talk about these elemental vibrancies. The silence of genocide and suspicion of New Ageism makes for a double taboo that needs to be challenged. And this silence is facilitated by the fact that such indigenous traditions are not reducible to a single systematic body of religion that can be neatly kept private and separate from the secular sphere. Because they do not represent a separable totality, they are often silently excluded from the dialogue of world religions, being relegated to anthropology or ethnology—"peoples to be studied" or "objects of inquiry."

RK: Or archetypal symbols of depth psychology.

CK: Right. And Jung, too, is taboo in academia. It is easy to dismiss the archetypes as Neoplatonic universals and disembodied abstractions. But they do try to articulate the intuition of a collective unconscious, ways in which we are all entangled—not just humans—in relations going all the way down . . .

RK: Through animality and terrestriality, entanglements that we still carry deep inside. We seem to accept this idea in genetics and epigenetics but have problems admitting it into the discourse of philosophy and theology. Though perhaps Buddhist karma is a way of articulating some of this in more Eastern religious terms—how we are all interconnected in what Thích Nhất Hạnh calls "interbeing."

CK: Do you know there is a historical link between entanglement and synchronicity? It goes back to Wolfgang Pauli, a young German physicist who worked with Einstein, Bohr, and Heisenberg and lost it at one point (family suicide, marriage breakup, alcoholism). So he went to Jung for help. Jung realized what he had on his hands, and while he passed him over to one of his colleagues for therapy, he continued a dialogue with him over the years, during which they fine-tuned the notion of synchronicity—a noncausal connecting principle—which is really a translation of the quantum theory of entanglement. I have a footnote on this in my book. More would expose my reading of physics to charges of New Ageism.

RK: Keller the crazy mystic who hangs out with Native Americans and Jungian mystics. Keller the witch!

CK: I'm flattered.

RK: But you are safe. You do so much hard-core scholarly analysis in your theology and physics chapters, you earn the right to slip in some mystical poetics from time to time. But it is sad that in today's academia there are so many no-go areas for serious discussion. Think of all we miss out on by dismissing these things.

CK: Well, *you* don't. In *Anatheism* you do manage to provide a dynamic matrix where different religious narratives (Abrahamic and Eastern) crisscross with philosophy, poetics, and politics. I read your work as a hub of hospitality between a series of overlapping axes, as mentioned at the outset. Our chiasmic crossings are akin, but I don't get around to the other religions as you do and see your work as supplementing mine in that regard. I had to forego certain connections for fear of being too promiscuous and spreading myself too thin.

RK: And, for my part, I feel your work on quantum physics and apophatic theology supplements my writing in all sorts of ways, pursuing directions I could only hint at. One can only do so much, and given our shared commitment to the folds of connectivity, the temptation is to open every door. Sometimes, intellectual hospitality means knowing which doors to open and which to keep closed. So that certain possibles are actualized, but not all, or at least not all at once. We are not Thomists in search of summae. Or Hegelians in search of encyclopedias. Those days are gone. There is a dark lining to every silver one. Inevitable limit and lack. Negation as well as affirmation. It is a delicate balance.

CK: Delicate. . . . Impossible, really. If the balance holds, it is betrayed, the affirmations run to positivism, the *via negativa* is cut off at the pass by the *via eminentia* and loses the force of its questions, the negations leer nihilistically back. But perhaps this hospitality that you offer anatheistically, that I find in the cloud of this very impossibility, does depend upon those self-limitations. We cut between possibles or we have nothing to offer, to actualize; we perform our finitude, yet we don't escape the entangling infinitude. From another perspective close to you, it appears as *chora*—the space of events, not a void between them. Roomy, womby, but dangerously indeterminate. Like the *tehom* that had preoccupied me in *Face of the Deep*, the not-thing that is not nothing, the biblical chaos of creation. In a kind of atmospheric circulation, the oceanic currents form the clouds. It won't give us directions. It lets us find them.

RK: I am glad you return to chora here. For that was, as I recall, where we began our first conversation many years ago. God and chora. Chora as the between—the "space of events"—which links the *tehom* of creation to the womb of Mary, and to Sarah before her, and many after her. Chora is the place of theopoiesis, where the divine becomes human and vice versa—as in the Greek inscription under the murals of the Madonna with child in the early Christian temples: *chora achoraton*, "container of the uncontainable." This is the site where the impossible becomes possible. As in the chalice-womb at the heart of Rublev's *perichoresis* icon, the female matrix at the center of the Trinity—without which it could never be, nor be kept in motion forever. Here we encounter a fourth dimension—before, between, and after the three. Ana-time and ana-space. Carnal precondition of the sacred. A cloud, if you will, where Word meets flesh and life begins over and over. Or one could also imagine it as a finite cave chamber where the sacred visits, happens, creates, procreates, recreates à l'infini. Chora as *in fini*. Where fear becomes love. Where "Do not be afraid" becomes "yes I will yes." The implications of this chora for a new feminism and new humanism—being worked out by thinkers like you, Irigaray, and Kristeva—are, it seems to me, hugely important.

4

Transcendent Humanism
in a Secular Age

Dialogue with Charles Taylor

The Canadian philosopher Charles Taylor, one of the finest intellectual commentators on Western culture and religion, has written widely on political philosophy, theories of social science, and the history of philosophy. He is best known for his narrative account of modernity's cultural origins and potential futures in *Sources of the Self: The Making of Modern Identity* (1989), and, most recently, *A Secular Age* (2007). Especially in the last book, Taylor has shown that modernity's rejection of religion is itself based on an assumed logic of history, or what he calls a "subtraction narrative"—the story that human progress in any culture necessarily involves the liberation from religion. Instead, Taylor suggests that religion has never left and is here to stay, but that religion itself needs to argue its claims within an "immanent frame," a modern, pluralistic, and disenchanted universe in which we can no longer simply appeal to the divine or transcendence but must argue for them. This arguing includes the recovery of traditional religious resources for our present modern problems.

Thus, like Kearney, Taylor is deeply committed to a hermeneutic understanding of secular and religious truths, acknowledging that human insights are conditioned by our history and language while maintaining a philosophical realism. As Taylor states clearly, the hermeneutic recovery of religious sources for human flourishing connects his own vision for peaceful coexistence of religious and secular citizens with Kearney's anatheism. Both thinkers can agree on the need for a "transcendent humanism" as a liberating alternative to exclusive, secularist humanism, on the one hand, and religious dogmatism, on the other.

This conversation took place in the host's home in Boston, in October 2013.

RICHARD KEARNEY (RK): In your conclusions to *A Secular Age* you mention two alternative scenarios. One is the continuation of the dominant narrative of exclusive secular humanism; the other is a new Christian humanism open to the transcendent—an attempt to "believe again." The first kind of humanism confines us to what you call the "immanent frame" of the modern moral order, ushered in by the Reformation and related revolutions in science and society. The second, more Christian humanism remains attentive to the quest for spiritual and religious "fullness." You recognize much of the former as positive and necessary, but you also want to add the second option. But why, some might ask, is atheistic humanism not enough? Why is a Christian or transcendent humanism so important for you, especially as a "believing again"?

CHARLES TAYLOR (CT): Well, I wish I had known of your term *anatheism* when I wrote my book. It would have fitted very well my idea of believing again—taken originally from W. H. Auden, as you know—after we have let go of our dogmatic certainties. There are different brands of dogmatism, as you point out in your book—atheist and theist. But let me try to respond to your basic question about humanism.

First, we need to distinguish between two kinds of secular humanism. One, which rules out any "beyond," is a kind of reductive materialism that recognizes no source of value beyond the immanent frame. Then there is another kind, which does acknowledge something else, some aspiration for something more, some "meaning of meaning," as the contemporary French thinker Luc Ferry puts it. But its notion of this surplus—for all its resistance to a general "flattening down" and unlearning of the great wisdom traditions—remains intramundane.

I think there are a number of frontiers separating both forms of secular humanism—open and closed—from a transcendent or Christian humanism. First, there is the basic notion of death (the most explicit divide); and then there is also some notion of a far-reaching transformation of human life—the kind that we find in the Christian understanding of agape or the Buddhist idea of nirvana and *anatman* (no self). Here, the notion of death goes beyond the normal secular understanding. It breaks out of the immanent frame and looks beyond.

RK: This kind of life transformation seems close to what you are describing in the final chapter of *A Secular Age*, entitled "Conversions." You cite the exemplary narrative "itineraries" of poets like Charles Péguy and Gerard Manley Hopkins. But some might ask—as they have asked me, in relation to my discussion of humanism at the end of *Anatheism*—why does the transformation of life require faith? What is wrong with the deep humanism of atheists like Camus or the brave pioneers of Médicins sans Frontières? Simone Weil raises a similar question in *Letter to a Priest*, when she writes that "All those who possess in its pure state the love of their neighbor and the acceptance of the order of the world, including affliction, . . . even should they live and die . . . atheists, are surely saved." And she goes on to cite the example of Matthew 25, when Christ does not save all those who say, "Lord, Lord" (that is, go through the motions of faith and observance) but rather those who give bread and water to a starving man, "without thinking of Him [God] the least little bit."[1] They do not even know they have given to Christ. In this sense they remain a-theist, or at least agnostic, in that they do the good even though they do not profess a theistic or confessional belief. Weil ventures the bold conclusion that whoever is capable of a movement of pure compassion towards a person in affliction possesses, maybe implicitly, yet always really, the love of God and faith. So an atheist or an "infidel" capable of pure compassion are, in her view, as close to God as is a Christian,

and consequently know him equally well, though their knowledge is expressed in other words, or remains unspoken.[2]

This perhaps comes close to Karl Rahner's idea of "anonymous Christians," but I think it is more radical still. It seems to me to be saying that
divine love is equally present in people of other religions—or of no religion at all—who practice compassion towards their neighbor. Hence
Weil's desire—one that I very much endorse in *Anatheism*—to see how
so-called pagan traditions like Hinduism and Buddhism are also bearers
of salvation. In *Anatheism* I call this basic bottom line of spiritual humanism, "hospitality" or "hosting the stranger" (*hospes*), loving the enemy
(*hospes*) as a guest (*hospes*). I find it extremely telling that the same word in
Latin, *hospes* (or *xenos*, in Greek), is used in both senses; and indeed, this
same term is repeated five times in Matthew 25 to identify Christ with the
outsider many of us ignore or reject. The stranger, therefore, appears as the
transcendent other insofar as he/she transcends our grasp, our possession,
our prejudice. As if claiming to know Christ is already not to know him
but only our idea of him as "Lord, Lord." I suspect that your reading of
Ivan Illich's take on the Good Samaritan, in *A Secular Age*, is moving in a
similar direction?

> CT: I share many of your anatheist sentiments here, Richard. This
> transcendent humanism that recognizes that there is something
> more is only possible, I believe, because there is already grace
> at work. Many extraordinary humanists, no matter how open,
> may reject the idea of a transcendent grace. Albert Camus is an
> example. And I respect that. But if one does accept grace, then I
> think one needs and wants to get closer to it through prayer and
> a certain faith practice (for me, personally, that is some form of
> Christian Catholic practice). But to say this is not to say, "We
> have the truth and you are all in outer darkness." Not at all.
> Salvation can exist outside the Church. And I think one of the
> good things about our modern age is that, after Vatican II, even
> reactionaries accept some kind of coexistence with atheistic
> humanism. They have to acknowledge that they cannot roll this
> back and that ecumenism is here to stay—as dialogue between

Christian religious and non-Christian religions and beyond, which of course also includes atheists open to some sense of the "meaning of meaning." I think that is perhaps close to your own sense of things?

RK: Yes. Anatheism, for me, is the space where an open theism and an open atheism can come into dialogue. Which is why—forgive the terminology—I propose that we can, for example, have both anatheist atheists, like Camus, and anatheist theists, like Simone Weil, who Camus described as the "greatest spiritual person of our time." In *Anatheism*, I also place philosophers like Merleau-Ponty, Kristeva, and Derrida in the first category, as I do writers like Joyce and Woolf. I place people like G. M. Hopkins and Dorothy Day, for example, in the latter category. I would tend to think that you and I are also closer to the second category, though I must confess there are days when I vacillate between the two. But that is allowed for anatheists! And neither position, in my view, excludes one from being a practicing member of a church as well as a genuine spiritual seeker—your third definition of the religious in *A Secular Age*, after Christendom and mobilizing faith. I am heartened, in this respect, by the Church's recent invitation of Julia Kristeva to participate, as a nonbelieving humanist, in the Assisi interreligious meeting in November 2011. This, for me, is a very welcome sign of a new openness to atheist brothers and sisters. The Assisi event witnessed, I felt, the promise of a real dialogue between a new humanism and a new Catholicism.

CT: Yes, this interreligious dialogue is crucial. It shows a kind of friendship and respect that can grow across barriers, keeping bridges open both within the churches and across the churches. Even Ratzinger (Benedict XVI), for all his narrow pronouncements on women and gays, encouraged this, and wrote some excellent theological work. We must recognize that God is much bigger than all the Church stuff, bigger than all the divisive definitions. We cannot put limits on God. Which is why we need to acknowledge that we are part of one hermeneutical family, accepting that we know nothing for certain about the transcendent— that there is always a certain messiness and fragility about all our efforts to get a hold on what is ultimately important here. Which doesn't mean we stop trying.

RK: In addition to the broad category of "spiritual seeker," would you agree that the search for "something more" can be greatly nourished by historical wisdom traditions which provide concrete possibilities of the sacred—namely, sacred narratives, times, places, rituals, liturgies, prayers, and sacraments? Doesn't the search for transcendence benefit from such acts of religious embodying and embedding—putting flesh on the otherwise rootless, faceless Word? This is what I call "sacramental incarnation," and I think it is close to your own emphasis on incarnation in *A Secular Age*, and your trenchant critique of "excarnation" (a term which I happily borrow).

CT: I believe this is indispensable. You see, I think people have difficulty here. We need to ask, Does it make a difference to be or not to be a Christian? Well, yes, because a certain kind of prayer is a certain kind of life. Not just a theory or theology but a whole way of being. It is at this existential, embodied, lived level that we find a difference. This is why I agree with Ivan Illich's idea of a *communio* or *conspiratio* based on a commitment to a life of agape which embraces the abject and discarded, as in the Good Samaritan story. This is faith in action, and compassion—faith incarnate.

RK: Your plea for a retrieval of incarnation as the genuine source of Christianity also seems to involve a desire to restore some sense of sacred festivity to our churches again, some access to liturgical and kairological time beyond the purely linear time of modern calculation and techno-scientific planning. You talk of carnival, for example, giving depth and height back to the life of faith. But you equally recognize that these same carnivalesque energies can, in a purely secularized society, be exploited or deflected in mass movements and events. It can go either way. I am thinking of your mention, in the final pages of *A Secular Age*, of the need for a reconciliation of Eros and the spiritual life. I completely agree. The great mystics and poets—and some of the early Christian communities—seem to have been able to do this, but real theo-erotic spirituality is largely lost today, isn't it?

CT: The Christian churches so often lose sight of the radical message of the Incarnation. Think of the sidelining of the laypeople and insensitive teachings on gays, sexuality, contraception, non-celibate or women clergy. The whole tradition of women and women's bodies as temptations of the devil! But look at France or other Catholic societies today, where there is such a desperate need for women to offer or officiate the sacraments and carry out the work of priests. And yet the Vatican shuts the door on that. It is happening in places like Brazil and Latin America, also, and has to unofficially for the Church to function.

RK: It has happened in my beloved Holy Nation, Ireland, too!

CT: Hence a certain hypocrisy, in a growing number of places, between official doctrine and unofficial practice. It is not healthy. And the tendency of the Vatican to appoint bishops who uphold this line is distressing. It simply refuses to accept that human sexuality is a very complex and often messy business, where absolute categories of pure and impure simply do not apply. But we are beginning to see in the lay church how human relationships between Eros and agape can be united in good ways and move things along again.

RK: How do you think that a new Catholicism, in dialogue with a spiritually open humanism, might work to bring a new Eros–agape relation into more common currency? How does one educate the body to spiritually flourish in consort with these twin forces of love? The Greeks had Aphrodite and the child god, Eros; the Romans had Venus and Cupid. But where are our stories? The Madonna is hardly a sufficient role model here, and one rarely if ever hears of the great tradition of mystical Eros in any of our Christian churches or catechisms today. How do we undo the excarnational character of our modern age and of our modern church?

CT: I totally agree that we need to revive and retell alternative or forgotten narratives. That is why I turn to the notion of "subtler languages" in the conclusion to *A Secular Age*, and the examples of poets and writers who do affirm nature, Eros, the body, and the notion of a living incarnate community. We need to retrieve and perhaps reinvent a new religious imaginary along these lines.

I am thinking, for example, of Charles Péguy's notion of "fidelity" to a larger believing community beyond the isolated individual, and his embrace of universal salvation for all living beings. Even animals are part of his eschatological vision! And, of course, Gerald Manley Hopkins's poetic explorations of dark nights of the soul and the epiphanies of earthly grace are also deeply felt upon the pulse of the senses.

RK: I see a sort of neoromanticism in your recent work, not only in the narrative of *A Secular Age* but also in your deep fascination with J. G. Herder and Wilhelm von Humboldt, in your current book on language. I know this interest goes back a long way—I remember you waxing eloquent on Herder when I was a graduate student of yours at McGill University, in 1976!—and I wonder if it might not have something to do with your appeal for a certain dialogue between monotheism and polytheism (so-called paganism) in the last pages of *A Secular Age*. It seems surprising, at one level. But then it makes sense in terms of your attempts to gesture towards possibilities of a new Catholicism, in its truly universal sense, which would be in dialogue with the more earthy and carnivalesque richness of certain non-Christian religions (think of Hindu temples and festivals, for example), where Eros and the body often do have a crucial role, without falling into facile syncretism or New Ageism. And perhaps this is, in turn, related to a tendency among young spiritual seekers today to revisit ancient pilgrimages like the Camino de Santiago in Spain or the Skellig monastery in Ireland or numerous holy places in India or Nepal. There is a hunger here, isn't there, that is often deeply interreligious without being spiritual tourism or consumer devotionalism?

CT: Yes, all this is deeply related to a response to the modern disenchantment of the world, which coincides with the strict and often legalistic codes of the modern moral order. Max Weber was right about the *Entzauberung* of our secular time, with its occlusion of any notion of higher times or sacred places.[3] This is a fact, though I think Weber used the term too loosely. It is precisely after having gotten rid of spirits that a number of people in the West today—and my analysis in *A Secular Age* is focused on the

North Atlantic culture and society—are interested in retrieving something that was lost but may be rediscovered in new ways, in terms of what I call reconversions to something new from out of the past. New forms of subtler languages which nonetheless might be able to reconnect with inherited narratives, imaginaries, and liturgies. And this, of course, is what you, Richard, call "anatheism."

RK: Yes, this is precisely what I would call anatheistic retrievals of the old as the new, in the sense of the double *a* of anatheism as "ab" (away from God) and "ad" (toward God). Philosophers like Ricoeur and Levinas agree, as you know, that one has to move away from the God of metaphysical power and conceptual idolatry before moving back toward a God after God, or a post-atheistic transcendence (which for me is a version of anatheism). Our common friend Ricoeur, in particular, spoke of a "hermeneutics of suspicion" (inspired by the critique of religion in Freud, Marx, and Nietzsche) accompanying a "hermeneutics of reaffirmation." And Levinas played on the double sense of *a* in *adieu*, meaning both farewell and welcome, to abjure and conjure, to revoke and convoke. This involves a messianic relation to the divine Other, where one is *contre dieu*, struggling with God in both combat and embrace—face to face, body to body—like Jacob wrestling with the angel (which is why I chose a Chagall painting of this scene for the cover of *Anatheism*). After the abandonment of God (*deus absconditus*) comes the possibility of a return to God (*deus adventurus*). Or, as Ricoeur puts it, "We must smash the idols so that symbols can speak anew." And, in this sense, anatheism is a series of hermeneutic retrievals of the sacred in new ways, in new symbols and stories—for example, the writings of Joyce and Proust, or the contemporary testimonies of people like Jean Vanier, Dorothy Day, Martin Luther King, and Gandhi, or, more recently, as you mention, of visionaries like Václav Havel or Aung San Suu Kyi. It's a new way of giving up in order to get back, a very ancient sacred cycle, so that disenchantments can lead, in turn, to reenchantment. Revolt to recovery.

CT: I fully agree with all that. But I worry about a certain danger in the whole disenchantment phenomenon of modernity—that it sometimes stops before any kind of reenchantment happens, and it can then end up in an appalling top-down moralism which dismisses the beliefs of popular folks as no more than primitive forms of bewitchment, superstition, and bigotry. So, while there is a genuine critical enlightenment taking place, there can also be a real narrowing of mind and spirit—what I call a "great unlearning" of certain wisdom practices and teachings, an evacuation of extremely rich spiritual traditions. Of course, the Reformation was right to expose the excesses of so-called pagan idolatry. But one of the unfortunate consequences of its more zealous campaigning was the exclusion of rich practices of the festive and the sacramental, linked to a "higher time" of repetition and reversal—practices witnessed in the sacred rites of passage and the transgression of the conventional moral order noted by Victor Turner and others.

RK: Mardi Gras and certain holy feast days in the Catholic and Orthodox Greek cultures would, no doubt, be remnants of such rites. And I suppose one secular equivalent of this would be Halloween (now the most popular annual feast in North America), where the spirits and ghosts of another time revisit us in uncanny and ceremonial ways. But this popular attempt at reenchantment—along with Christmas and other popular holidays—is all too frequently reduced to commercial vacations. One easily forgets that Halloween was the Eve of All Hallows and that Christmas was the Mass of Christ! But, as you and I have both argued, the secular takeover of the sacred can also express itself in violent and murderous ways—Hitler's Nuremberg rallies, mass killings in Rwanda, and other forms of populist scapegoating and bloodletting. The past is never past, as Faulkner said.

CT: I concur. Disenchantment was not just a trait of exclusive humanist secularism but also of the Christian churches themselves, to the extent that they sought to deny this very powerful dimension of the sacred. And once repressed, it can come back, as we know, in all kinds of perversions. To dismiss completely the festive in its original form of "reversal" risks depriving people of a special time and space where they might realize that the established moral and social order is not some kind of perfect code but an interlude between different kinds of codes, none of them perfect. Carnival was a time when things could be stood on their head and great secular powers put in their place. The problem with the modern moral order is that it can sometimes ignore that it is an interlude and instead take itself for an end in itself—the final, fulfilled stage of social evolution, culminating in our present secular age. This is the kind of teleology you find in theorists like Fukuyama or Huntington and to which I am deeply opposed. They cannot think beyond the exclusivist limits of the immanent frame. And, in a far more dangerous and extreme form, one witnesses the effect of teleologies of "perfect societies," imposed by various totalitarian regimes, fascist or Stalinist. We'll make everyone beautifully and definitively happy—and everyone outside our perfect order is impure and primitive, to be dismissed, or worse.

RK: When this kind of supersessionist thinking is found in religions it is also extremely disturbing. "We have the one absolute truth and we have it absolutely!" I see genuine Christianity as going in an opposite direction (not that it is the only religion to do so). For, if Matthew 25 is correct, Christ came as the least powerful of strangers and consorted with the most impure and abject members of society. We both agree that Jean Vanier and Mother Teresa represent this original kind of Christian witness, as does someone like Ivan Illich, with his startling reading of the Good Samaritan story and his critique of the authoritarian betrayals of his own Christian church as a corruption of the best—"*corruptio optimi est pessima*." Here he is following not only Matthew 25 but also Dostoyevsky's chilling critique of "The Grand Inquisitor."

CT: Yes, I have personally been very influenced by Illich's interpretation of the Good Samaritan. He sees it as not simply expressing the *principle* that we should reach out to someone in need, regardless of origin, belonging, etcetera, but actually as a *practice* of reaching out, by way of starting a new relationship. Agape founds relationships; the act extends the network of agape that the Church should ideally express. Illich constantly reminds us that the church as institution—with its rules, exclusions, and

chains of command—is always in danger of traducing and dena-
turing this network, of making rules and authorities hegemonic.
This is the *corruptio optimi*, which is the worst kind of ecclesiastical betrayal. The Good Samaritan opens a different path, a path
of action which keeps the Christian message constantly open to
new relationships.

RK: Can I come back, finally, to the connection between anatheism
and Auden's term "believing again," which we have both used in
our thinking about a God after atheism? Does this mean, in your
own story, a return to a certain "Catholic" tradition, and if so,
how would you redefine this?

CT: First, let me say what I find so good about your reading of this
"believing again" idea, and then I will add something about my
own sense of retrieving a Catholic tradition or traditions.

Regarding your own work: I enjoy reading *Anatheism* enor-
mously and was struck to see how many common themes we are
working on, even if at times in somewhat different languages. Let
me mention just two main themes for now. First, and not surpris-
ingly, is the ana- theme. This is profound. I think the "believing
again" idea is crucial for our age. Auden first used the phrase, of
course, but it is even more relevant a half century on. There are
many people who still believe that the religious tradition they
want to belong to has remained forever what it is, as it has been
handed down to them, and they feel they have to defend it at all
costs, in every aspect and angle, in order to remain true to it. And
there are, happily, a growing number of believers who understand
their itinerary differently—namely, as a journey they are returning to out of a provisional or early alienation, and in which they
are rediscovering a new wealth of possible itineraries that can
lead to where they are hoping to go. You can start from a number
of different paths in order to arrive at your goal.

RK: A bit like the Chemin de Saint Jacques de Compostelle, which
actually comprises multiple different *chemins* leading to the pilgrim
destination, with multiple starting points going back centuries—
Dublin, London, Kraków, Prague, Bordeaux, Vézelay, Le Puy, and
so on. The various "ways" converge or diverge at different junctions
on the journey, but they are all heading in the same direction.

CT: Yes, it is a matter of not equating beginning and end, the terminus a quo and the terminus ad quem. And then, in the twentieth and twenty-first centuries, we find many people, again, who follow itineraries that seem to have no immediate or earlier models behind them, no obvious maps or charts. And if one follows the possibilities of the ana-, one realizes that there is room for different mappings. And you can look back at the tradition and see how various figures actually opened up new routes and paths through unchartered terrain.

Take a figure like Saint Francis. He may reappear in your life because what's striking about Francis's story is that he is not just accepting the way he has been offered; he is starting a new one. And that is why, in the last chapter of *A Secular Age*, I chose a number of modern figures we have already mentioned—Péguy and Hopkins, for example, who, even though they are less dramatic examples than Francis, are also ana- people. They are people who came back to faith in their own way, who believed *again*.

Now, the second main ana- theme I want to stress relates more directly to the question of the sacred and the secular. It is this: the placing of any faith position—my own, your own, others'—within the whole gamut of faith positions. Because one of the key arguments of my book is that what is essential to modern Western secularity is this immense gamut of choices, the nova effect of choices that are expanding, increasing, generating new possible ways of combining or recombining or not combining earlier positions, and therefore opening up a larger palette of itineraries and allowing for a wider variety of what I call, in the final epilogue to my book, "conversions."

RK: Which might more accurately be called *re*-conversions? But I am curious for you to return to my question about how all this relates to your own faith journey as an "ana-theist"—if I may be so bold as to include you amongst the ana- people! How do you see yourself as someone who believes again by "repeating forward," by giving a new future to the past?

CT: OK, regarding my own sense of recovering Catholicism, I would begin by saying that I am happier with the notion of Catholic intellectual traditions in the plural. In addition to the usual understanding of a mainline tradition running from Augustine and Aquinas down through the scholastic and neoscholastic movements, I personally have been influenced by other Catholic readings—for example, Blondel's philosophy of action, Péguy's social philosophy of "creative renewal," Fergus Kerr's Wittgensteinian rethinking of Thomism, as well as the whole rich phenomenological revisiting of Catholic theology and philosophy—Karl Rahner, especially. I think we need to see how these various intellectual itineraries can overlap and converge in all kinds of creative ways.

RK: And what about ecumenist retrievals and overtures? What about Catholic thinking opening up, after Vatican II, to new currents in Russian and Greek Orthodoxy—which stress the importance of the heart prayer, rich liturgy, and the living of the holy in our everyday life—or to Protestant and Jewish thinking, with their strong emphasis on the ethical? I think of the wonderful exchanges between Ricoeur and Levinas with Catholic philosophers and theologians at Castelli, Louvain, Cerisy, and elsewhere. Not to mention the importance of Catholic input to interreligious conversations with Hindu and Buddhist thought. The Jesuits, Benedictines, and Trappists have a great amount to offer here, don't they? Teilhard de Chardin, Abhishiktananda, Thomas Merton, Bede Griffiths, Sara Grant. I am personally convinced that pioneering thinkers like these—who I like to call ana-Catholics or radical Catholics, in the sense of honoring the shared ontological heart-source (root *radix*) of wisdom traditions—are giving birth to a whole new generation of Catholic thought, deeply engaged with other religions, which have challenged, deepened, and enriched our own. The current emergence of "new monasticism" movements is yet another signal of this promissory reawakening.

CT: Yes, absolutely. And I would just add that in addition to "opening out," there is also a very important movement around Vatican II of "opening back." If it is essential to open outwards to the very different ways in which the Church is experiencing faith in the Incarnation (an enduring Christian core principle) in different continents, like Africa, Asia, and Latin America, it is equally important to acknowledge the rich differences in time; that is, the multiple ways in which the Christian Incarnation was understood and lived in very diverse historical periods—ancient, medieval, modern, contemporary. Each generation brings something new, and these new concerns, anxieties, and challenges call for renewal and *resourcement*. Here I have in mind thinkers like Yves Congar and Henri de Lubac—a huge inspiration for Vatican II—who saw a way of prizing open the somewhat congealed tradition by revisiting and revising some of the great insights of the early patristic thinkers who conceived of things in refreshingly interesting and surprising ways. This retrieval of such ancient and ignored spiritual and intellectual traditions enabled a number of Vatican II thinkers to go beyond the sterile obsessional debates around modernism and antimodernism, Reformation and anti-Reformation. It broke from these recurring disputes and jolted the Tradition into a rich plurality of traditions.

In my own case, it was reading the work of the brilliant French Dominican Yves Congar, even before Vatican II, that taught me, as a young man growing up in Montreal, that the Catholic Church was not some timeless depositary of absolute, unchanging truth but a living body capable of constant renewal. Congar spoke of a new spiritual age of "subjectivity," which very much fits in with what you and I—and other recent authors, like Roger Lundin (a Protestant)—understand by Auden's line about "believing again." Not "believing still," as if nothing has altered in one's faith, but coming back to faith after periods of doubt, questioning, loss, or alienation and rediscovering something infinitely more rich—what you, Richard, call anatheism.

> RK: And what Ricoeur (also Protestant) calls a "second naïveté," a faith *after* atheism. As I mentioned above, I find his dialectic of religion–atheism–faith chimes very much with our respective notions of believing anew in the wake of disbelief.
> CT: Yes, I too always feel very close to Ricoeur.
> RK: And Bonhoeffer (yet another Protestant), murdered by the Nazis, had a similar notion of "religionless Christianity," intending the term *religion* in the specific sense of a narrowly

conservative and self-referential institution. In my own view, the Catholic tradition you and I hail from can rediscover itself as a plurality of traditions precisely through encounters with radical and innovative thinkers like this, often from other Christian denominations—Anglican, Evangelical, Methodist, etcetera. This ecumenical crisscrossing between Catholic and non-Catholic currents of thought enables the former's appreciation of sacramentality to cross-fertilize with the latter's privileging of prophecy. I am thinking particularly here of David Tracy's distinction between the "sacramental" gift of Catholics and the "prophetic" gift of Protestants—the former celebrating the inherent epiphanies of incarnational life, actions, rituals, gestures; the latter declaring a new mission that breaks iconoclastically with the past and opens up messianic horizons of hope and salvation. Catholicism and Protestantism need each other. And I think they both need Eastern Orthodox spirituality to remind us of the ancient tradition of "heart prayer"—that special realm of mystical interiority and liturgy.

And, I repeat, I see such an ecumenical openness within Christianity to be utterly compatible with an equal openness to non-Christian spiritual and intellectual traditions. As we witness in the example of the Sacred Heart sister Sara Grant, who, in the late 1970s, in Mumbai and Pune, engaged with her Hindu neighbors in interreligious prayers and sacraments inspired, as she saw it, by Vatican II's idea of "inculturation." Grant worked closely with the Benedictine pioneers of interreligious dialogue in India—Dom Henri Le Saux (Abhishiktananda) and Bede Griffiths—and the fact that she was a woman was also, I think, an essential part of retrieving yet another dormant resource for renewal within her Catholic community.[4] In her groundbreaking work, *Toward an Alternative Theology: Confessions of a Non-Dualist Christian*, Grant notes the revolutionary importance of the great paradox that "divinity is immanent transcendence"—something she believed was a common insight of both Advaita Vedanta and Christian Incarnation. She even offered the theological thesis that the Hindu Shankara and Christian Aquinas were intellectually reconcilable in their respective views of the cosmos as sacrament. I was personally very moved by her description of a ten-day Easter Vigil in 1975 with a Ramakrishna monk in her Prema Seva Ashram as an event of "deep calling on deep," where outward differences were "simply transcended, while each remained what they were—Hindu and Christian." She spoke afterwards of a transreligious epiphany which taught her that unity between religions is not realized by eliminating differences but by surpassing them to a unity that precedes them and exceeds them. And she adds that this sense of passing beyond or beneath confessional divisions is experienced both as a desolation (the fading away and absencing of distinctions) and, simultaneously, as a joy at the presencing of a "harmony with all that is or ever can be."

Whether one is a Christian or Hindu or any other religious seeker, once one taps into what interreligious mystics like Grant—and before her, Ramakrishna, Ramana, and Vivekananda—call "the cave of the heart" at the center of both the universe and each human person, a hidden source wells up and continues after in the background of one's being, "like the muted roar of some great river in spate." I find this extraordinary—as an idea, an image, and a claim to deep spiritual experience. Both Grant and her Hindu counterparts argued that such interreligious epiphanies operated at the level of the heart-womb-belly (*guha*) as well as the mind. It calls for "subtler languages," as you say.

I just take Grant here as one example—encountered on my own particular journey—of what I believe is an expanding Christian rediscovery of religion's potential as a "hospitality towards strangers"—including alien, foreign faiths.

5

New Humanism and the Need to Believe

Dialogue with Julia Kristeva

Julia Kristeva is a Bulgarian-French philosopher, literary critic, psychoanalyst, sociologist, feminist, and cultural theorist. Her most recent work on "post-Christian humanism" overlaps significantly with Richard Kearney's anatheism. Kristeva defines this humanism, with Nietzsche, as "a process of permanent refoundation."[1] According to Kristeva, European culture is undergoing an unprecedented existential crisis concerning the definition of what it means to be human. We no longer know, "What is a man? What is a woman?" In her view, this crisis calls on the human sciences and humanism to reenvision human structures by creating new languages in literature and the creative arts for a renaissance of our humanity. This new humanism's task is "to reinterpret the moral codes built throughout history, without weakening them, in order to problematize them, to renew them in the face of new singularities."[2]

Kristeva's new post-Christian humanism recognizes the absolute need of human beings for ideals to endow life with meaning (the need to believe), and the tension of these ideals with our desire for knowledge, for hard-nosed realism (the need to know). In secular terms, Kristeva recognizes the same tension Christianity has historically problematized as the relation of faith to reason. For her, religious ideals are important not least because they point to important failures of secularism in address-ing human social needs. One of Kristeva's most insightful remarks, for example, is that secularism lacks a proper discourse on womanhood in general and on motherhood in particular. Christianity offers resources in figures such as Mary and Teresa of Avila, but such ideals must be creatively reappropriated for our time. In short, humanism must be a feminism.

Thus, Kristeva's project closely resembles Kearney's anatheist work of speaking "once again" about religion, but in a recuperative, hermeneutic mode of applying religious traditions creatively to current cultural issues. Kearney's conversation with Kristeva touches on three main themes: the new humanism and psychoanalysis, the search for a new politics to meet the challenge of social disintegration, and the relation of faith to fiction.

The following exchanges took place during several meetings in Boston and Paris, in 2013 and 2014.

RICHARD KEARNEY (RK): My main interest in these conversa-tions is to tease out the religious implications of your recent writ-ings on mysticism, humanism, and what you call the "incredible need to believe." More precisely, I want to explore with you the implications of your new humanism for an anatheist understand-ing of faith.

Let me begin with your recent book, *Teresa, My Love*, where your literary protagonist, Sylvie Leclercq, claims that Saint Teresa of Avila represents the true "*humanity* of Christ." Your character talks of a new interreligious (or postreligious) humanism capable of reconciling the singularity of each desiring subject with a plural-ity of diverse beliefs. I quote her vision of things to come: "I imag-ine a humanity concerned with the desire for the Other in every other, looking through and with the history of all—Jews, Chris-tians, Muslims, Confucians, Shintoists, and others—without ignoring their hostilities, reducing their differences, or submit-ting to their institutions." For your protagonist, as for Teresa, "the Other in us comes in varied forms." So my question is whether one of these forms might be what I call the anatheist God after God? For surely Teresa's theoerotic encounters with the mystical Other surpass the old God of metaphysical immutability and theodicy? Do they not embrace a sacred stranger within and without?

I found this related passage in your *Teresa* book equally intriguing: "Through love of Christ's humanity, you continually receive from him your freedom. Continually, without solution, without end, infinitely free. Is this humanism?" And I wonder how all this might relate to a theme dear to us both: the affirmation of the sacred "thisness" (*haecceitas*) of everyday things—what Teresa calls the "pots and pans," what you call "singularity," what I call (after Joyce and Hopkins) "epiphany."

> JULIA KRISTEVA (JK): Let me begin with your last point. The importance of the category of thisness or singularity is as central to a new humanist ontology as it is for your own anatheist ontology. My recent readings of Teresa, in addition to the developments and impasses of modern secular humanism, led me to revisit a key notion of Christian humanism—namely, Duns Scotus's concept of haecceitas. This is also key to your own writing on micro-eschatology and the "god of little things." We know today that, if the modern sense of happiness is freedom, freedom is not necessarily integrative, collective, and standardized, but that it is concomitant with the singular. Duns Scotus [1266–1308] had already maintained this against Thomas Aquinas: truth is not in the universal idea, nor in opaque matter, but in "this one"—this man here, this woman there; whence his notion of haecceitas, of *hoc, haec,* or again, *ecce,* "this," the demonstrative indexing of an unnamable singularity. Moreover, it is maintained that the discovery of Duns Scotus goes back to his reading of the words that God addresses to Moses: "I am *the One* who is." The unpronounceable calling of the name would be the index of utter singularity.

I am interested in developing a Scotist ethics based on this incommensurable singularity of each person, disabled persons included. What is a Scotist ethics? That is *the* question to ask at the crossroads of theology and of philosophy. Is it a more "mystical" ethics (some, such as Gilles Deleuze, have said "atheist"), while that of Thomas Aquinas would be more "social"? In an ethics of Scotist inspiration, at any rate, singularity could be thought of as the only positivity, I would say today, the only value. Beginning with the positivity of beings, Duns Scotus extended it to Being itself, to God, as the *causa singularitatis* (cause of singularity). God would be singular, and

Christ quite particularly so, because the God-man develops the density of his singularity through the test of his passion unto death, and as far as his glorification as a wounded-crucified survivor, since this is neither a reparation nor a satisfaction but precisely the evidence of his singularity.

> RK: A central aspect of anatheism is the attention paid to the "least of these"—the forgotten and estranged. What I call hospitality to the stranger. In your own recent work, and especially in your book with Jean Vanier, *Leur regard perce nos ombres*, you apply the Scotist ethic of thisness to the disabled. Could you say more about this, and most especially about how ethics, humanism, and religion might overlap on this question?

> JK: An activist for the rights of disabled persons in the United States, Nancy L. Eiesland [1964–2009], takes up, without knowing it apparently, this Scotist idea in her book *The Disabled God*, when she describes Jesus as the only "disabled God." Does he not appear to his apostles, even in his glory, with an "impaired" body, a damaged body? Here the wound is not a lack, because it is an integral part of his glory, itself given and perceived as a singularity.

In the different fashion of modern humanism, the ex-canon Diderot took up for himself this "positive singularity" when he undertook to transform the disabled person into a political subject—for the very first time in the world. In his "Letter on the Blind for the Use of Those Who See" [1749], he basically suggests that disabled persons have all rights, "are born free and equal in rights." And the Declaration of the Rights of Man will need a lot of time to put into practice this principle that transforms into efficient positivity, finitude in act in the disabled person. The right to "personalized compensation" in France, in the law of 2005, is an outcome of this.

Nevertheless, to achieve this ambition of modern humanism, political will and jurisdiction are not enough. It would be necessary to reinvent the *corpus mysticum* (mystical body) that Kant himself evokes at the end of the *Critique of Pure Reason* [1781], in order that the singularity of the person with disability would be able to transform the norms into a dynamic, progressive concept: reinvent love as the union with the singularity that is completely other. In other words, for the inclusive solidarity with the weak, it is a matter of substituting the love of singularities. What love? Love as desire and will, so that the singular might clarify, be recognized, and develop in sharing its own singularity. Much more than solidarity, which has great difficulty sustaining itself, it is only this love that can lead the positive (and not "deficient") singularity of the one who testifies to mortality to blossom in a society which is founded on the norm without which, as I said, there is no bond, and which can also lead to the evolution of norms.

> RK: Would you say that this new humanism of the singular is gesturing towards a certain anatheisitic retrieval of Christian spirituality after the death of God?
>
> JK: You are asking me about the relation between my project for a new humanism and your attempt at an anatheist revisiting of the sacred "after atheism." Let me try to respond by first developing some reflections on the new humanism that I delivered at an interreligious meeting in Assisi in 2011. Le Parvis des Gentils is a forum for dialogues between believers and nonbelievers that was initiated by Pope Benedict XVI in March 2011. There I presented a speech entitled "To Dare Humanism" ("*Oser l'humanisme*").[3] This was already several years after I had written *This Incredible Need to Believe*.[4] The Assisi meeting was entitled Days for Peace and Justice in the World and was an ecumenical gathering for all the religions of the world, and included a delegation of non-believers. In this last capacity, I delivered a second paper, entitled "Ten Principles for a Twenty-First Century Humanism," in front of an assembly almost entirely male—colorful, wearing suits, with hair styled in a thousand and one ways—a true *cour des miracles*!

In his speech, Pope Benedict welcomed our presence and, as is his duty as pope, described us humanists as beset by suffering, since we had not found, according to him, the true God. Anxiety in the rows of nonbelievers! Nevertheless, very quickly, the philosopher that he is, avid reader of Nietzsche and Heidegger, pointed out (it seems that it was also the meaning of my speech) that for us truth is a "path," a "continuous interrogation," an "interior struggle." And he spoke to the believers, giving us as an example, in a way, and enjoined them to never forget that "no one is the owner of truth." Forgetting this, the world would inevitably go to war and there would never be peace. We could only adhere to his words and note that we witnessed a major political act for European humanism and its continual recasting.

Upon my return to France, I wondered, with the leaders of the Collège des Bernardins, how to continue this exceptional encounter at Assisi, in the context of a resurgence of anti-Semitism, racism, and Islamophobia with the Merah affair,[5] but also in the context of the sentiment of incomprehension that Catholics share. The project of creating the Montesquieu reflection group, which includes representatives of the principal French religious traditions and nonbelievers, as well as men and women who come from universities and the media, was born in this way. We attempt to carry out in-depth debates about diverse aspects of identity conflicts, which lead us to take up concrete positions in actual life. The group is only in its beginning stages, and already it includes women like the philosophers Blandine Kriegel, Elisabeth de Fontenay, and the Rabbi Delphine Horvilleur. We will converse with experts who work on teaching ethics at public schools. I would also like Mrs. Latifa Ibn Ziaten, the mother of one of the victims of Merah, to be invited.

You see, these reflections on the necessity of rebuilding an ethics emphasize time, in my writing and my engagement; they are incorporated in *Pulsions du temps*, a collection that presents a reflection on temporality.

RK: Why time? How does the question of temporality inscribe itself into the ethical relationship between your writing (philosophical and literary) and your commitment to the new humanism? You seem to see a critical link here between your own story and the larger history.

JK: Born in Bulgaria, of French nationality and an American adoption, I consider myself a European citizen. I lived the consequences of the grand catastrophes of the twentieth century, the holocaust and the gulag. I witnessed the messianic return of a certain number of hopes tied to the perspective of a democracy for all. I see today a new religious revival. In this history, the religious revival seems to me the most alive, and perhaps best able to respond to the endemic crisis stemming from our cultural heritage. It is not about a return to "causes." Causes, after all, have been deconstructed as much as "origins" and "truth"; they no longer speak to us.

Saint Augustine invited a "retrospective return"—that is, a questioning and problematization of the tradition. And, for me, this vision is coextensive with European culture. We already find it in Greek philosophical thought and in Plato's dialogues—the culture, together with a questioning of it. In another manner we find it in biblical history; the Talmudists do not cease to question the "I am that which is/was/will be," from Yahweh to Moses. Finally, this vision impregnates my own conception of humanism, which is not the cult of man "writ large" in the place of God, or a theomorphism, but simply (if I may say so) the evolution of philosophy of the last two centuries that poses "a big question mark concerning that which is most serious," according to the Nietzschean formula; that is to say, concerning God.

The entire journey carried out by my generation around phenomenology, passing through Marxism, Freudianism, linguistics, structuralism, and psychoanalysis, led me to interrogate the legacy of human and social crises. It also led me to be interested in the human microcosm and the history of religions.

RK: I would like to hear you say more about the relationship between your humanist project and a possible post-atheist recovery of the sacred, liberated from the metaphysical trappings of the God of theodicy and power. What are the gains and what are the dangers?

JK: Tocqueville and Hannah Arendt tell us, in essence, that an event occurred in Europe—and nowhere else—that "cut ties with the religious tradition." This unprecedented event, the death of God, had been prepared by the Greco-Jewish and Christian traditions. But "God is dead" can expose two faces of modern nihilism. On one side, there are those who hope to go without an ethics: they make politics a comprehensive moralism, managed by the secular, watching over possible/impossible solidarity in a period of austerity, and by the legality supposedly capable of providing a blueprint for all. On the other hand, there are those who make religion a tool, if not a political weapon, because it is in this way that fundamentalisms develop today. But, as Hannah Arendt anticipated, those who use God for political ends are nihilists, and perhaps even more so than professed nihilists.

Are we thus in conflicts of religion that go along with clashes between traditional moral codes and their denial by unrestrained freedoms—clashes which are spurred by scientific and technological development? Or are we at the crossroads of clarifying the need to believe and its corollary, which is the desire to know? This, for me, is *the* question of the twenty-first century. It is impossible to respond to this without continually rebuilding this other space of thought and life that pulled away from life, which is precisely that of secularization and humanism.

RK: Some might say that this crucial contemporary relationship between the need to believe and the desire to know is specific to a current Western crisis, arising particularly from upheavals in European humanist culture.

JK: Well, it is true that a new humanism developed in Europe since the Renaissance and the eighteenth century, with Erasmus, Diderot, Voltaire, Rousseau, Goethe, and several other rebels, up until Freud and his successors, who inspire my thinking. I understand "humanism" to be an infinite work, that is exorbitant and drawn out over time. Its work involves a "transvaluation of values" in the Nietzschean sense. It is effectively about taking seriously the crisis that shakes the world and that, far from being entirely economic, political, and social, is an *existential* crisis that confronts us with a major unknown: What is a man? What is a woman? Echoing de Beauvoir, I have written, "One is born a woman, but I become a woman." I would add, "One is born human, but I become human."

RK: How? How does this transition from "one" to "I" occur? You are talking about mutations in identity aren't you?

JK: Yes. The never-ending answer to this question is, in my view, associated with the current crisis, the crisis of *Homo sapiens*. It is about a sexual, ethnic, racial, national, religious, and familial identity crisis. The crisis certainly calls upon the human sciences, which developed and expanded following the decay of the theological continent more than two centuries ago. But this response depends so much on the possibility or impossibility of creating new languages, new literature, new art.

In the dawn of the Renaissance, Dante Alighieri [1265–1321] in his *Divine Comedy* (canto I, 69) looked for a language capable of "disregarding" the human; he spoke of *transhumanar* (transhumanization), thus creating a neologism in his new style. Faced with the profound crisis made manifest by current events, a religion—ancient or new—cannot save us. The continual rebuilding of humanism appears to be a radical gesture that the new human comedy requires, the radical gesture of a *transhumanar* that humanity needs. We do not know what this new humanity—brewing in the cloning laboratories and the stomachs of pregnant mothers, in the death drives of disadvantaged teenagers and the rush of Web surfers towards supermarkets of spirituality—will be. But, on the couch, I hear the revolt of my clients—a new space of the "enraged," as was said in May of 1968—who demand the impossible. They reevaluate an intimate region of the religious continent, intimate experience. I hear the disconnection of teenagers lacking ideals and incapable of distinguishing "good" from "bad," new actors of radical evil who inhabit this fecund breeding ground of "gangster Islam." Do you remember the Merah affair and the killing of a soldier by youths in London on May 22, 2013? Do you remember the boy who stabbed a soldier to death at the Défense three days later?[6] I see the media first worrying about these events and then taking pleasure in bombarding us with "shady portions" of political men engaged in "business" at the head of the state.

> RK: Your new humanism seems deeply, perhaps even ominously, coupled with a neopessimism that borders on nihilism. Yet it seems to me that you are also pushing for something that comes "after" nihilism and the death of God, aren't you? Something that brings the human to its limits—and perhaps beyond.
>
> JK: At the risk of appearing apocalyptic, I claim that today we witness extremely disturbing phenomena that reach the limits of the human, as you say. If we are not capable of looking them in

the face and clarifying them, of being with them and surpassing them, we will not be able to build this new version of humanism that asks us to "exceed" the human, which is in crisis—to always and constantly go beyond. It is not about creating voluntarist plans but about reevaluating the historical memory of moral codes that came before us and surveying the psychosexual and social discontent of these new political actors who are in crisis. I use the phrases "deconstruction of the human" or "crisis of the human" wittingly, because they attract attention to the fact that *homo sapiens* has reached a certain limit, and that we nevertheless have the capacities to be conscious of this limit and to think through this situation. The crisis was perhaps latent in the past, but today, with our hyperconnected societies, all becomes very visible, because the means of satisfaction are very violent (mafia, weapons, drug addiction, aggressive religions) and the need for satisfaction is heightened by images of hyperconnection. It is about a radical phase of nihilism. Is this not a reason to lose hope in our epoch? I am a resolute pessimist.

RK: I can see where you are coming from in general sociopolitical terms. But could you ground this in some particular examples, especially relating to the crisis in Western Christianity, which you have written about recently? And, most particularly, as it relates to the body. This interests me greatly in terms of our work together on the project of carnal hermeneutics.

JK: I will give you two examples of what I mean. I will make reference to adolescents and mothers, according to a humanist interpretation of Christianity as "a thinking through the body," but without the space between thinking and the body—rather, a "thinking with the body."

First, the example of adolescents. There is a neologism for speaking of certain adolescents—NEET ("neither employed nor in education or training"), according to European terminology. In France, young people who are neither employed nor in school or training number 1.9 million. A lot of them sink into delinquent behavior and extreme violence. Their acts presuppose a destruction of personality that essentially touches young people from displaced populations, such as immigrants who have not assimilated and who live through serious familial crises. But this disintegration does not spare teenagers from nice neighborhoods; anorexia, drug addiction, kleptomania, suicide are all rampant.

The need for ideality is immense in adolescents, and this ideality constitutes the adolescent as a believing subject, different from the child, who is playful and curious. The child-king who sleeps in the "infantile" inside each one of us is a researcher in a laboratory; with all his senses aroused, he looks to discover where children come from. The adolescent, on the contrary, is a *believer*. We are all adolescents when we are impassioned with the absolute. Adam and Eve, Dante and Beatrice, Romeo and Juliet are its emblems; we are all adolescents when we are in love. Nevertheless, our drives and desires are ambivalent, sadomasochistic. This belief that the ideal object exists is continually threatened when it is not kept in check. Thus, passion in search of the ideal object reverses itself into punishment and self-punishment. You have deception—depression-suicide, when it is not under a form more regressive and somatic, such as anorexia; or even, in an adequate political context, the destructive force of self-with-other that I have named the "kamikaze syndrome."

Because the adolescent believes that the ideal exists (romantic partner, profession, ideology), he feels its impossibility as cruel. From then on, structured by idealization, adolescence is a malady of ideality—either the adolescent lacks ideality, or the ideality he forms in a given context is neither suited to the postpubescent drive nor to his need to share with an absolutely satisfying object. Adolescent ideality is always necessarily demanding and in crisis; it rebels against norms and impossibilities. Adolescent belief inexorably contributes to adolescent nihilism. Why? Because paradise exists (in the unconscious), but "he" or "she" disappoints me (in reality). I can only want paradise in "them" and take my revenge on them; delinquency ensues. Or, since this paradise exists (in the unconscious), but he or she disappoints me or fails me, I can only want this paradise in me and take my revenge on myself against them; mutilation and self-destructive attitudes ensue.

Civilizations that are called "primitive" or premodern had initiation rites for satisfying and containing these maladies of ideality. Then we had Christian fasting, particularly that of medieval times, whose ascetic rites absorbed and heroized anorexic behavior. Later, a literary genre, the novel, was created as an initiation story about the adolescent hero, a lover and adventurer. The romantic ideologies of the nineteenth century and the proletarian revolutions and third world movements of the twentieth offered their harbors to adolescents in love with ideals. Contemporary secularism is the only civilization that lacks initiation rites for adolescents, despite the existence of these rites in prehistory and, currently, in organized religions. Could this be because we deny the need for ideality? Sharing the syndrome of ideality specific to the adolescent, the psychoanalyst has a chance to lift resistances and bring the adolescent to an analytic process that adolescence rebels against.

> RK: You attribute a very important role here to psychoanalytic work—both as a listening and a working through. Work on society, you are suggesting, needs to be supplemented by work on the psyche, for the new humanism to have a chance. Is that so?
>
> JK: Yes. You see, psychoanalytic listening allows us to approach the new actors of humanism—liberated passions in women, mothers, teenagers, among others—whose eruption in culture and politics today embarrasses traditional ideologies that are about revealed religious dogmas or the failings of humanism.

One cannot say enough that humanism is a feminism—from Théroigne de Méricourt to Louise Michel and Simone de Beauvoir. However, women's access (still incomplete) to the freedom to love, to procreate, to think, to undertake a project, or even to govern, can only make us forget that secularism is the only civilization that does not have a discourse on motherhood, although an important part of research in contemporary psychoanalysis today is devoted to the early mother–child relationship. What is a mother? She is an actor of that which I will call "reliance" (*reliance*). The mother constructs a sensitive code with each newcomer, a prelanguage, and transforms the tactile for bringing the infant to language.

Before the "need to believe" that crystalizes the primary identification with the father of individual prehistory, maternal reliance is the dawn of the psyche, in this way preceding the need to believe that religions institutionalize. Could a woman subject—lover of increase and each day more necessary, professionally—say "I" at this crossroads of maternal passion/ vocation? Religions either forget her or make her a goddess, a queen. "The free woman has not yet been born," writes Simone de Beauvoir. The free mother still less so, and there will not be a new humanism without mothers knowing how to speak. One wonders whether there must be a saint like Teresa of Avila for building a different motherhood, that she defines in this way: "not only to enjoy the self and to enjoy for the self," but "to think from the point of view of the other" and "never have her hands tied."

But if humanism is a feminism, it is also adolescence. Why are these teenagers, who are anorexics, depressives, drug addicts, arsonists, or else dreamers, pioneers, liberators, and romantics, so fascinated and afraid? Because these are lovers lacking ideals, who believe, firm as iron, that the absolute love object exists. Since they do not find it, these Adams and Eves, these Romeos and Juliets become nihilists, drug dealers, kamikazes. Secularism is the only civilization without initiation rites for its adolescents. Will psychoanalysts, educators, sociologists, and parents know how to decipher these "maladies of ideality," these needs to believe that betray, for example, their erotic excesses and their deadly (*thanatic*) acting out?

> RK: Can you say more about how the search for a new humanism relates to your psychoanalytic reading of the "incredible need to believe"? This seems to me to be at the very heart of our discussion. I am interested to know how this therapeutic work is individual and how much is social and political—that is to say, work at a more communal or collective level.
>
> JK: The need to believe, which I consider fundamental to human existence, is encountered by the analyst in two kinds of psychic experience. Let me say a word about each.

The first relates to Freud answering the appeals of Romain Rolland, and is described, not without hesitation, as an "oceanic sentiment" [in *Civilization and Its Discontents*]. It could be about the intimate union between the self and the surrounding world, felt as an absolute certainty of satisfaction, of security, as well as the loss of self for the benefit of that which surrounds us and contains us—for the benefit of packaging. It relates to the personal experiences of the infant, who has not yet established boundaries between his self and the maternal body. Indisputable and not shareable, given only to "some" for whom "regression can go far enough," and however authenticated by Freud as an original experience of self, this prelinguistic or translinguistic personal experience, dominated by sensations, could be at the heart of belief. Belief, not in the sense of a supposition but in the strong sense of an unwavering certainty—a sensory fullness and ultimate truth that the subject feels like an exorbitant after-life, at once sensory and mental. Strictly speaking, ec-static.

Certain aesthetic works show this. I see it particularly in the work of Proust. The narrator creates a dream state without images ("the dream of the second apartment"), woven of pleasures and pains that one believes to be (he says) unspeakable and that mobilize the extreme intensity of the five senses, and that a waterfall of metaphors alone could attempt to "translate." According to the psychoanalyst Frances Tustin [1913–1990], the story of these dreams interprets this as a triumph over the endogenous autism that lives in the very depths of the unconscious of each of us. Will the writer succeed where the autistic one fails?

My second example is "the primary identification with the father of individual prehistory." Take Psalm 116:10, for example: "*He'emanti ki ada-ber*" (אֶדבֵּר כִּי הֶאֱמָנְתִּי): "I had faith even when I said, 'I am truly unfortunate'; I said in my misfortune, 'All men are liars.' " In response, Saint Paul, in his second letter to the Corinthians, 4:13, goes back to the Greek translation of the Psalm: "*Episteusa dio elaleissa*";[7] in Latin: "*Credidi, propter quod locutus sum*"; in French, "*J'ai cru et c'est pourquoi j'ai parlé*"; in German: "*Ich habe geglaubt, darum habe ich geredet*"; in English: "I believed, and therefore I have spoken."

Some lines before this statement, the psalmist evokes the merciful audience of God, the loving Other, and assembles the diverse interpretations of the Hebrew term *ki*: "and," "because," "despite." I thus hear the verse in this way: "Since You speak to me and listen to me, I believe and I speak, despite the unspeakable."

The context of the psalm is very explicit. It associates faith or belief (*emuna*, where one hears the root *amen*), which commands the act of speaking, with these precise, ordinary comments, in this deceptive instance: "I am unfortunate," "Men are liars," etcetera. Faith—that is to say, certainty ("There is the Other to whom I listen and who listens to me")—holds the key, the condition and profound meaning, to the act of speaking itself, which is that of a complaint. Because I believe, I speak. I would not speak if I did not believe. To believe what I say, and to persist in speaking, follows from the capacity to believe in the Other, and not at all from strongly deceptive existential experiences (misfortune and lies).

But what is it, to believe? The Latin *credo* goes back to Sanskrit, *kredh-dh/srad-dhā*, which denotes an act of trusting in a God, implying restitution in the shape of divine favor accorded to the faithful. Secularized, financial "credit" also stems from this: I deposit a good while waiting for a reward. (Émile Benveniste has analyzed this development in great detail in his *Vocabulary of Indo-European Institutions*.) Belief is a credit; it is not surprising that the two are both in crisis today.

> RK: Those two examples are fascinating. But could you say more about the first, psychotherapeutic reading of "belief," which seems to me to be your ultimate hermeneutic model when it comes to understanding the whole question of religion and the sacred? This is clear in the case of your Teresa book. But I am curious to see how you would apply it to more everyday, clinical, nonmystical instances.
>
> JK: Psychoanalytic experience of the child and the adult display a crucial developmental moment where the infant (*infans*, the one who does not speak) projects itself onto a third party with which it identifies: the loving father. Primary identification with the father of individual prehistory—dawn of symbolic thirdness— replaces the fascination and horror of dual interdependence between mother and child. This trusting recognition, which offers me a father loving the mother and in love with her, and which I devote to him in my turn, changes my stammerings into linguistic signs whose worth is determined by him.

Freud writes that the words of language as signs of objects—but above all as signs of my joys and terrors—transform my anguish into "a believing waiting" (*gläubige Erwartung*). Loving, paternal listening gives meaning to that which could be, and without this, there is an unspeakable trauma—an unspeakable excess of pleasure and pain. But it is not me who constructs this primary identification, and it is no longer the loving father who imposes it on me. *Einfühlung* with him—this point zero of becoming one with the third—is "direct and immediate," like lightning or a hallucination. It is through the intermediaries of sensibility and the speech of the mother loving the father—a mother whom I still belong to and with whom I am still inseparable—that this "unification" of me-in-the-other-who-is-a-third is transmitted to me and establishes me. I do not speak without this propping-up that is my "believing waiting," addressed to the loving father of individual prehistory who possesses the attributes of both parents—this father who was already there, who was there before Laius was, before the from-then-on famous Oedipal father came to formulate his prohibitions and his laws.

An imaginary father emerges in this way who, in recognizing me and in loving me through my mother, makes me believe that I can believe, that I can identify with him. Freud even uses the term *investissement* (*Besetzung* in German; *cathexis* in English): to believe and/or to invest, not in him as object of need or desire but in the representation that he has of me and in his words—in the representation that I make of him and of his words. "I believed, and I spoke."

This foundation of my need to believe, thus satisfied and offering me the optimal conditions for developing language, could be accompanied by another capacity, corrosive and liberating: the desire to know.

Who does not know the jubilatory trance of the child asking questions? Still situated on the border between the flesh of the world and the kingdom of language, the child does not cease to bring us back to this inconsistency of names and beings, of Being, that no longer terrorizes him but makes him laugh, because he believes that it is possible to name, to make names. The question, the dawn of thought, and of revolt. . . .

RK: To shift this in a slightly new direction: I am very interested in your reading of Arendt's openness to a "new politics of incarnation."[8] Such a move, you suggest, would oppose the fundamentalist return to archaic origins with a "refoundation of the authority of the Greco-Judeo Christianity that gave the world the desire for a common world" (a new sense of human plurality and subjectivity). But what exactly would it mean to reinterpret this "gift"—as you call it—and to invent such a "new politics"?

JK: At a practical level, your question of the new politics brings to mind the question of the indigenous uprisings in the Arab Spring, Tunisia, Turkey, Syria. How are we to regard these new political actors? I have no competence for commenting on the complexity of these situations, but I would like to examine the meaning of revolt—as it applies here and also to our European tradition—and of the necessary rebuilding of humanism in the context of globalization and global conflict.

For at least two centuries, the rich and complex meaning of the term *revolt* has been mainly political. But we should note, in passing, that the old etymologies of *revolt*—"wel" and "welu"—indicated a traditional act leading to the denomination of exterior, protective, technical objects, giving meanings of "return," "discovering," "circular movement of the planets," the Italian "turn-around," the "volume" of a book, the French "vaudeville," and even the rolling "Volvo" of Sweden. Today, we understand "revolt" to mean a protest against norms, values, established powers. Since the French Revolution—to respond to your question of a new politics for Europe—political revolt is the secular version of this living conscience, when it tries to stay loyal to its anguishes and freedoms. Revolt is our mystical synonym for dignity.

But something has changed since this endemic crisis. For the first time in history, we realize that it is not enough to replace old values with new ones. This is not a solution for us in the West because every solution (the "free" market, consumption, security, hyperconnectivity) that becomes a value and claims to replace old remedies (charity, class struggle), in its turn, congeals into dogmas and dead ends that are potentially totalitarian. Under the pressure of technology—of the image and of the acceleration of information—we forget that the speaking being is actually living, provided that one has a mental life. And yet this life only exists if it is a perpetual questioning of its norms and powers; of its own sexual, national, linguistic identity; of its desires, its sufferings, its loves, and its hates. It is rebellious men and women who are threatened by the misfortunes in civilization, not political systems. I think, for example, of the university president in Argentina who told me he wanted to transform the young people of bad neighborhoods—into researchers. He proposed that they do research on the why and the how of drugs, arms trafficking, and prostitution in their zone. This man had done his thesis on Meister Eckhart, a mystic of the thirteenth and fourteenth centuries who asked God to let him be free of God.

My point is that, all in all, before revolutionizing the city, revolutionize oneself! The means for this are varied. As an analyst, I consider that psychoanalysis is obviously one of them. But artistic experience and the anatheist rediscovery of religious experiences of the past, even when one is an atheist, are others.

Protesters have the impression of rebelling against the norm, against the wealthy, against obscurantism, against dictators, against non-Muslims. But, frankly, who rebels if power is dependent on global, all-embracing finance? If this global management lacks a course or vision? If power is incapable of discussion and questioning? And who is going to revolt if the revolutionaries are reduced to the freedom of merely "changing channels"—"patrimonial people" at best, owners of nothing, dispossessed of what was formerly the inner self?

> RK: How does this notion of revolt relate to the question of contemporary nihilism and the "conflict of religions" that you have spoken about elsewhere? You have written much, recently, on the question of violence, of the death drives which are no longer containable within traditional religious categories and institutions. How do you propose we deal with the death drive, once a culture no longer defers to religious traditions and laws?
>
> JK: To examine this closely. . . . Often it is not a person who revolts but an unstoppable pressure that bursts forth, a remainder of desire reabsorbed by the death drive itself, that explodes the person and obstructs his absolute satisfaction. This pressure is dangerous; it is ready to explode itself in order to explode other people. We are in the outpouring of a death drive. I return to these outpourings of violence that one calls in another sense "revolt," while, on the contrary, it is about a more radical phase of nihilism that is brewing below conflict of religions. This explosion of violence is more serious because it grasps the impulses of civilization in a more profound way—the destruction of this prereligious need to believe, which is constitutive of mental life with and for other people. Adolescent gangster-fundamentalism suddenly reveals that, from now on, the religious treatment of revolt finds itself discredited, insufficient to ensure the heavenly aspiration of this paradoxical believing—strongly nihilist because pathetically

idealist—that is the disintegrated and desocialized adolescent. Psychoanalysis ventures into this profound disorganization of the person—this disconnection ("I" does not exist) and cutting of ties to the other—until one succumbs to a disobjectification ("the other has neither meaning nor value") where the death drive alone triumphs, the malignancy of evil.

We are thus confronted with a new form of "radical evil." What is radical evil? asked Hannah Arendt, after Kant. It consists in declaring the superfluity of human beings and carrying out their killing, she answered. Is radical evil without a "why"? Mysticism and literature say so, in their own manner. But the political pact cannot leave it here. With psychoanalytic experience, I look for the logic of extreme evil to refine interpretation in transference–countertransference. We discover that, with reference to familial disintegrations and social breakdowns, the need to believe collapses in an empire of disconnection and disobjectification, which is accompanied by an insane pleasure, or in the void of apathy.

We must make a distinction here. Yes, evil exists—first, as an evil that results from conflicts between values, which in turn result from divergent or concurrent libidinal interests, and which underlie our conceptions of good and evil. Religious man and moral man are constituted by this. More or less guilty and rebellious, they live on this, are concerned about it, and hope to elucidate it, possibly to *hear* one another in place of killing one another.

In addition to this evil, there exists another evil—extreme evil—that sweeps away the meaning of the distinction between good and evil and, in so doing, destroys the possibility of accessing the existence of other people as oneself. These limited states do not take refuge in hospitals or on couches but unfurl through sociopolitical catastrophes, in the abjection of extermination—the holocaust, the horror that defies explanation and reason.

But new forms of extreme evil spread throughout the globalized world today, in the wake of maladies of ideality. Contemporary psychoanalysis—because it consists in a lively searching—tries to understand by going right up to these borders of dehumanization. Politics (in theory and practice) finds itself in front of an historical challenge: Is it capable of facing this crisis of the need to believe and the desire to know that the box of religion cannot contain, and that at bottom affects connections between humans? In these times of "excess," anguish that congeals opinion against a background of economic and social crisis expresses our uncertainty in front of this colossal issue.

> RK: In your recent exchange with Jean Vanier on the life of the disabled—*Leur regard perce nos ombres*—you seem to acknowledge that there is some element of the spiritual–sacred–sacramental that the new humanism needs to incorporate, or at least take note of. There appears to be an appreciation of the special role of agape—love of the abject, contingent, accidental, and wounded—that we find, for example, in the stories of the Good Samaritan, Saint Francis or Teresa, or indeed of Vanier's L'Arche movement, which responds to the call of the disabled as inspired by the suffering-healing servant, Christ himself. This surplus element of *caritas*—of impossible love—seems to be largely missing from the "exclusive secular humanism," which Charles Taylor identified with the modern moral order (including the politics of welfare states, which is, of course, indispensable).

Do you agree that there is a certain incarnate Eros and agape of Christian love—or something equivalent; there are other names for it—that the normative frame of the new humanism could be informed and deepened by? Would you embrace some element of pathos which goes beyond the necessary work of moral–juridical–statutory legislation towards an "impossible love" that exceeds the immanent frame of civic rights and duties? (And let me repeat that I take it as agreed that such institutional rights of state legislation are utterly necessary in any just, decent democratic society.)

My question is basically this: When it comes to disabled persons or young citizens undergoing psychosocial crisis in today's culture of market exchange and simulation, does our new humanism not need to remain open to an anatheist order of "grace" tied to "need," of "impossible love" tied to "justice"? I put these words in quotation marks to signal that we are not talking clichés here.

> JK: Has love become impossible? You mention my exchange with Jean Vanier. There are a number of factors which make us fear

the disappearance of love, or at least mutations so deep that they completely reshape the psychic map of the human being. There is the fear that disability triggers (in spite of laws of integration and changing perceptions), the traps of hyperconnectivity that bring risks (the abolition of time, the encouragement of immediate satisfaction, proximity that is only virtual, etcetera), along with unprecedented advantages (speed, abundant information, instantaneous responses). There are many young Internet "addicts" today who find themselves in a no-man's-land without safety net. The Web is not a support but a virtual mirror with holes in it; it breathes in and out, connects or abandons, but does not allow the shaping of an identity or a world. Hence the search for ways to adapt. The Web surfer consumes information, facts. He diminishes when he relinquishes his abilities for understanding a meaning, and he lacks the time for appropriating and problematizing that meaning. Without his own space and without time, the Web surfer rushes toward the latest trend of "toolboxes" and toward supermarkets of spirituality. During a conference held at Louvain, in April 2013, I argued that the need to believe is not satisfied in our secular, market society, where young people are Buddhists one day, Taoists the next; then they add a bit of Islam, a pinch of Catholicism. Sociologists view this religious patchwork as a temporary solace that calms the need to believe. But, fragile and integrated, it is on this ground of unsatisfied demands that fundamentalism will make its mark.

Moreover, contemporary reality confronts us with other phenomena that a new humanism must engage—without sectarianism and without naïveté. What do we make of the radical conversions of young Catholics to Islam? How do we understand women's attraction to the chador? I cannot answer these questions, which are beyond my competence, but only offer some thoughts that come from my feminist and psychoanalytic practice.

The society of consumption and of the image has replaced the word *freedom* with the word *choice*. Women who veil themselves tell us, "The veil, it is my choice." They forget that this is also—that this is first—the choice of their fathers, their brothers, and their husbands. But also that

freedom consists in a continual surpassing, that freedom is a risky experience that risks itself first in the encounter with someone else, and in a different way in singularity. Freedom is not at all equivalent to replacement
(merchandise) or power (familial, religious, political).

In the spirit of the Simone de Beauvoir Prize, we have proposed that the
Academy of Paris start a program in high schools that includes extracts of
Beauvoir's writings on freedom, for young girls and boys to comment on,
hoping that this will happen. I evoke notions and experiences like "self,"
"other," "encounter," "surpassing," "desire," "man," and "woman." Christian
humanism and secular humanism developed and deepened these notions
and operate according to their logics. They are rewarding, emancipatory,
risky, and very demanding. Are converts to fundamentalism won over by
the aggressive, combative visibility of certain currents of Islam? Or do
they ignore the prodigious complexity of European culture? Or else, is
this complexity poorly transmitted—transmitted blandly, without conviction, or even with shame for its faults and crimes, without emphasizing
its high points that are, all told, the truth as journey, the questioning of
identities, the concern for the other and for the encounter?

Sometimes I hear that women choose the veil because it allows them to
escape men's desires. Unless this is another manner of seducing, secretly
and quietly, signifying that there is something seductive to see—in certain circumstances alone—therefore another strategy of desire, which is
supposedly for the particular purpose of gaining security. Always, security
and the permanent protection of motherhood. "Married in polygamy,
perhaps, but mother and wife nonetheless," say certain converts.

This objection brings me back to the point that secularism is the only
civilization that does not have a discourse on motherhood. Several texts
in my last book, *Pulsions du temps*, are devoted to this. I propose that a
maternal eroticism exists, which is not the eroticism of the lover. I reha-
bilitate the word *réliance*, in a to-and-fro between Old French, French,
and English. *Reliance: relier* (to connect), *rassembler* (to reassemble), *join-
dre* (join), *mettre ensemble* (put together); but also *adhérer à* (adhere to),
appartenir à (belong to), *dépendre de* (depend on); and, in consequence,
faire confiance à (trust in), *se confier en sécurité* (confide in security), *faire
reposer ses pensées et ses sentiments* (rest one's thoughts and feelings), *se rassembler* (to gather), *s'appartenir* (to rely on oneself). Between biology and
meaning, between violence and separation, and the tact required for the

transmission of the affects and language of the other, maternal reliance specifies the passion mothers have for their children. We believe we know what a "Jewish mother" is; the Virgin mother is an example to Catholic believers. But modern humanism—up until the most recent waves of feminism that timidly venture there—has deserted this territory.

> RK: So how would you propose to rehabilitate this very challenging and almost taboo notion of reliance? How do you hope to represent it in today's society or find a place for it in the social pact? It seems to me your new humanism calls here for a new feminism— at least as it relates to this question of reliance.
>
> JK: You are right. This question about the contemporary import of reliance is crucial. It is concerned with eroticism, which the social consensus denies by reserving the range of sexuality for only idealized or pathological "love." The persistence of eroticism is so vulnerable that only a maximal tact could avoid these two interpretations that distort it all along human history. Is man capable of desacralizing maternal eroticism? Women themselves take pleasure in it, with their obvious libidinal advantages. The "heroism" of Freud ventures there, until he writes that, for the woman, the only manner of "freeing" herself from "respect" is to "familiarize herself with the representation of incest."

Today, two versions of the maternal contend for the profound logic of maternal eroticism, requiring it without sacralizing it: the gesture that traces the movement of flesh toward the image on this side of and beyond sound, with its childlike freshness in the "Chinese mother"; and Sarah's laughter (when God tells her she is pregnant with Isaac). The laugh that changes Sarah shows her doubleness—incredulous and/or trusting. He keeps her available in the fissure between believing and not believing. The disease of civilization today is in the hands of these two variants of maternal eroticism: the calligraphic ease of the Chinese mother in the global current and the wisdom of Sarah, ready to die for laughing at fertility and immortality.

We used to believe that women want to be free by stopping themselves from being mothers. We realize now that they want to be free to decide to be mothers or not. Many of those who desire to be mothers gladly bring in reproductive technologies, without prejudice. Is this because reliance, presubjectivity, makes familiar this dispossession of self that science imposes on the most intimate with new forms of "assisted" maternity or maternity "for other people"?

"The free woman is just being born," writes Simone de Beauvoir in *The Second Sex*. There will not be a free woman as long as we lack a maternal ethic. It is just being born, and when it is it will be an ethic of reliance. While waiting, the desire for motherhood will look for refuge under veils and in the obscurantisms that call the exclusion of women from the freedom to think "protection."

> RK: The question of maternity and maternal reliance is not the only controversial issue you have addressed in contemporary European, and indeed international, debates on gender and sexuality. There is also the vexed and contested issue of gay marriage, which has been particularly heated in France recently. And which raises questions about the resurgence of a certain Catholic conservatism—allied, it appears, to a special kind of French exceptionalism.

> JK: It is true, the recent French debate on "gay marriage," where a generation of new Catholics suddenly appeared, surprised public opinion. This is a euphemism. I do not agree with those who classify this current as based on fundamentalism alone. Numerous are those who return to tradition with a need to believe and with a no less intense desire to know. One can hope that the Church of France hears this, that it helps to appropriate the tradition in the sense of a journey. "God is he from whom we learn that sometimes that which we believe to be our own is foreign, and that which we believe to be foreign is sometimes ours" [in Augustine, *Soliloquies*].

Taken to court and destabilized by the decision precipitated by a marriage law for all, the social body actually responds: hopes and despairs, laughters and angers. Was it about a French exception, while other nations—wise or resigned—evolve and adapt? French passions, as ardent as they have proven themselves to be in the course of their history, have been directly hit. "Neither God nor Master" opens to a life where nothing is prohibited; it is impossible to impede or prevent the revolutions that play out in laboratories without borders. The whole world knows it. The question is no longer there. In addition, while jurisprudence manages the "situation," the French symptom—excessive, enthusiastic, or anguished—wonders, Where do we stand on the human?, in the face of a surprised world, indifferent, that does not ask more of France—for the moment. We are here in front of a new and different configuration of our question about love and justice, limits and transgressions.

In a recent colloquium of the Paris Psychoanalytic Society, I hypothesized that the majority of men and women who support gay marriage do not do so simply because of legal equality. They support it because they recognize homoeroticism as an ordinary psychosexual constituent. Ferenczi and Freud have observed that homoeroticism participates in the psychic construction of all speaking beings, by eroticizing the similar (*la mêmeté*), idealizing projections onto the other oneself, and, thus, participating in the discovery of the other sex. Religions, notably those that are monotheistic, retain and celebrate homoeroticism. Abraham does not consume Isaac after having attempted it, Jesus rejoins his Father, and the faithful consume the Father in the Eucharist.

Homoeroticism, legalized in this way and rid of all perversion, appeared to the majority polled as the mirror of their own "identity," inherent in social bonds, in the value of equality, and in universalism itself. It is as if, counteracted and even discredited, Freudian analysis, which postulates that the social bond is homoerotic, won the game and installed itself in our consciousness. Homoeroticism does not scandalize us; we recognize it as our own, say the majority of those polled, while at the same time homophobia persists and mobilizes those who do not accept their homoeroticism and struggle against their repressed homosexuality, such as skinheads, dealers, etcetera.

RK: For some, as you know, the introduction of gay marriage/marriage for all represents a challenge to the traditional paradigm of heterosexual marriage. And, at a more general level, it raises the whole question of sexual and gender identity. How would your psychoanalytic-humanist perspective hope to address these critical issues in a way that goes deeper than the usual ideological response?

JK: Is this to say that gay marriage/marriage for all means the failure of heterosexual marriage? I believe that this idea reveals in all cases an extraordinary fragility, which is perhaps not separate from its seductive character. At the same time, it reveals the central and unavoidable role of the norm that it continues to incarnate across the original fantasy of the primal scene, that persists in spite of the decoupling of procreation and sexuality.

Listen to the desires that are expressed in defense of marriage for all. One looks in vain for where the "values" are. As if the heterosexual couple and its family were the measure of these values! Even if conventional morality has trivialized them and our globalized television programs represent them to the point of caricature, our fantasies converge on them: test tubes, frozen eggs, sperm banks, even women's bellies that one buys for the time of a pregnancy.

Although evoked by opponents of the law, the French debate lacks an analysis, a defense, and an illustration of heterosexuality. It does not reside only in the anatomical difference between males and females. Heterosexuality can no longer be invoked as the most reliable means for transmitting life, or of guaranteeing generational memory. It reveals the extreme intensity of eroticism, from which it receives an unbearable fragility. We needed Freud's genius to formulate what we all know intimately: the procreation that haunts humans is not a natural act, and it is even less a sovereign one. And we needed the genius of Georges Bataille who, in *Eroticism* [1957], exposes the fragility that lives in the fury of the primal scene—original and universal fantasy if there is one: fusion and confusion of man and woman, vivid loss of energies and identities, life's affinity for death. Heterosexuality is not only a discontinuity ("I am other, before the other") normalized by continuity (fusion for "giving" life). Heterosexuality is a transgression of identities and codes, that does not proceed from terror but from anguish and from a desire for death carried by the promise of life across death.

"All against" the familial institution, the genitality dramatized by the primal scene is the asocial face of the family. Transgression of prohibitions, sublime disorder of obscenity, the revealing of "antagonism between sexual love and social connection," and the coupling of man and woman, disrupt the community—"race, national divisions, and social class"—and "accomplish culturally important operations."⁹ The original fantasies of the speaking beings that we are congeal on this glowing hearth of the primal scene, and not on the stability of test tubes or enchanted loves—homo or hetero—for one does not know what the next day will bring. Shakespeare, Joyce, Céline, help!

The Freudian analyst, whether man or woman, explores, I dare say, more than ever, the psychic spaces of our contemporaries and knows that the capacity to make sense (to speak, focus attention, reason, think, create) necessitates a cohesion–coherence–identification–unification. Up to now, there is the One, there must be the One, in order to speak and make sense. Could it be this that monotheism celebrates, accentuates, exaggerates, capitalizes on, while using and abusing it? The role of the father in the traditional patrilineal family could be that of guaranteeing and optimizing this function, this emergence. The loving father of primary identification; then the severe father of prohibitions and law. With the mother and her "reliant" eroticism, with the analysts who listen to us today and, even more, with the symptoms of disconnection and disobjectification that bring extreme evil, we encounter a new version of the paternal that is neither totem animal, nor Laius–Oedipus, nor Abraham–Isaac, nor Jesus and his Father forsaken and resuscitated. In the love-hate of transference, the father is not only loved and hated, put to death and revived, but literally annihilated on our couches and nonetheless incorporated by the analysand. Like in the primal scene? Perhaps, if one thinks of it as the explosion of identities and norms where the coupling of man and woman disrupt the community and join themselves with the zenith of their rebirth (re-naissance)—of procreation.

It is this continuous dissolution-recomposition, life's affinity for death, of which the analyst likes to think of himself as guarantor, that makes possible our understanding of addictions, somaticizations, criminality, and other borderlines. The subject of these "new maladies of the soul" reappears with a paradoxical identity that evokes the Brownian movement of Pollock's "drippings" entitled *One*. This takes root in a gesture of dispersion and plurality.

So what happened to the One, if the beginning/self-beginning is a dissemination? Am I still One when I analyze or am analyzed? Assuredly yes, my identity exists ("There is One"), but it remains indeterminate, deprived of a fixed center and freed of fatal repetition—a little like serial music, or like an improvisational dance that is supported by an underlying order, in the opening. Neither the dead father nor "führer," authority disappears in analysis; nor in a reconstructed society in transformation. My identity scatters in the two parents' permanent adjustment of this other scene of fecundity in the new beginning that is bringing up, educating, and passing on to their progeny.

I have not forgotten "marriage for all." It will not be the pious voice of a republic cut in two, divided between the "moderns" and the "traditionals"—the gays (the reconstituted), test tube babies, surrogates, etcetera, on the one side, and those nostalgic for the norm, on the other. Instead, a genuine patchwork quilt takes shape, the improvisations of the one borrowing models from the other, and vice versa—interfering, innovating, disastrous and festive, with new and specific forms of child rearing. It comes from accompanying each project of family, adoption, filiation with a personalized attention, case by case. Like always? More than ever.

The persistence of the biblical family and the Chinese family compete for the destiny of the millennium to come; there is no other choice for Europe and America. Without giving in to the temptation of a politics of psychoanalysis (which would be a negation of its deontology), perhaps psychoanalysis alone has the capacity to respond to this new urgency—not the disappearance but the dissemination of the One in its incommensurable uniqueness. If we are persuaded of this, we will succeed in making ourselves understood.

> RK: The encounter between biblical and Chinese paradigms of understanding seems to be central to your cultural project for a new humanism. How does this dialogue between East and West (the latter understood in the broad sense of Greco-Roman, Judeo-Christian culture) help us address our contemporary crisis of identity, both spiritual and somatic? We are back to the question of the "psyche-soma," which you write of in your *Theresa, My Love*. Some, like Huntington, speak of a "clash of cultures," but you seem to prefer (as do I) the hermeneutic model of a "conversation of cultures"—albeit deeply critical and challenging.

> JK: The question of the survival—or not—of the Christian notion of love in globalization cannot avoid the challenge that the

meeting of cultures and, within this, the meeting of the body
and Chinese social order, puts to our post-Christian humanism.

Blaise Pascal had already, in the seventeenth century, drawn attention
to the inevitable encounter between our two worlds, since he wrote in his
Pensées, "Which is the more believable of the two, Moses or China? It is
not a question of seeing this in a basic way; I tell you that there is something that obscures and something that clarifies. We must put papers on
the table."

Several anthropological and cultural facts attest to the space between
Chinese psychosexuality and that of the Greco–Judeo-Christian tradition:
the strong survival of the matrilineal family paralleling patriarchal Confu-
cianism; the duality of yin/yang commissioning a psychic bisexuality; the
imbrications between language, music, and writing; etcetera. In addition,
many developments of our culture seem to develop according to a Chinese
logic. Are not Ezra Pound, Colette, and Sollers Chinese among us?

First, I maintain that there exists a real heterogeneity, which we should
highlight in order to clarify, between our modes of living and thinking
and Chinese modes. There is an irreducible singularity with which the
Chinese woman and man approach experiences as fundamental to psychoanalysis as body and soul, mother and father, women and men, but
also language, writing, or even meaning and signification.

I will say, second, that the psychoanalytic transvaluation of these experiences and categories already gives us the possibility of approaching the
"Chinese gaps" not as enigmatic strangers but as facets of psychosexuality, admittedly centered on Oedipus but also opening to other configurations, when speaking is lived as an experience.

However, I will conclude that the best knowledge of Chinese male and
female analysands invites us to better learn these "gaps" and to keep count
of them, in order to avoid the temptations for normativism and reduc-
tionism that can tempt psychoanalysis, and to diversify this listening to
human singularities that specifies the ethic of psychoanalysis.

Contemporary with the Jesuit mission to China, Leibniz believed,
along with these priests, that the Chinese not only did not know "our"
God, but understood the concept as something endowed with a sort of
intelligence and a kind of law, *li*. And the mathematician makes himself
the visionary of a Chinese humanism whose mystery still escapes us and

that we do not hesitate to stigmatize as "arrogance." Could this be because it appears to suit the logic of enterprise and of connection, where the self is reduced to an intersection between infinite cosmic and social folds (today clearly national, and that manages to revoke it)? Moreover, could the continuous destruction/construction, inherited from Judeo-Christian monotheisms, that distinguishes European humanism in its universal aspiration, be a disability that risks impeding our entrepreneurial competitiveness?

On the contrary, in claiming to ignore the logics of interior experience, one risks seeing the anguish of finitude and the explosion of violence that thwarts connectivity in all instances—this ideal world's cooperation and mending by "homeotechnics" that we promise the "New Alliance" in its complexity. Globalized humanity looks for an encounter between, on the one hand, Chinese adaptability to cosmic and social intelligences and, on the other, Greco–Judeo-Christian psychosomatic complexities.

> RK: This seems to be where your notion of "multiverse" comes in—as a way of reconciling our contemporary need to retain a certain universality of the One while safeguarding the equal desire for singularity and dissemination. In my conclusion to *Anatheism*, I try to address a similar question in the contemporary challenge of interreligious dialogue, by proposing a hermeneutic model of "translation" between host and strangers, the one and the other, the unifying and the diversifying. But you are currently looking more to the model of contemporary astrophysics for your model of multiverse, are you not?
>
> JK: In a time where astrophysics reshapes our understanding of the human, "multiverse" is a metaphor that I willingly borrow from what is called superstring theory—of quantum physics that proliferates possible universes, and of the flood that drives them to exist. A meta-law governs the whole: there is a universal humanity, whose concept and practice issued from a universalist monotheism and from the rupture with this monotheism, but the singularity of each of its parts—of each person—is of such a fineness that the general law has different modalities.

In this spirit—and while a wind of uncertain and imperious liberty blows through the Arab world—a reflection of the chief rabbi of Great

Britain reveals to me a meaning of the sacrifice of Isaac that exceeds "narrow particularism," giving voice to the "dignity of difference." The alliance will be a "bond of trust" that makes manifest the "tender concern of God," since the alliance believes that "one bond does not exclude other bonds" and that, as a result, the traditional enemies of Israel—Egypt and Syria—can be "elected together with Israel." The alliance would thus mean not a reduction of diversities in the unique, but a doubling, tripling, multiplying ad infinitum?

I note: the One-All (of biblical and evangelical monotheism) is reversed, extraverted, returned in the Universal. But, in the face of the emergent diversities which I just described—singular "faces" or "worlds"—it is a multiversal humanism that tries to find itself today. And I conclude by asking, Is this possible? Reality makes me skeptical. But if it is, it could only be possible with our traditions of the Universal and their modifications, which testify to the leaps and crises of secularism.

RK: A final question concerning your recent work on Teresa of Avila and the critical rapport between faith and fiction. I would like to hear you say more about your idea of "writing therapy," which recurs in several of your works, not just on Teresa but also on figures as different as Proust, Duras, and Colette. I am fascinated by your suggestion that writing can actually be a way of transforming "folly" into "sense," psychosis into sacrament (in the case of Teresa)—a way of creating a new relationship between what you call "love-thinking" (*pensée-amour*) and a new "body-thinking" (*corps-pensée*). You often cite eucharistic motifs here and are clearly fascinated by the theme of writing as "transubstantiation" in writers like Joyce and Proust. Do you feel some resonance here with your own writing?

JK: Teresa and Proust are particularly interesting to me in this regard. Born of an "old Catholic" mother and a Marrano (Jewish convert) father, Teresa "writes (her) fiction so as to be understood." She constructs herself in this way and becomes—through writing—a famous author, a political woman, decisive in the politics of the Church that will make her a saint. But it is Marcel Proust—born of a Jewish mother and a Catholic father, himself ironic and sardonic, subtle analyst of homosexuality and society, neither Jewish nor Catholic and both at the same time—who brilliantly describes the experience of writing as transubstantiation. (I try to address this in some detail in *Le temps sensible: Proust et l'expérience littéraire* [1994].) "Let us suppose Catholicism dies out," he writes, while protesting against the closing of cathedrals, and actually assimilating his experience of writer to transubstantiation.

RK: But how is this possible? What did Proust mean by adopting and adapting this pivotal mystery of Catholic theology? Do you agree that there is something of an "anatheist" retrieval going on in Proust, something I argue in the third chapter of *Anatheism*?

JK: Yes. Proust understood transubstantiation, in Catholic fashion, to refer to the Eucharist, where the bread and the wine, by the consecration of the mass, are not signs or figures of the body of Christ but actually become the flesh of Christ, transformed into his "real presence." Hence, for Proust, this transformation—this metamorphosis of life into human words—is fulfilled in the act of writing. And it is the metaphor that realizes—for those who want to read it with this sensorial lining—the transubstantiation which the novelist dreams of.

In a letter to Lucien Daudet, Proust mentions a "certificate" of his baptism and first communion. If the baptism actually took place on August 5, 1871, at the Church of Saint-Louis d'Antin, no trace of a certificate of communion exists in the family archives, nor in that of the Church. Moreover, a letter by Father M. Fillard, archivist of Saint-Louis d'Antin in the 1990s, when I wrote *Le temps sensible*, confirms that the parish registers did not mention first communions in Proust's epoch, and no certificate had been delivered on this occasion. The style taken from Proust's letter—where he goes so far as to mention an "archbishop of Saint-Louis d'Antin"—implies that this "certificate" is only an exaggeration designed to convince L. Daudet of his Catholicism. A photo of Proust taking his first communion could have authenticated the allegations of the correspondence, but it does not seem to exist in any public documents. The biographies mention, however, the young Proust's catechism course, which his mother could have judged too strict for the fragile sensibility of her child.

We must resolve ourselves to think that the minimal element of Proustian writing is not the word-sign, but a doublet: sensation *and* idea; represented perception and incarnate image. Proust savors his sensations as the essence of things, provided that they are associated with conflicting desires of a personal history; he lives from a "transformed intelligence incorporated into matter." And might not this transformation of energy, where the thinker disappears and drags things in front of us, be the first effort of the writer toward style? Which is no less than a definitive "matter, cool and pink." Could this style be a flesh? Because he reveals yours to you?

According to Proust, writing is a transubstantiation because it is an "experience," in the double sense that this term has in German: *Erlebnis* and *Erfahrung*. It makes a new object emerge, immediately grasped. First appearance and brilliance (*Erlebnis*), it becomes a secondhand knowledge of this emerging, patient learning (*Erfahrung*).

Whether a repressed emotion or an active synthesis, or even both at once, experience runs through the subject's carnal and verbal manifestations and completely modifies his psychic map. And experience is inseparable from desire and love. In them and through them, it feels like a conversion. As psychology *and* representation, experience signals a fragile hyphen, which is painful or joyful, between the body and the idea which makes these distinctions null and void.

Proustian experience is, I would argue, doubly transubstantial. It is memory found again, under ideas and words—the opaque force of a sensorial shock that immerses the speaking being in Being and includes the whole universe in a subjective imaginary. The art of metaphor and that of the sentence consists in transmitting this adherence to the ontological—the communion of the psyche with the world, the outside reinvested in the inside that takes pleasure in it so as to speak about it.

Concurrent with this imaginative incorporation of the world, this absorption of the ontological, Proust gives his body to literature and, through literature, to the world. Suffocating in a dull room on Hamelin Street, without food and without sleep, deathly ascetic, he offers his dinner guests the example of a dying person in the middle of assuring his resurrection through a book. All those who knew him during his last years had been struck by the mystical vigor of this transmutation of a body into literature, beyond the assumed snobbism and the often fetid odor of complacent friendships. Devouring the world to the point of blending with the palpitation of things and with the foibles of socialites, the writer wholeheartedly lets himself pour out in his work, which takes the place of infinite Being like grace. He joins a Christlike ambition with Greek sensualism; the passion become man sacrifices himself to the last cult—that of literature—which seems to him the only thing capable of closing the loop, of leading the Word to flesh.

However, this finale would have been too pathetic, and thus not at all Proustian, if it were not preceded by the interminable spirals of an ironic interpretation—anatheist, painful, disabused, and returning endlessly to all of its movements, of which one could trace the unconscious filiation to the Talmudic penchant for unmasking. Similarly, inhabited by violence and biblical remorse, Proust does not separate affection from desire. This confusion, which is a revelation, admittedly engenders a lot of misfortune for the characters and the narrator. But all along, misfortune—interpreted in all its sensorial parts and under all the corners where the characters could live—recedes in poses, deceptions, appearances, impressions, points of view. The heart of the pathetic spectacle turns out to be "the immense edifice of memory." The only dignity that is of value here is the position of this voyeur incarnated in the objects of his named senses—the narrator.

"Reality, this waste of experience," writes Proust. Allow me to add that only an experience can save us. From this point on, the gods who have permitted the dignity and the decay of men make themselves too inaudible or too restrictive. Ethics rarely creates joy. But loves, when we encounter them, and hates, when they do not immediately destroy us, always arouse needs and desires for which we lack places and times. Experience is the single configuration by which we reach a jouissance.

At the limits of the body, in the silences or the excesses of sex, between the world and what I can say about it, experience is this process of love and hate that makes me a living person. In the confines of a faith—Catholic, Protestant, Jewish, Muslim, Buddhist—or even in my solitude in Being, with its meanings and figures, or still in the humility of a devotion, the taming of an egoism, the excesses of an effort—experience is extreme. It opens me to myself, it drives me to the end, it makes me leave myself; and finally, it is a place where I can encounter others or lose myself. One chance.

We approach psychic death because the death of values that we complain about risks reaching a point of no return. What is the best antidote to this laziness, to this eclipse of a civilization, if not to let ourselves be devoured by and incorporated by time, to absorb it, to come back to life exorbitant, like the sentence whispered from a refound memory, to come up against this exquisite edge where the world makes itself sense and where sense becomes sensible? In search of jouissance, in search of experience —isn't this *In Search of Lost Time*? Can we still read it?

RK: I believe we can.

—Translated from the French by Jennifer McWeeney

6

Anatheism, Nihilism, and Weak Thought

Dialogue with Gianni Vattimo

The Italian philosopher and politician Gianni Vattimo is best known for his concept of "weak thought" (*pensiero debole*). Weak thought is Vattimo's term for his hermeneutic ontology: human existence and perception are interpretive all the way down. In his most recent work, Vattimo has argued for a "hermeneutic communism," a communism stripped of grand metaphysical assumptions that seeks to stem the tide of capitalism by working on concrete issues—in particular, historical communities. While Vattimo derives his thinking from Nietzsche, Heidegger, and Gadamer, in the works *Belief* (1999) and *After Christianity* (2002) he has also articulated weak thought in terms of his own Christian tradition, as incarnational thinking.

As he makes clear in the following conversation, incarnational Christianity means that God exists only in memory, only within our particular story, through the historical tradition that shaped how we perceive reality. Vattimo goes so far as to call his incarnational faith "atheistic." For him, atheism is precisely the conviction that God does not exist as a Supreme Being, nor as any kind of "real" presence. In fact, his radical refusal of any philosophical realism makes him wonder whether Kearney's notion of returning to "epiphanies" of religious experience constitutes a regress into metaphysics, as if some reality rewarded the anatheistic return. By the end of this dialogue, however, both Kearney and Vattimo agree on an anatheistic hermeneutic according to which truth, God, and justice are a matter of "endless democratic interpretation."

The following conversation took place in Vilnius, Lithuania, in July 2013. Their exchange is prefaced by Vattimo's general response to Kearney's book *Anatheism*, which provided the context for their conversation.

> GIANNI VATTIMO (GV): Responding to Kearney's excellent work means I have to take a stand toward the book. This attitude of hermeneutic responsibility certainly won't displease Kearney; from this stand I have to understand and attempt to let others understand the importance of this text, and why it is worth reading and meditating. I can sum up what I have to say in two words: *anatheism* (which is the title of the book), and *kenosis*, a slightly lesser-known Greek term, which, however, should be well known to specialist and nonspecialist readers of Saint Paul's letters and the tradition of Christian mysticism.

ANATHEISM

Anatheism is the religious attitude Kearney promotes and recommends for the spirituality of our time; kenosis is the term Saint Paul uses in a famous passage from the letter to the Philippians to designate the meaning of the Incarnation. Making himself human like us, the Son of God "lowered" and humbled himself to the point of being treated like a criminal and suffering death on the cross.

At first blush, the Greek prefix *ana-* could be understood negatively, as if Kearney's point were a negation of atheism, the way the prefix is used in the Italian word for "alcohol free," *analcolico*. However, *ana-* means both "ascent" and "return." Kearney does not emphasize both of these meanings. He prefers the second meaning, return.[1] However, I would not say that the first meaning, "ascent," is entirely absent. As the reader will realize, for Kearney the return always implies some moment of full illumination, some kind of reaching the summit, which certainly coincides with the dark night many mystics recount, but nonetheless retains the character of a decisive moment. Kearney conceives of this moment as a sort of evidence, in keeping with the tradition of phenomenology he inherited from his mentor, Paul Ricoeur. Therefore, the meaning of the prefix *ana-* is not only a philological issue but also a philosophical one; it seems to me that it marks the slight but not insignificant difference through which I penetrate Kearney's discourse, and in so doing, it indicates the only interpretive path I wish to indicate.

The culture in which we happen to live is inclined to think of itself as the point of arrival of a development. In the prevailing philosophical schemes (whose origin is Hegel but is also generically positivistic and inspired by the Enlightenment), such development is conceived as originating in primordial phases characterized by theism and by a religiosity not infrequently superstitious. Then, progress evolved through science and technology toward Nietzsche's "death of God" (the idea of God revealing itself for Nietzsche as a lie no longer necessary for the techno-scientifically developed man); that is, toward an increasingly generalized theoretical and practical atheism.

Kearney starts off denying validity to this historicist Enlightenment narrative, in light of both his personal experience and what he rightly considers a widely spread resurgence, or survival, of the problem of God beyond all atheistic decrees. This is not only because of what we could call the performative self-contradictions of "progress" (such as the nuclear bomb or the holocaust) but also because of the uncertainty and the experience of finitude that characterize our world. These experiences awaken our world to that sense of void and suspension of all certainties Kearney calls anatheism. Once again in keeping with his phenomenological training, Kearney conceives of this mood along the lines of Husserl's *epoché*, the suspension of the "natural" attitude toward things that enables the elevation to a vision of essences.

We move beyond the "natural" atheism of our world when we experience the void, which is also the openness to an epiphany, an illumination, which opens us anew to the experience of God—whatever God it is. The void and the uncertainty that open us to anatheism and to a new possible encounter with God include the modern and late-modern awareness of the plurality of religions, as well as the problem of interreligious dialogue and the manifold ways that intersect and sometimes clash in it. Kearney's anatheist is a person of dialogue with foreign gods—the gods of strangers. The religiosity regained in the suspension of theistic and atheistic absolutes is also characterized by an openness toward the other. This openness has always been unavailable to faiths that haven't gone through the mystical and cultural dark night of which we moderns are both the offspring and the products.

In the frequent autobiographical digressions of the book, Kearney recalls his long fights against the authoritarianism of his own church and of other churches and sects he came across. In this way, anatheism is not only, at bottom, the moment of suspension and void geared toward finding anew a "full" faith more or less akin to traditional faiths, but also an attitude that has to accompany every faith regained. (It almost looks like we are talking about the Kantian "I think"!)

Every faith, in whatever way it has been regained, has to entail a prayer asking for help to believe: "Lord, I believe; please help my unbelief." This, as Kearney reminds us, was also Mother Teresa's prayer. And we could also think of Pascal, who recommended to nonbelievers to pray in order to obtain faith.

Thus, anatheistic faith comes very close (perhaps too close for ecclesiastical orthodoxy?) to poetry and poetic imagination. On this point, however, one could object to Kearney that his conception of a kind of phenomenological evidence that would fill the void of anatheistic experience runs the risk of coming dangerously close to a reprise of metaphysical religion. There has to be "something," some kind of essence that we run into (more or less realistically), when in the anatheistic suspension one experiences some kind of illumination, a sort of dialectical reversal of darkness into light. Otherwise, what would be the difference between the poetic myth and the religion which one "believes"?

There are many myths today. In the pluralistic world in which we live, it is hard not to notice it, alongside the inevitable repercussions this has on one's faith, be it theistic or atheistic. Kearney decides to choose narration as his working method. Do the many, often fascinating literary examples found and presented in Kearney's book, then, offer an answer to the theoretical question concerning the capacity to live an anatheistic faith? To live a faith, that is, which is not merely born anew in the moment of radical openness, of the epoché or phenomenological suspension of all putative obviousness and certainty, but which, on the contrary, can be continuously lived as non-absolute?

KENOSIS

At this point, we can find the other term that I suggested as a guide in reading the book: kenosis; i.e., God's lowering and self-humbling, divine abandonment of majesty and transcendence. Kenosis is in fact central for Kearney, too. From my point of view, which is otherwise thoroughly sympathetic with Kearney's anatheistic proposal, his phenomenological assumptions lead him to expect that the moment of suspension and emptying is preliminary to some kind of fulfillment, thus potentially misleading him into thinking of kenosis only as a provisional stage, as if God humbled himself temporarily in order to recall us to him and finally let us partake in his triumphant plenitude.

God's lowering would thus be a pedagogic device, a kind of communicative strategy, which leaves entirely unchanged the traditional metaphysical picture of God as the self-subsistent being. Even the proximity of religious experience to poetry, and even (especially) the rebellion against the absolutism of dogmas and churches, risks falling back into the shadow (or light) of God's provisional self-humbling, who nonetheless remains the indefectible supreme reality of our traditional faiths.

The questions arising from this possible interpretation of Kearney's book are numerous and not at all trivial. For instance, Kearney's decision to refer to atheism and theism within the context of Abrahamic religions is in a sense historically and hermeneutically compelling. However, won't this decision have different meanings depending on how kenosis is considered? Is the God humbling himself only one among many pictures of God offered by known cultures? Do we abide with it only because we were accidentally born in the Judeo-Christian tradition, with the understanding that in the end we have to get rid of it (like Wittgenstein's famous ladder in the barn) in order to get to God as he really is? If on the contrary, as Christians are supposed to think, kenosis is a story that pertains to God himself and not only to one of his culturally conditioned images, how will anatheistic faith be configured in its actually lived form?

Thus, modern secularization can be perceived as a mere historical accident that—qua epoché, void, experience of being lost—prepares us for a new religious plenitude, or else as a vocation that has to be lived in all its implications, to the point of thinking, with Bonhoeffer but perhaps even beyond him, that "there is no God who is there" (*un Dio che c'è non c'è*). This would imply, for instance, that one worships God exclusively in the form of service to others, not only without dogmas and holy offices but also without churches and rites, most of all without hierarchical divisions between clergy and laymen, and so on. Perhaps we could say that, for essential reasons, an authentically kenotic God can only be experienced in an anatheistic or, more simply, anamnestic religion. The God whom Moses can only glimpse from behind while he is departing gives himself to us likewise only in the form of a memory, which never refers to a past or future presence. We are not far from the childhood images of Christmas, the Child Jesus, the things that we "remember" on certain festivities and in some periods of the year. Memories, in fact.

Only those who lose their soul—not just temporarily, in order to then gain eternal life—shall save it. Let us acknowledge that a religiosity of this kind is hard to conceive, even before being hard to live. This goes to show that it is impossible to be religious without some kind of institutionalization—and then discipline, dogmas, and, in the end, hierarchies. These are the historically inevitable conditions, perhaps so far—or forever—of the theistic–atheistic tradition, of religious wars, of opposed absolutisms. With respect to kenosis, Kearney (who is so kind as to cite one of my books) remembers the French Passionist Stanislas Breton, who reads the kenotic ethics as sharing the destiny of the "damned of the earth" who fight for their liberation, and at the same time thinks that at the lowest point of lowering (including the ethical lowering of those fighting to the last) there is a kind of paradoxical bouncing back, an "exulting ascent up to the point of origin."

"What else otherwise?" one could legitimately ask. Kenotic ethics can be lived in a monastic form—in the literal sense of the word: remaining outside of the world—or else by becoming poor among the poor and the outcast (obviously, without them having any benefit from it; rather than another little brother of Father Charles de Foucauld in a favela, a wealthy and skillful entrepreneur is better). But how could one enact kenotic ethics politically? How make of it the principle of a revolution? And why would we, if the point is still preparing for the encounter with that God who, if one doesn't take kenosis seriously enough, is still the unmoved mover of medieval theology?

An intensification of interreligious or interethical dialogue does not seem like a plausible conclusion of Kearney's discourse; after all, this is not really the solution he proposes. As we bitterly learned, among other things, from the recent experience of the economic crisis, globalization— I think also in the case of ethics, of doctrines, etcetera—only masks the domination of one part of the world over the others. Who can really set out to build a global ethics without abiding or installing oneself in a standpoint of sovereignty? Does anyone know of mythical cultures having theories about multiple mythical cultures? Such a theory, as much as global ethics, requires a perspective of sovereignty.

In this respect, too, it is better to practice an anatheistic religiosity as a way to side with the "last and least of these," upholding a position of moderate ethnocentrism (such as Rorty's): I am aware of being within a particular perspective, and I try to live it in an open, hospitable, and tolerant way as much as possible, knowing that in the multitude of interpretations the only one that is certainly false is the one that claims to be identical with the truth. In politics, too, I will choose to fight with those with whom I find myself mostly (and reflectively) in consonance (proletarian with proletarians, anatheist Christian with anatheist Christians, pacifist with pacifists), without ever thinking that I am fighting for the truth, nor that "God is with us." In so doing, I take it that if there is a God (even in the Bonhoefferean way of not being there) he is anatheistic like me.

RICHARD KEARNEY (RK): Let us return to the word *ana-* ("after" in English, "dopo" in Italian). The question of what comes after— after God, after theism, after Christianity. How does the "after" inform the relation between the sacred and the secular?

GV: I love your idea of ana-. And I suppose my initial thought is this: Why should I speak of something after God if I believe that Nietzsche is right to say that God is dead? Well, first, I would say that it is in the Gospels themselves that we learn that it is because God is dead that we can be both Christian and atheist. It doesn't mean God disappears but that there is an incarnate God who dies. This incarnate God signals the end of the traditional metaphysical God. So we live in the epoch of nihilism because the death of God, in Nietzsche's sense, means there is no longer one supreme value; there is no longer a supremely existing God, a Supreme Being. This is what we mean today when—after

Heidegger and Nietzsche—we speak of the "end of metaphysics." I would say that, today, it has become both possible and necessary to become anatheist, to become postreligious. Because, as a matter of fact, there is no foundational structure of Being we recognize, there is no ultimate or ulterior Being in itself, no noumenal substance hidden behind phenomenal appearance. That is why one is Christian rather than Kantian.

RK: So you would hold to the term *Christian* or *ana-Christian*?

GV: Yes. For instance, the difference between me and Derrida here is the question of history. He is deeply and seriously a Jewish thinker who does not believe that something happened in history. I believe that something happened in history. And here I am closer to Hegel than to Derrida, or to Kant. For Kant believed in a transcendental ego that is timeless and universal, always the same; but after Hegel, Dilthey, and Heidegger, we can no longer believe in such a timeless truth outside of history.

RK: How does this relate to your understanding of nihilism? When you say nihilism you do not, of course, mean nothing at all. There are different kinds of nothing, right? Or as Samuel Beckett puts it, "Nothing is more real than nothing."

GV: When I speak of nihilism I do not speak of a structure of Being which reveals itself as "nothing." No. I speak of a history in which the supreme values have lost their value—in the sense that the old God no longer exists. But not in the sense of nothing exists. Nihilism doesn't mean we sink into nothingness. It must be understood as a story, the story of a history.

RK: And Christ is one of the characters?

GV: Yes. And Saint Paul is another. I don't say this story is History, with a capital *H*—The History, the Only History. No. It is *our* story, *our* history. We are related to our particular cultural and historical provenance. And in this sense I, like you, am deeply hermeneutic. For hermeneutics is a philosophy made possible by the fact that we live in a web—today a worldwide web (www) of communications, travels, multiple cultures and values, particularly since the discovery of new worlds, several other worlds, a plurality of hitherto unknown continents. The hermeneutic motto—"There are no facts, only interpretations"—would not be possible without such interconnections and involvements with a complexity of worlds and values. And I believe that all this is a central part of our nihilistic history as Christian history.

RK: We share a deep respect for the German pastor Bonhoeffer, murdered by the Nazis. As you know, I cite him as an exemplary anatheist with his call for a "religionless" Christianity. And I suspect you, too, have sympathy with his call for the integration of faith in a secular world. Especially when he speaks of a God without religion and metaphysics and asks: "How do we speak in a secular way about God? In what way are we religionless secular Christians?" Or again, when he claims that "With God we live without God. For God is weak and powerless in the world and that is precisely the way, the only way, in which he is with us and helps us."[2] Would you go along with this secular reading of the divine, which I myself seek to develop with Bonhoeffer in *Anatheism*?

GV: I would, but I would express it more ontologically. The way to understand the "nothingness" of nihilism—the "without God"—is to realize that Being is not something that "is" but something that "happens." And so it is not something we possess as a presence but something we remember as past.

RK: As what has passed and passed away?

GV: Yes. Weak thinking (*pensiero debole*), as I formulate it, is a history of rememoration of what has been forgotten. Why? Because metaphysics—which has dominated so much of our philosophical and theological thinking—is, as Heidegger noted, a forgetfulness of Being. So, for me, hermeneutics is an attention to the claim that Being is what happens. Being is event. But is that all that I can say? It is true that I cannot directly describe the fact that Being *is not*, but happens. No. So the only way to think Being in relation to beings is to remember what happened. But remember what? Remember all? Everything? No. Remember what was forgotten.

RK: So when Being that was forgotten is revealed as nothing, nothing, no-longer-being (that is, as discarded, excluded, occluded), *only* then *can* Being that was forgotten be remembered? In other words, we must remember the forgetfulness of Being that has been forgotten in order to remember Being? Is that what you are saying? And if so, would that apply equally to the forgetting and remembering of God?

GV: If I don't remember what is forgotten, I simply go on considering what "is" as Being, as all that there is. And the same applies to the being and not-being of God. Here, Heidegger's critique of metaphysics as ontotheology is right, but it is not enough. It needs to be complemented and completed by Benjamin. Forgotten being, as Walter Benjamin realized, is the silence of the losers. Heidegger offers interesting hints about retrieving lost being in his last major lecture in the 1960s, *On Time and Being*. But we have to resist the lure of mystical metaphysics, of some primordial forgotten secret.

RK: Some magical *Geheimnis* where *Geschichte* (history) is masked as *Geschick* (destiny).

GV: Exactly. For such a mystified original Secret can easily ignore the ordinary historical call of forgotten human beings. We should, I suggest, understand Heidegger's Silence of Being in terms of Benjamin's silence of the silenced.

RK: The voice of the voiceless. Or, as Saint Paul says—a phrase you cite in several of your writings—"the nothings and nobodies." Forgotten being is about the power of the powerless, isn't it? The power of the weak? Or what Jack Caputo, after Paul, calls "the weakness of God"?

GV: My idea of weak thought is precisely that—the thought of the weak.

RK: A thinking *of* the weak, which is also a thinking *about* the weak—understood as the vanquished, oppressed, disinherited, excluded.

GV: Yes, and so the reversal of the metaphysical model of Being echoes the reversal of the idea that history belongs to the victors. "*Vae victis*! Woe to the vanquished." Weak thinking takes the side of those who have nothing against those who have (or think they have) everything. Just ask yourself, who are the ones offended by the declaration that the God of Supreme Being and Might is dead? It is not the weak. It is not the meek. It is those who claim that Being *is* and that it is *theirs*—their foundation, their authority, their power. So, in a way what I am calling for is a new "weak" way of rethinking nihilism and communism—and Christianity. Weak thought is not popular with the winners, with right-wing news media. The winners cannot accept that what is theirs now, in the present, is not eternal, endless, sanctioned by divine right, blessed by God. So what we need to listen to—if we are to free ourselves from addiction to present power, present presence, present Being—is the forgotten.

RK: The as-yet-unpublished story of the losers?

GV: Exactly. For, as Benjamin says, what makes real revolution is not some glorious, luminous idea or ideology but the suffering of the lost ones.

RK: Paul Ricoeur calls this as our "debt to the dead" in his conclusion to *Time and Narrative*. So revolution becomes a negation of negation, an unforgetting of the forgetting.

GV: Yes. And when people ask me what I am *for*, I tell them first what I am *against*: the forgetting of the weak and suffering. There is a verse of Eugenio Montale, written during the fascist period: "*Codesto solo oggi possiamo dirti: ciò che non siamo, ciò che non vogliamo*" (The only thing we can say to you today is what we are not and what we don't want). This is the attitude of revolutionary nihilism. Or, as I often like to say, "Now that God is dead we can love one another!" Or as Aristotle is alleged to have said, "I am a friend of Plato, but I am more a friend of truth."

RK: This brings us back to the question of the ana-. What comes after Being and after God?

GV: You and I are very close on this. But there are also some small differences in our readings of "after," as I tried to point out in my preface to the Italian translation of your *Anatheism*. On my first reading of your book—perhaps I feel this less now—I felt that for you the "after" is a void in which positive illuminations and affirmations can come to us. And this seems to me a bit too mystical. But now I tend to agree that listening and attending to what arrives or emerges in the space and time of ana- is also a way of accepting that certain illuminations may come—which are not just a return to the old God, the old Being, the old presence. I think I understand better what you mean. I subscribe to

Hölderlin's sentiment that "Only at times can our kind bear the full impact of gods. Ever after our life is a dream about them" [*Bread and Wine*, seventh stanza]. This was the epigraph for my first book on Heidegger, *Being, History, and Language*. I agree that clearings, lightings, *Lichtungen* happen. But I like to stress that we live this mainly as a dream after the events, never in their immediacy, or positive presence or return to presence. Illuminations of being are always what is already gone. If it is not gone, it is because you still claim to have it now, in the present, as presence or re-presentation, and you are a metaphysician. Heidegger fell back into metaphysics when he became a Nazi, because he erroneously believed that national socialism promised a luminous new beginning, which might replay and replace the original beginning of pre-Socratic Greece—Greece before metaphysics.

RK: So his seduction by Nazism was, ironically and tragically, a metaphysical nostalgia for the lure of a premetaphysical origin, a regressive nostalgia for the pure name of the first beginning. What Freud might call melancholic longing for the "lost object." A sort of metaphysical hankering for something that never actually existed in the first place. A mistaken desire to recover something in its lost plenitude. The illusory lure of a lost illusion.

GV: Yes. And I would say here that Heidegger forgot his own great insight into the ontological difference. He mistook Hitler for the new Heraclitus. After 1934—and especially after "The Origin of the Work of Art," in 1936—Heidegger never engaged in or commented on politics anymore. But he kept going back again and again in search of the originary words of the poets and thinkers, particularly pre-Socratic thinkers like Anaximander and Heraclitus. He kept trying to recapture the originary event of Being-coming-into-truth in forms of poetic thinking, replacing political acts with works of art. He was obsessed with rediscovering new ways of beginning, of radical novelty, of pure Being.

RK: And what is politics for you today? How does your work as an active member of the European Parliament relate to your own "weak thinking"?

GV: What I am trying to do is the opposite of Heidegger. I want to make politics *practical* by opening new horizons and paradigms in very concrete ways. That's what it means to be a hermeneutic communist, as I explain (with Santiago Zabala) in *Hermeneutic Communism.*[3]

RK: You are rereading Marx in a revolutionary way through Benjamin and Paul—in the name of the lost ones. But can one do the same with Christianity? It seems to me that you reread the "nihilism" of the death of God in a way which retrieves and reinterprets key Christian notions like kenosis, the kingdom, *caritas*, the least of these. These terms frequently recur in your recent writings. There is more here than an embrace of the void.

GV: In philosophical terms it is a rejection of reduction, a refusal of the positivist reduction to the preconceptions of objectivity. When Jesus speaks of the *Parousia*, he speaks negatively, warning us not to believe those who say prematurely, "Here is the Messiah." He resists objectification. He refuses to say positively what or who he is.

RK: "Who do you say that I am?" as he quizzes his disciples. One might say that Jesus is a perpetual giving which refuses to become a given. He is messianic by disappearing as soon as he appears. *Noli me tangere.* "I must go so that the Paraclete can come." He reveals himself as the one who cannot be captured, fixed, determined, the one who is always already gone and always still to come.

GV: Yes. I am giving a lecture shortly on the question, Does a real hero exist? I will claim that all heroes in our culture are always dead. You never encounter a hero. They don't exist in the now, only in the past tense. You tell the story of a hero, the story of the history of a hero. But the hero is already dead and gone. I think this is what Heidegger hints at in *Being and Time*, when he writes: "Being not beings, insofar as there is truth." The event of Being, when it happens, only happens at sunset. It is always twilight.[4]

RK: The owl of Minerva has already flown, as Hegel says.

GV: I think that there are traces of a residual apophatic Christianity in Heidegger. Being gives itself insofar as it retreats. And his view also chimes with Anaximander's phrase, "Whence things have their coming into being, there they must also perish according to necessity; for they must pay a penalty and be judged for their injustice, according to the ordinance of time." For Heidegger, death is the shrine of Being. Dying is an opening of space for others. I confess that I personally believe in some kind of eternity. I still believe that my loved ones live on somehow. But perhaps in the sense of my friend who said, "Is there a life before death?"

RK: I was very struck, on reading your *Not Being God*, how you continue to believe in ideas like eternal life and the hope of somehow seeing your loved ones—your aunt, your lover—again; and that you say compline prayers and invoke basic Christian notions of love, compassion, kenosis from the Gospels and Paul. And yet you say, again and again, "Thank God I am an atheist." A nice performative paradox! So I am curious to know what kind of "atheist" you are. As you know, there are several other contemporary philosophers rereading Paul in recent years—Agamben, Badiou, Kristeva, Žižek—and all claim to be atheist. And Derrida, as you are also aware, repeated the fact that he "rightly passes for an atheist." How to you understand your own atheism? I personally think you are an anatheist atheist!

GV: For me, the answer to the question lies—as I suspect it does for you too?—in listening to the others, in listening to the history of the forgotten. Even the pope, when he meets the Dalai Lama, must listen to his other, mustn't he? He doesn't behave as if the Dalai Lama's soul is lost. *Extra ecclesiam nulla salus*! No. Even the pope nowadays is an anatheist—at least he appears so in dialogue with others, in welcoming strangers, as you would say, Richard, with your notion of anatheist hospitality. As I often put it, sin means not paying attention, not listening to the other. As when we say in Italian, after letting something go unnoticed, "*Che peccato*!" What a pity! What a shame! What a sin!

RK: One has something similar in colloquial English, when one says, "I missed it!" I didn't listen; I didn't see or catch it while it was there. I didn't pay enough attention—and so the moment passed me by. I missed the boat!

GV: Exactly. So *Andenken,* for me, is a way of thinking back, paying attention to what was lost; it is going beyond what is merely present to remember what is past, to undo our forgetting.[5] That is why to make a revolution you cannot be a Stalinist, for Stalin did not remember. He paid no heed to what was missing and missed, to what was lost and gone. He was too bent on victory, triumph, power.

RK: The lure of the New Soviet Man. Pure presence. If Stalin had been capable of weak thought he could not have murdered those millions.

GV: Stalin simply adopted the capitalist-military-metaphysical model of power and gave it a different name, a different color.

RK: To come back to the question of anatheism and atheism . . . I am reminded of a "weak" reading of the Greek Orthodox notion of *perichoresis*. Rather than reading this as a triumphal icon of pure presence between the three persons of the Trinity, I like to hermeneutically rethink the *chora* at its heart—the empty space which allows the three persons to constantly move, each leaving a place for the other, as in the Latin translation *circum-in-cessio*, where "*cedo*" means to cede one's place to the one coming after you, to the stranger, the placeless one. So that the Trinity may be rethought as a constant dynamism of mobility and desire, giving something to the other from out of the space of nothing, from the free place one leaves open, from no-place, *u-topos*.

GV: And this giving space you describe reminds one of Anaximander's word about "giving time."

RK: What I wonder is this: Can we rethink Christianity "weakly," in terms of giving time and space? Abandoning the place of the Master to become a "suffering servant," washing feet, healing the sick, listening to the forgotten—the Samaritan, the crippled, the excluded, the weak, the *alienigena*, as the healed "foreigner" is called in Latin in Luke 17:18, when he returns to give thanks. Attending to the "lost sheep." Wasn't Christ himself an exemplary "loser" in your sense? An alien stranger, an *alienigena* like the healed leper who returns to give thanks. Hence the irony of the Church triumphal turning the servant Christ into a king and master! Something Dostoyevsky understood so brilliantly in his "Grand Inquisitor," and so trenchantly analyzed by Ivan Illich as "*corruptio optimi est pessima*," the corruption of the best is the worst.

GV: I would have liked to discuss all this with our new pope, Francesco! I almost met him in Argentina last year for an interreligious conversation between a rabbi, a Muslim, Bergoglio [Francesco], and myself. But he was elected pope and had to leave!

RK: *Che pecatto*! You missed him!

GV: I did. But I think he has started his new job well.

RK: So you think the church is retrievable? Is it possible to have a weak, communist, nihilist, hermeneutic Christianity? Or, in my terms, an anatheist Christianity?

GV: I think it is not impossible. But first the church must become accommodated to secularization. The temptation is to look for the future of the church in a return to some kind of original, pure Christianity, as the Vatican has tried to do in Africa, for example. They sought to revitalize the church by going back to some illusory beginning, an originary time of miracles. And then one finds people like Monseigneur Emmanuel Milingo, a bishop who practices black magic and refuses to engage with secular society. So there is the danger of a new spiritual primitivism, an obsession with pure origins, which the Western Catholic church identifies with Africa. I distrust this attempt to reconstruct a presecular spirit, or any attempts at big conversions, as when kings of old converted entire populations by dint of power.

RK: As here in Lithuania, where we are now speaking—the last European country to be evangelized, in the fourteenth century. They were given the choice by the invading Christian emperor, to become Christian or die. But to come back to an earlier question: In what sense do you remain an atheist?

GV: In the sense that I do not believe that God exists as a Supreme Being.

RK: In that sense, I too am an atheist.

GV: What I like about atheism is it weakness, its smallness. *Ateismo è bello*! Atheism is beautiful, just as small is beautiful. So why am I still a Christian? Because I was born one. Many believe that, to be a Christian, you need proofs of the existence of some metaphysical Being, evidence of a first cause of the universe. The inaugural moment of the big bang. The so-called God particle [Higgs]. What interests me is not that but what happens *after* the beginning, the history that comes after the big bang. And that includes Jesus. And I am part of that history. I don't need to go back to some first origin—physical or metaphysical—and I don't see why any theory, argument, or evidence of that kind should deny the history of events which follow after, and which include Christianity, the story in which I find myself.

RK: So you resist the idea of a single account of the universe—metaphysical or scientific—in favor of a hermeneutics of narrative? An ongoing hermeneutic conversation in which we play our respective historical roles, with all the responsibility that involves for remembering those who have passed away—edited out of history—and acknowledging the stories that have been preserved and passed on?

GV: Exactly. I do not consider myself a member of Humankind. I am not a subject of some abstract Humanity. I am a single human being who has a part in a history of other human beings. We have to abandon the idea of a sovereign "Universal View from Nowhere." That is a form of normalization, capitalization. I want to cultivate a belief that is not universalist in that abstract, homogenizing sense. My only sense of the universal is the shared hope in the new ones coming.

RK: And who are these "new ones"? Neighbors? Strangers? Are you espousing a form of communitarianism?

GV: I am a communitarian in that I am against predetermined universalism. Often, when I visited North America and was confronted with identity politics, I saw communitarianism as a risk of narrow provincialism and nationalism. But now I think, if it is a legitimate resistance to capitalist universalism, why not? When the Israelis are struggling to create a country, I am with them; but when they become dominant and repress other groups struggling for their country, it is not good.

RK: How do you see your hermeneutic communism playing a role in the European Parliament?

GV: Today, Europe is experiencing a crisis where everything is subject to a kind of economic terrorism. There is a new disciplinarian ethos of fear, austerity, obedience, submission, security. Europe is living in a kind of half light. It risks becoming a big internationalist bank. It needs to become socialist. Lenin said communism was electrification and the soviets. But what we have now in Europe is electrification without soviets. Communities are without power.

RK: It reminds me of what Alasdair MacIntyre says at the end of *After Virtue* about the need for a new Trotsky and a new Saint Benedict. Though in your case it might be more a new Lenin and a new Saint Francis?

GV: I like MacIntyre. He did good work in the early days, on religion and secularization.

RK: He wrote a book on that with Paul Ricoeur.

GV: I especially like Ricoeur's *The Conflict of Interpretations*, and was even tempted at one point to write something called *The Play of Interpretations*, incorporating Gadamer's notion of *Spiel*. But my difference with Ricoeur was that he often drew a sharp distinction between the secular and the religious, between philosophy and theology. Who decides? I don't think he sufficiently theorized the connection between the secular and the sacred. They are not worlds apart. The religious is inextricably bound up with secularization.

RK: I agree. Indeed one of my repeated claims in *Anatheism* is that the sacred is in the secular, though it is not of the secular. One cannot simply separate the two. They are inside each other, and Christianity itself has a deeply secular meaning in its affirmation of everyday life (*secularis* as temporal), as Charles Taylor points out in *A Secular Age*. It is part of our hermeneutic history.

GV: This is where I have a difficulty with Derrida at times. For him, the messianic is about the arrival of some absolute Other, something unprecedented and surprising. But Hitler, too, was absolutely new, unprecedented, surprising. My answer to Derrida is, "Jesus." The Messiah is already come and gone. Part of our history. And that is why we need *Andenken*. Again the "an-" of *ana-*: the hermeneutic thinking back, the rememoration called for by Heidegger and Benjamin. As mentioned above, events are not totally new but things forgotten that are remembered— we recognize an event by remembering to remember it has passed, as past. *Andenken* is attending again to what is missed, remembering what is forgotten. Being is not what is there—a being or combination of beings, givens, actuality—it happens (*es gibt*) as an event that is always just missed, lost, passed. Being is what happens but is only grasped as what has already happened, since it is never present, possessed, given—it is never presence but always a temporality of *différance*.

And that is why I repeat that, when Heidegger bids us listen to "the silent calling of Being" (as what withdraws and conceals), this ontological listening needs to be supplemented by a political listening to the voices of lost generations, those who were muted and masked by the injustices of history, erased in the official version of history—the triumphal account written by the mighty and powerful (empires, kingdoms, churches, victorious states or statesmen). Or, in our modern times, we might speak, with Adorno, of the "total administration" of things—capitalism, technocracy, consumerism, globalization. Ana-thinking, by contrast, is listening to the losers, to the stories that are forgotten in the civilization of winners (namely, those who defend the ruse of reason and destiny, theodicy, metaphysics). The silence we need to listen to today is the silence of the silenced.

So, the ana- of re-membering does not mean remembering everything, every event, but the events of the losers. That is what the ana-, the "re-" of revolution, demands and promises. Nihilism is revolutionary to the extent that it affirms that Being is insofar as it is not. As I mentioned before, for Heidegger, "There is (*es gibt*) Being—not beings—only insofar as truth is." In other words, don't take beings, givens, facts, actualities as the last word. Overcome them towards what is more, other, forgotten by beings. Or, as Zabala put it in his book *The Remains of Being*, being is the "remnants of Being."[6] Nihilism in this sense is refusal: the nihilation of presence as a dominant power. Nihilism is antimetaphysical, if we understand metaphysics as the claim that Being is what "is"—namely, a total being (*Seiendes*).

> RK: So how, finally, might one translate this hermeneutic nihilism of being into a Christian thinking about God?
>
> GV: I come back to Saint Paul and his notion of *hos me*, "as if they do not" [1 Corinthians 7:29–31].This is a Pauline equivalent of the

ontological difference: being is other than what it is. It is nihilism defined as a certain respect for distance and difference. Like Max Scheler says of the phenomenological epoché, it gives us a form of "moral detachment," a form of freedom of negation and suspension. Heidegger had a similar appreciation of phenomenology, early on, a quite Pauline and Christian one, but when he became a national socialist he betrayed this view. He became a Nazi when he stopped reading Paul (and Husserl) and started reading Hölderlin. His initial impulse as a Christian hermeneut was to reject the old metaphysics of Being and a certain Calvinist doctrine of predestination. He wanted to save Being—and God—from theodicy, to rethink and remember them (*Andenken*) instead as event. But the lure of Hitler was the temptation to return to a metaphysical politics of pure origin—as so many of the German Romantics fantasized in relation to ancient Greece, the great beginning when all was one. He thus betrayed not only his revolutionary Pauline Christianity but also his great insight into the historicity of Being as event, as a happening of difference, as gift (*es gibt*).

So, if I am a Christian, it is because I refuse to abandon my historicity and history. Christianity is my childhood—my childhood religion, our childhood religion. It is what has shaped and formed us. And while, as I said, I am very critical of the authoritarianism of the Roman Catholic Church, I also recognize that, without it, I would not have this Christian history, either in terms of what I learned and received growing up or as a member of a historical–cultural community.

But, I repeat, I make no universal claims for my Christianity—no bird's-eye view that this is the only religion, the only true reality. Truth differs from reality in that it is not absolute but always in relation to this or that belief. And once we acknowledge religious truth as a matter of belief or commitment (troth), we also acknowledge the element of unbelief. "I believe; help thou my unbelief." Here we recognize religion—in my case Christianity—as a play of interpretations, of beliefs and disbeliefs, as weak faith in the strongest sense of the word (*debole*). Truth is to be recognized as a series of interpretative paradigms (in Kuhn's sense), not as correspondence to some objective "reality" out there. The truth of Being is not what is but what is not. And, applied to religion, this means, as Bonhoeffer reminds us, that a God who exists doesn't exist. God—like Being—is not an object. God "is" not. Divinity announces itself by subtractions, withdrawal, kenosis, free negation, as when Christ speaks of gaining one's soul by losing it. Or when Paul speaks in the letter to the Philippians of the truth of Christianity as kenosis, divine self-emptying, the privileging of the nothings and nobodies, the "least of these." Here we have a God who ceases to reign as Imperial Father, renouncing sovereign power in order to become our brother as Christ, not a master but a friend and servant. The temptation of the Church is to take God or itself for some kind of timeless Supreme Being—and yet we need the Church for the transmission of the history, the story, the testimony of Christ through time.

RK: How would you define, in sum, an anatheist hermeneutics?

GV: I would say it is neither idealist nor realist. Idealists cling to metaphysical illusions of first beginnings, while realists are reactionaries clinging to a metaphysical model of Reality. They refuse hermeneutics because hermeneutics proposes the model of truth as agreement, discussion, dialogue, conversation. Hermeneutics leads to a politics, or a church, of pluralism. Why? Because it constantly poses the question, "Who says that?" It challenges authoritarians by asking, "According to what authority do you decide this?" Take the absolute authority of economic science in today's world politics—in the EU or US. Who are the economists who decide? This is a question of ideology, and it calls in turn for a recognition that truth—Being, God, art, justice, science—is a matter of endless democratic interpretation. Hermeneutics refuses to believe that one person, science, or doctrine has the truth. It suspects Power as One, the One, the Official Truth. The only truth is "troth," the play between beliefs and disbeliefs. Praying to believe. That, perhaps, is a good motto for anatheist hermeneutics.

7

What's God? "A Shout in the Street"

Dialogue with Simon Critchley

Simon Critchley is a British philosopher and public intellectual who is now Hans Jonas Professor of Philosophy at The New School for Social Research in New York. Critchley's interdisciplinary research interests range from continental philosophy, literature, and psychoanalysis to ethics and political theory. After his first major book, *The Ethics of Deconstruction*, on Levinas and Derrida, Critchley published an essay collection on literature, death, and ethics, entitled *Very Little . . . Almost Nothing*, in which he first articulated what he called "atheist transcendence," a theme that returns in his most recent work, *The Faith of the Faithless*.

Critchley's basic assumption is that social and political engagement always requires faith of some kind, some vision and commitment that go beyond evidence and certainty. He argues that "even those who cannot believe still require religious truth and a framework of ritual in which they can believe."[1] Even the faithless must thus have faith, and such faith cannot be self-generated but requires an infinite external demand. With Levinas, Critchley insists that this infinite demand has to be ethical, has to arise from personal relation, and thus cannot ever put an abstract cause, such as a revolution, for example, above human beings. Religion is often misrepresented as worshipping certainty, but Critchley argues that genuine religious thinkers can actually teach us that faith has to do with very little, almost nothing. As the following conversation demonstrates, Critchley's atheist transcendence aligns with Kearney's anatheism on this level of faith as a wager rather than a certainty.

This exchange took place at The New School, New York, in May 2013.

RICHARD KEARNEY (RK): You, Simon, talk of a faith of the faithless while I talk of a God after God. My question is, "How different are these two positions?" Let me start with a distinction we both make between "belief" (a propositional believing that something called God exists or does not exist) and "faith" (as an infinite demand, desire, hope, trust). You talk of faith as a supreme fiction, but I'd like to know what content, what substance, what truth, such a creedal fiction claims—if any? Your faithless faith is clearly deeply linked to mysticism—as is my notion of anatheism—but if one pushes what you call "mystical nihilism" and "mystical anarchism" to the brink, what do you end up with? Something (theism)? Nothing (atheism)? Or would you be open to the possibility that you could end up with something in between or beyond both? Both theism and atheism; neither theism nor atheism. What I call anatheism? In short, if faith is not a "believing that" but a "faith in," what is it a faith in?

SIMON CRITCHLEY (SC): It can be very simple, as when I speak of faith in another person, the other person. So, at one level, the claim is very basic: whatever meaning religion has—or transcendence has—the content of that is found in the human relation. Here I remain bound to Levinas by the hip. And so I distinguish not just between belief and faith but also between religion (understood as the bond which ties me to others in community) and theology (a discourse founded on a transcendent metaphysical deity, which I remain very suspicious of). There is a moment in *Ulysses*—and I know you have thought and written about this—where Stephen Dedalus is talking with the teacher, Mr. Deasy, and he mentions God. . . .

RK: What's God? "A shout in the street!"

SC: Exactly. It is a shout from outside. It is a cry from outside, heard but unexpected. So the simple answer to your question is that the content of faith is "other." But the difficult answer is to acknowledge that faith is more complex and subtle. What if you *don't* hear the shout on the street? Or you hear the shout and you say, "Shut up! Stop shouting! I'm having a conversation here!" What if you don't hear it as a call? So, in order for faith to have a content, there has to be some subjective disposition towards it.

RK: A disposition to receive the call, to listen, to receive.

SC: And what I guess interests me in people like Paul and Augustine is that theirs is a weird mix of the internal and external. I was thinking the other day about conversion. About the relationship of faith to philosophy, especially in Augustine's *Confessions*, where there is a special subjective moment of turbulence and turmoil, and Augustine is subjectively inclined towards a radical experience of doubt. Then various things happen, and he withdraws from the house and hears a call: "*Tolle lege!*" (Take up and read!). Augustine goes back into the house and opens the Bible at random and reads the passage by Paul which says something like, "Do not fornicate, do not be a bad person," etcetera—and then he is at rest. What does it mean to hear that call? What makes Augustine ready to hear it and to convert, then, at that particular moment, and not at another?

RK: And why call it God? Is not poverty a cry in the street? Sex is a cry in the street. Revolution is a cry in the street. Why God? In other words, why not interpret the cry as ethics or politics rather than religion? Why would you not let go of religion altogether—as so many modern thinkers have done after Freud, Marx, and Nietzsche—and call it humanism?

SC: Because what interests me about the call—in the visceral register of subjective and intersubjective life—is to be found in religious thinkers like Paul, Augustine, Pascal, and Kierkegaard. These people, it seems to me, are asking exactly the right questions in the right way—even if I cannot accept their theological conclusions, their answers.

RK: So you are saying religious writers are telling us "more" about the human—subjective and intersubjective—than nonreligious writers?

SC: Yes, in a way. And in answer to your question about humanism, I would say it all depends on what you mean by that. If you mean liberal humanism wedded to an idea of progress based on a faith in scientific development—for me that is a "theological" dogma that needs to be confronted and challenged by something like faith.

RK: So you would oppose faith to that kind of secular dogmatism?

SC: Yes, and what I consider to be a very pernicious secular theology, which believes that truth is reducible to naturalistic accounts of what it means to be a human being, and that people who don't believe that are stupid or sort of inhuman!

RK: Yes exclusive secular humanism (as Charles Taylor calls it in *A Secular Age*) can be very intolerant at times.

SC: Like all dogmas in different periods.

RK: Religious or irreligious.

SC: Exactly. So it's a question of trying to recover the subtlety, complexity and depth of thinking about the human that one finds in genuine religious thinkers. I only really find it in the religious or mystical tradition, and that, for me, has always been the case. The philosophers who some people no longer consider philosophers—such as Levinas and Heidegger—are thinkers who are thinking very deeply out of a relation to the religious, and that is why, for example, I devote a long chapter to Heidegger's reading of Paul in *Faith of the Faithless*. You can read *Being and Time* back and forth, up and down, and talk about its relationship to Kant and its methodological debt to Husserl or as a rereading of Aristotle, etcetera. But, for me, that is all completely irrelevant without the essential "drama of conversion" that this extraordinary book is all about.

RK: I agree. But you could say that what is religious or Pauline about *Being and Time* is really its "structure" rather than its substance—conversion as a structural event of subjectivity, to use Badiou's kind of language. But for something to be called "religious" generally implies some dimension of divine alterity or truth, some sense of a transcendent or sacred call, doesn't it? And I am not sure that this alterity is present in *Being and Time*. Unlike Levinas, who does speak in such terms, in *Totality and Infinity* and elsewhere. And you do, too, in *Faith of the Faithless*, when you talk of love and hospitality and the infinite call in ways not found in *Being and Time*. You refer to Kierkegaard's "work of love," to faith as a troth-pledge underwritten by love, to Saint Paul's power of the powerless as a radical hetero-affectivity and infinite wanting, and so on. So my question here again is, *Who* calls when the call is infinitely demanding? Is there someone in the "no one" that calls? Is there something in the "nothing" that infinitely demands?

SC: Yes. There is something that calls, but it has to be *heard*. In someone like Levinas, as you know, ethics is a relation with the Other, a relationship of infinite responsibility—so the "content" of the ethical relation, which is also called the religious, is the Other. But if one looks at Levinas's later work, he actually seems to be arguing that what is primary is actually some kind of subjective structure, which he calls "substitution," the Other in the Same, persecution. So that it is almost as if, in order to be able to hear that call, there has to be some kind of conversion in our subjectivity.

RK: A sort of reversal or rupture, a turning around? Something like the Socratic *periagoge* or the biblical response to the summons, "Where are you?"

SC: Yes. So I think there has to be two things going together. There needs to be a content—a call—but also a reception of the call. You may or may not hear the call—as in the classical debates about the empty tomb or the resurrected Christ.

RK: I see what you are saying in terms of the Levinas analogy. But to come back to the "cry in the street," there are, I think, very different kinds of cries as well as very different kinds of responses. Right? One kind says, "Where are you? Feed me! Clothe me! Give me water to drink! Help!" Another says, "*Schnell*, into the gas chamber!" There is a difference between "Hail Mary" and "Heil Hitler," after all! They are not ontologically or ethically the same, or similar, or equiprimordial. Granted, they are all *structurally* cries, but each is delivered, uttered, shouted in a radically different "spirit" in each case. I am using "spirit" here in the sense of Ignatius's hermeneutic "discernment between spirits." There is a huge difference, in short, between the cry that kills and the cry that loves, the cry that takes life and the cry that gives it, the cry that calls for yes or no.

You yourself do not shy away from talking about an ethics and politics of "love." Stephen Dedalus's "cry in the street," as I read *Ulysses*, eventually becomes Molly's final cry of love: "yes I will yes I will yes." Her desire for life gives a future to her past, opens her memory (which she recalls in her half-waking matinal rememoration of the day) to future possibilities of Eros and agape, contained in the promissory note of her closing words: "I *will* yes." As Joyce wrote in a letter to his friend Valery Larbaud, "*Pénélope, le dernier cri.*"

Now, I don't believe for one minute the infinitely demanding call in your ethics, politics, and religion of love—even the famous "love for nothing," which you celebrate in your *Hamlet* book, *Stay, Illusion!*—is *neutral* on this. The specific character, intention, and *sense* of the cry matters hugely. Love is not hate! I don't see how one could escape all evaluative discernment regarding the nature of the Other who calls and cries. The ethical call is to love and justice—which, as Levinas says, defines the religious call par excellence. Isn't that so? It is the call of the widow, the orphan, the stranger—at least in the Jewish-Christian tradition, but also in Buddhism and all the great wisdom traditions. So where is the "Good" in all that? Where is God in the cry that infinitely demands?

sc: I see what you are saying. Tricky. The call can ask for help or make a threat. And my response to the call can be compassionate or violent. I really don't think there is a logical or philosophical procedure to sort these things out. I think we have to accept—and this is something difficult I learned from Levinas—that there is something irreducible here. The Other is the only being I can wish to kill. Why? Because the other person refuses to be negated. If I drink my coffee or eat a banana, I internalize them and negate them as Other. These Others yield to me. But the other human being is not of that character. And therefore I wish to totally negate the Other. There is always this difficult but unpalatable fact—to do with the proximity of love and hate, of peace and violence.

RK: But again, here you are talking about a subjective interpretation or action vis-à-vis the Other. And here is my problem with Levinas, too—the lack of discrimination and discernment with regard to different *kinds* of Others. For Levinas, they all seem to be lumped into one. As with Derrida, who follows him in saying that "every Other is every Other" (*tout autre est tout autre*). The Other can be a god or a monster, but for Levinas it makes no difference. All that matters is how I (the accused/abused self) experience it—how the human subject suffers the Other as substitution, hostage, kenosis. The Other does not have to be good in this kind of ethics, but "I" do. It's all down to subjectivity again! But what about the "transcendence" of the Good, which calls *prior* to the good of my response?

SC: Levinas does talk of the prior transcendence of the Other.

RK: He does. And here I am using Levinas against Levinas. Neither you nor Levinas seem to be advocating some gnostic God of good–evil (as in Jung's *Answer to Job*), nor a theodicy (à la Leibniz), which sees evil and violence as part of some ultimate holistic good. Your infinitely demanding call is basically the good calling the good for the good, is it not? You don't talk of the infinite demand for torture, for example, only the demand for love, for faith, for justice—right? I see *Faith of the Faithless* as fully consonant with *Anatheism* in the repudiation of any kind of metaphysical omni-God or theodicy. And we both invoke mystical examples for our model of faith. We share a fascination for figures like Eckhart or the beguine mystic Marguerite Porete, burned at the stake for writing a love poem about God—especially your take on her notion of "ravishing far/near" (which I also wrote a catalogue essay about, for Sheila Gallagher's recent art show).

You are constantly hovering around terms like *mysticism* and *infinite demand, conversion* and *love*, in a "strong" sense. It is not a case of casual or cavalier mentioning. It is not a soft-centered, New Age, Alain de Botton humanism. Don't your notions of mystical atheism and anarchism open up something else? Something more? Something infinitely other or could we say divinely other?—beyond the old God of metaphysical sovereignty—what Heidegger called ontotheology? I try to move in this direction too, as you know, when I talk of the double *a* of anatheism: adieu as both a turning away from (*ab deo*) and a turning towards (*ad deum*) God. And here I feel very close to Levinas, when he talks about Judaism giving atheism to the world, as a separation from pagan fusion and power (*le sacré*) in favor of an ethics of the holy (*le saint*). And I think this double movement is a sort of double atheism in a way: the atheism of atheism, adieu to adieu! Or you might say a double nihilism, a nihilating of the nothing which, it seems to me, opens onto something— something else, something other, "something rather than nothing"!

> SC: This is what I call "conversion"—a turning around and a turn-
> ing towards. For me, it's the turning towards the sound in the
> street. But let me give another example: I was thinking again
> recently of the famous Grand Inquisitor episode in *The Broth-
> ers Karamazov*. You know the scene, where Christ appears after
> an auto-da-fé in Seville, in the sixteenth century. And the Grand
> Inquisitor has Christ arrested, and the scene unfolds, and Jesus
> doesn't say a word, and then the Inquisitor unfolds his story. And
> what is clear from what he says is this: it is all right for Christ to
> go into the desert and resist the three temptations of the devil,
> but, having tried that too, the Inquisitor decided that human
> happiness was greater than human freedom. And this is where
> the debate gets interesting. The position of Christ, which would
> appear to be a faith in God, is actually an affirmation of freedom.
> Faith is only faith insofar as it freely affirms itself as such. And
> that is the paradox of faith. If faith is more than that, it isn't faith,
> because I don't choose it.

So what Christ calls us to is the radical affirmation of freedom in relation to the "fragility" of our relationship to faith. The Grand Inquisitor
story contains the utterly sincere avowal that Christ's message was not sus-
tainable and so had to be replaced—by the Church triumphal—with the
well-being of the faithful, a well-being of consolation and contentment

brought about by the three temptations of "miracle, mystery, and author-ity." That's the countermessage of the Church, which the Inquisitor has pledged to administer. And so we find ourselves in the midst of the whole intriguing question as to whether the fragile and radical faith delivered by Christ—the freedom of genuine faith—is compatible or not with the political and ecclesiastical institutions of earthly power. For me, the whole point of the story is that Christ does not come back as an all-powerful, omnipotent figure. He reappears as a fragile human being who is arrested and taken away—we are not sure where. The story ends with his leaving the room.

RK: And the kiss. Doesn't Christ kiss the Inquisitor on the lips? And Dostoyevsky tells us that this kiss "burned on in the Inquisi-tor's heart."

SC: Yes. And then we presume that Christ will be burned at the stake as the worst of heretics. So I think what Dostoyevsky brings our attention to is the necessary "weakness" of faith, right? Very Pauline, as you say. And to ask more than this is to ask for the wrong thing. Faith is a kind of commitment and conviction—but not a certainty. And I think this is what a lot of nonreligious people get wrong about religion. There are certain religious people who claim certainty, but I think that's flawed. The truly religious disposition is the affirmation of faith that takes place through doubt. So the enemy of faith for me is certainty, and the fuel of faith is doubt. You say as much in *Anatheism*. And I always think that nonreligious people think there's some hidden secret, some magical, invisible ingredient that's going to trans-form things. But faith is actually the other way around. Faith is about doing with less, not more. And that's more interesting.

RK: So, paradoxically, the genuinely religious attitude deals with uncertainty, whereas the antireligious seeks certainty—and if it doesn't find it in faith, where it doesn't belong anyway, it rejects it out of hand. Faith is *not* about power, magic, and authority, as Dostoyevsky reminds us. That is the temptation, the error of the Inquisitor, the lure of the omni-God. Whereas, as Dostoyevsky said, "True faith comes forth from the crucible of doubt." I think that what Keats has said about "negative capability" is also

relevant to both imagination and faith—the ability to find oneself in the midst of "uncertainties, Mysteries, doubts, without any
irritable reaching after fact and reason."[2] That "irritable reaching"
is a temptation for both the religious and antireligious dogmatist.

SC: Yes, I agree that is a far more interesting way of seeing things.

RK: Well, two things come to mind here. Let us come back for a
moment from Dostoyevsky to Joyce—curious how we are resort-
ing to literature so much here, as elsewhere when we discuss faith.
Wallace Stevens and Oscar Wilde are so central for you—indeed,
you get your "faith of the faithless" idea from the latter. Joyce, Virginia Woolf, Proust, and Hopkins are central for me in *Anatheism*.
So, to return to Joyce's "shout in the street" for a moment, I am
interested in three ways of reading this cry; namely, as *sacred*, as
erotic, and as *ethical*. Since we have already touched on the sacred
cry above, let me say a word more about the other two.

Molly's erotic cry of love crowns the book. Her final "yes" is charged
with the amorous sighing of the Shulamite woman in the Song of Songs,
mixed with her own personal longing for passion, pleasure, and Eros. It is a
comic-erotic cry which opens up a future. It is heard by Stephen Dedalus,
perhaps, as he exits the Blooms' garden, back onto the street. And by all us
readers. Then there is the ethical cry of the widow, orphan, and stranger
that reverberates throughout the book: feed me, clothe me, care for me,
remember me—in short, where are you? Echoes of Isaiah, Matthew 25, for
example, in the Eumaeus episode (the cabman's shelter) and other scenes.
Of key importance, also, is the cry of conscience, which Stephen Dedalus
experiences as "agenbite of inwit," from the Old English term for guilt—
in his case the ghost of his mother, whom he refused to pray with on her
deathbed, but also the "mothers of memory" who cry out to be remembered, the "Daughters of Erin," who recall the famished and forgotten of
the Great Famine (a cry also echoed in the pleas of the Liffey washer-
women in *Finnegan's Wake*—"mememormee, mememormee"). These
cries of conscience—often transgenerational—are what Ricoeur and Vattimo (in our dialogue in this volume) name the silenced voices of history,
voices which recall our "debt to the dead." The ancient cry of "Zakhor!"
(Remember!). And the dead here include not only Stephen's mother, who
recurs as a ghost, but also Bloom's departed émigré mother (who gave him

a potato as memento, which he carries in his pocket) and his prematurely departed son, Rudy. That whole recall of conscience—ethical, political, personal—to honor the buried and forgotten, seeps through Joyce's work.

> SC: It is our solidarity with the dead, historically and individually. I think especially of the nighttime episode, where the call of the dead son (Rudy) is so moving and pervasive.
>
> RK: The call to remember, between father and son, is key for Joyce. As Haines says at the beginning of the novel, it is all about "the Father and the Son idea. The Son striving to be atoned with the Father." And Stephen's revisiting Prince and King Hamlet's ghost scene is pivotal: "Remember me!" So, if God is a shout in the street, this can be a variety of summons—of need, Eros, memory, conscience. But if it *is* a divine cry, it cannot be a cry to murder or hatred.

I think that the roles played by "God's cry" in your faithless faith and in my anatheist faith have a lot in common. But there are differences. And I suspect that one of these differences may center on the question of sacredness. I don't want to have to rid faith of its sacramentalities and scriptures to have it serve as a mere "structure" of subjectivity. Sometimes you seem, as we discussed above, to go more for the structure than substance of faith, yet you constantly invoke certain traditions of Christianity (Paul, Augustine, Porete, and the mystics). Your notion of faith does not come from nowhere, ex nihilo, out of your own mind! You're repeatedly inscribing yourself in specific hermeneutic traditions and mystical narratives—and I am completely with you on this.

> SC: Right.
>
> RK: Let me stay with the pivotal role of narrative in faith. I want to take the very practical and therapeutic example of AA (Alcoholics Anonymous). Here, as you know, addicts undergo a process of healing, going from an admission of utter "helplessness" to some form of "recovery" by handing over to a "higher power."
>
> SC: The language is very religious.
>
> RK: It is. In fact, it is a bit like a Quaker meeting—open to both the faithful and the faithless. We'd both be very welcome! There is

no contract, no identity cards or medical charts needed to enter, no payment involved. You simply listen to the cry of the Other and they listen to yours—and something happens. Healing happens. And statistics indicate that it happens far more effectively through AA twelve-step programs than through any other clinical, medical, or psychiatric procedure. If there is faith here—in what AA calls "a higher power, however you may wish to define it"—it is not a propositional *belief that* a metaphysical first cause or Supreme Being exists somewhere up there. It is, rather, to return to our opening discussion, about *faith in*: faith as troth, as trust, truth, betrothal.

SC: And as practice. There is a progression. Twelve steps, right?

RK: Right. And the practice is about a journey of abandonment and recovery. A common religious story, but one also open to atheists or nonbelievers who are ready to let something else come to their healing aid. The higher power invoked can be, as mentioned, "however you define it." One can define it, with Levinas and yourself, for example, as the trace of the Other in the face of the other person. So might it not include Simon Critchley's faith of the faithless? I think yes. What do you think?

SC: I agree. One of the most exciting moments of my life was last year when I got an e-mail from Wayne Kramer, one of the founders of MC5, the legendary Detroit punk band. When I was a punk, there were three bands we'd listen to: Iggy and the Stooges, Velvet Underground, and MC5. MC5 was the first and the most radical; they were revolutionary communists. And Wayne Kramer, who lived in New York and was a serious junkie and alcoholic, wound up in prison; and while there, he educated himself, became a serious AA member, and became sober. Well, he sent me an e-mail because he'd read *Infinitely Demanding* and thought we had stuff to talk about. So we met and talked and it turned out that he, a man of immense moral seriousness, is now doing a thing called Jail Guitar Doors, where they bring guitars into prisons and help inmates.

My point is that there is a proximity there, between us. And so I want to come back to the point you made about Eros and the sacred and the various different cries in *Ulysses*. For me—and other people have said this—*Ulysses* is a book about Home Rule, and the impossibility of Home Rule. The politics of the book are complicated, as you know, because Joyce didn't take the easy path.

RK: He always carried a British passport and was very critical of ethnic or tribal nationalism—mocking Kathleen Ni Houlihan as an "old gummy granny."

SC: Stephen cannot return home, and home is not home for Bloom. There is the final scene where they urinate together in the garden and the arcs of their urine cross—and then they part. But that kind of intersection is not a reconciliation in some happy home.

RK: It is not Hegel.

SC: No. It takes place under the windowsill of the bedroom where Molly Bloom languishes, with her very different sense of desire and Eros. And that, for me, is the very nub of the book—and its mystery. Because on the question of love, when I think of love, I don't mean a sentimental idea of love but an erotic one. As Lacan says, the question is whether you can love and desire in the same place. We are very good at loving and desiring in different places. We desire in relation to all kinds of profane and perverse stuff (we don't need to go into), and love is so often sanctified and sanctimonious. The big cultural issue that Joyce—through Molly—raises is how love and Eros cross. *Ulysses* is about that. Molly is trying to love and desire in the same place—in relation to Bloom with his male impotence, to her dead child, to her adulterous lover.

RK: "As well him as another," as Molly says about her recalled lover under the Moorish wall in Gibraltar. It's a classic instance of "metonymic desire," isn't it? But laced with loving affection for that first lover and her subsequent ones, including Bloom himself—who, "childman weary . . . in the womb," accepts Molly's Eros with "more abnegation than jealousy, less envy than equanimity."

SC: We agree about so much of this. But I think there may be an interesting difference between us in terms of Catholic and Protestant attitudes. In a sense this is odd, since I don't really think in these terms at all. But what interests me, in all the religious figures who fascinate me, is religion as an anti-institutional force which refuses the sacramental authority and tradition of the church. Now, in Paul—we agree—we are not concerned with the repudiation of Judaism; rather, he is retrieving the old in terms of the new. But in someone like Martin Luther or Marguerite Porete there is *protest* there, an antinomian contestation. The concerns of religion that compel me are those of radical protest and refusal, right up to certain nineteenth- and twentieth-century expressions of American Christianity.

RK: I presume you would include the heritage of nonconformist movements like the Quakers and Shakers in that, as well as the Mormons, whom you interestingly defend in a recent *New York Times* piece.

SC: Yes, and the whole history of black Christian emancipation in the US, which I have been studying a lot recently. I am doing a reading and research study with an African American student at The New School, and he's getting me to reread James Cone's *Black Theology and Black Power*. Cone has this amazing argument that black power is the only consistent experience of Christianity. It's close to Bonhoeffer's idea of a radically iconoclastic faith.

RK: What Bonhoeffer calls "religionless Christianity."

SC: Right. Faith and faith alone. And that means we don't just turn over the tables of the money changers but we erase the temple altogether, and the churches as well. I think that is the direction I am going in.

RK: I am not sure I would want to erase as much as you would—anatheism is about trying to retrieve and reimagine what is still life-affirming and emancipatory in tradition—but I certainly share your sense of protestation. Both Ricoeur and Bonhoeffer's radical prophetic Christianity—expressed in the idea of a post-religious and post-atheistic faith—plays a crucial role for me in *Anatheism*. Besides, my mother came from Protestant stock.

SC: And my mother from Catholic!

RK: So we are both theological mongrels! But I am with you in your critical revolt against authority as triumphal ecclesiastical power—but I do not want to get rid of the sacramental altogether. That's why in *Anatheism* I come back to Joyce, and Merleau-Ponty's notion of profane sacramentality—Joyce celebrating the sacramental epiphanies of the carnal, erotic, quotidian; Merleau-Ponty claiming (with Paul Claudel) that there is not a god beyond us, but *beneath* us. God as transcendent Word made flesh, descending into the immanence of the world, the sacred in and through the secular (in the true sense of *saecularis*—ordinary time and space). The sacramental as eucharistic incarnation—*amor mundi*. And I would add Gerard Manley Hopkins to this list, with his wonderful Scotist poetics of "thisness." The divine in the very *haecceitas* of things. The sacramentality of the everyday. Here I part company with Levinas's allergy towards the "sacred" (with its blindness to animality and nature) and a certain form of Protestant Puritanism, which evacuates the sacredness of the flesh, voiding and avoiding the grandeur and mystery of sacramental surplus, excess, sublimity. I am suspicious of the puritanical distain for the jouissance at the heart of everyday existence (what Yeats called "the foul rag and bone shop of the heart"). I have a lot of sympathy for Hester Prynne!

SC: In Levinas's case, this allergy to nature was also informed by historical and political reasons—his horror of the totalizing fusion of paganism and national socialism's cult of the body and nature.

RK: Which he linked with the Hitlerite cult of blood and soil (*Blut und Boden*) and even with a certain Heideggerean nostalgia for pre-Socratic *phusis*.

SC: Yes, and this drives Levinas to formulate an ethics of the holy (*le saint*) divorced from any idea of the sacred (*le sacré*), understood as nature, irrationality, animality.

RK: That has a particular charge in Levinas's case. But the alterity of nature is something that several kinds of Western philosophy, based largely on Platonic metaphysics and ethical monotheism, have denied or dismissed at their peril. This is something with huge implications for our understanding of the divine (not to mention the environment)—what is or is not truly sacred. It has led to what Charles Taylor rightly calls our contemporary culture of "excarnation." Our long abuse of nature and animals in the West does not augur well.

SC: Unless you become a Franciscan. In Francis there is an "infinite demand" extending across all creatures and all beings—human and nonhuman.

RK: Right. And, in keeping with Francis, I want to give an "earthiness"—both Christian and Dionysian—back to the God after God, so that it does not dissolve into apophatic abstraction or into nothing at all. So instead of the X sign of "nothing"—the nothing that infinitely demands and solicits but is never there in the flesh—I want more radical, everyday incarnation. Eucharists of the everyday, available to anybody and everybody in a totally unrestricted sense.

So I am putting two things out there for you: one, the sacramentality of the flesh (Molly Bloom and Francis being my patron saints!); and two, the alterity of a "higher power," as invoked in twelve-step journeys of healing and recovery, which is of course the "power of the powerless" in its most radical and extraordinary sense. Both of these—the sacramentality of thisness and the transcendence of healing—point to something beyond the power of the human subject, cogito, subjectivity. They point beyond the "human" *tout court*, but in a way that celebrates and enlarges and vivifies the human. I am not talking about some metaphysical God "up there" in the Platonic sky but a God arising after the death of God that is nonetheless "somewhere"—somewhere beyond my ego and yet before my senses!

SC: Me too. It is surrender to Height. Absolutely. And surrender cannot be unfree. Freedom is crucial. That's the difficulty. What does it mean to freely submit? That is the question, and I agree with you on this. But the "God beneath us"—perhaps this is a difference between us.

I remember being in a lecture about fifteen years ago (in Louvain), when Didier Franck spoke. There was a huge cross suspended behind him, and when he was asked a question about Merleau-Ponty, he replied that when he thought about the body in Merleau-Ponty he thought of *le corps glorieux*—the mystical body of Christ. It's as if in Merleau-Ponty there is a God beneath us, an endless, seamless field and flux of the flesh of which we are all a part. This is a sort of ontological version of the mystical body of Christ. I admit it is a great doctrine, but I have a problem when it is applied to a phenomenology of the flesh. This might be a difference. I'm not so trusting in the God of the flesh beneath us and have always been more drawn to those religious and spiritual movements that are distrustful of the flesh—for reasons I am not totally in control of. Though I don't personally believe in the Cathars, I feel a fascination for them. It is a kind of early ultra-Protestantism—a complete refusal of the flesh of the world and an affirmation of the beyond. But then I disagree with them to the extent that this is bound up with a certain cult of perfectionism.

RK: Which smacks of gnostic dualism and asceticism.

SC: Yes. So, for me, it is always a question of the relation between *sarx* (flesh) and *pneuma* (spirit). I always want to affirm a certain ambivalent position where we have one foot in spirit and another in flesh. We are amphibious beings, moving constantly in two elements. We are eccentric creatures with regard to ourselves. So any affirmation of pure spirit can go too far, and any affirmation of the pure immanence of flesh is a falling back. . .

RK: Into a form of fusion.

SC: Yes, and I want to maintain some kind of gap between flesh and spirit. So another interest of mine is the question of humor, where I oppose people like Bakhtin and Eagleton who celebrate laughter as a carnivalesque eruption of lower material bodily structures. It's a great story—laughter as revolution of the flesh!

RK: A sort of Rabelaisian excess!

SC: Exactly. But what interests me in humor is not this comic carnival but the "difficulty" in our relationship to the flesh. So I think of someone like Bergson, where the experience of "humor" flows from the ambiguity of knowing whether we are dealing with the human or the mechanical, a person or a thing. That's complex and puzzling. Or, as Beckett says, in an almost logical proposition, "If I had the use of my body I would throw it out of the window. But perhaps it is the knowledge of my impotence that emboldens me to that thought" [*Malone Dies*]. It is a perfect example of what

Beckett calls—I think in his long essay on Proust—a "syntax of weakness." Neither one nor the other. The body is all over Beckett. His texts are full of bodies, but bodies as oddly inhabited by voices. Now, I would love to say yes, yes to Molly's yes. But there is something almost too triumphally carnal about Joyce for me. It is great at one level—you read Joyce's letters to Nora; he really loved the flesh! But at another level, it's too much.

RK: In this sense I agree I am probably more Catholic and you more Protestant. But I like the idea of a fecund tension or mix between the two. I think it's a salutary and creative. Joyce the Catholic, Beckett the Protestant—with a bit of each in the other. They are both tragic-comic at heart, or "jocoserious," to use a favorite term from *Finnegan's Wake*. But I think one can find this same creative tension in certain religious figures who interest us both. Marguerite Porete being a case in point, with her mystical notion of the "ravishing far/near." The far is the Height, the vertical, the transcendent—the infinite call that comes from the Other and never lets up. The near is the flesh, the thisness of the here and now. The cry comes from out there, but out there *in the street*, not in the heavens. The infinitely demanding cry of the stranger comes from above, granted; but it is welcomed, nourished, heard by us here below. The "far" incarnates in the "near," which for me is the theoerotic ecstasy of the flesh, utterly immanent and carnal. And maybe we should even talk of two cries: the "far cry" of the outsider, which is one of radical alterity; and the "near cry" from within—that is, from the excess of interiority and immanence (not unlike Heidegger's call of conscience, *Gewissen*, or Descartes's infinite idea within us).

And what I find so intriguing about mystics like Porete, Teresa of Avila, and John of the Cross—especially in the *Spiritual Canticle*—is the mix of radical eroticism with radical asceticism. John and Teresa were reformers in launching the discalced orders; they were protesting against the sclerosis and laxity of the Church, even if they were also, subsequently, celebrated as "saints" of the Counter-Reformation. During their lives, John was incarcerated in a tower and Teresa (a Marrano) was investigated by the Inquisition. Porete, as you well know, was burned in Paris, in 1310, as were other women mystics in the beguine movement supported by Meister Eckhart.

And what interests me in all these dissident mystics is that they were radical reformers while also being claimed by the call of the immanent universe, of the mystical body—what Porete described as the "ravishing combustion" of rapture when far crosses into near, as swiftly as a "lightning flash." Porete's ecstasy, expressed in her love poem to God, was a flame of both amorous passion and sacrificial passion. Carnal bliss and annihilation. A double passion. An explosive collision of transcendence and immanence, desire and love. You offer a beautiful reading of this in *Faith of the Faithless*.

SC: Thank you. That is certainly what I am after. As others have pointed out, for the female mystics, the experience of the sacred was absolutely bodily. And, with the exception of Saint Francis, only women produced stigmata—

RK: Don't forget poor Padre Pio!

SC: The female body is usually the place where this happens. We have Julian of Norwich putting her fingers in Christ's wounds and, as the blood flows, there is a sort of jouissance of the flesh. But it is already a transsubstantiated flesh, a spiritualized or sacramentalized flesh.

RK: As in Margaret Mary Alacoque's transcorporation of hearts—when she puts her hand into Christ's chest and exchanges his heart for hers!

SC: Extraordinary. And what interests me—I am never sure why what interests me interests me—is how this mysticism of Eros is related to the question of asceticism. Let me try to explain. I think my interest is bound up with the flatness of desire in the contemporary world. We have the idea that bodily desires are there, complete. You can perfect them, you can go to yoga, go to the gym, and medicate yourself in various ways. The body is something that has to be served. Pain must be avoided at all costs. This kind of attitude makes a good deal of the past history of the body unrecognizable—where religious traditions, from Saint Anthony and monastic movements onwards, were concerned with the reorganizing of the flesh, with rethinking and reexperiencing the body. What the female mystics are doing is a more radical version of that—and it leads me to the question of what mystical asceticism would mean now. I suspect it has gone off into practices we would describe as disorders—anorexia, piercing, cutting, bulimia, whatever—to be "treated." Whereas, before, these kinds of practices could be fashioned as spiritual exercises.

RK: But surely that was because there was a "discipline" of practices—a tradition, a narrative, which guided and hallowed such habits. Whereas now it is often a matter of whim or caprice, an untutored experiment or self-willed project. A sort of *ascétisme sauvage*, if you like. Something to be tried out, tried on, then pathologized or fixed.

SC: Yes. I am reminded of the stories of female mystics like Margery Kempe or Christina the Astonishing, figures who didn't write their own works but were followed around by mendicant friars and brothers who recorded their teachings and lives. I am intrigued by the movement of the Beguines in Belgium and the Netherlands. Their lives became the stuff of extraordinary narratives. For example, Christina the Astonishing threw herself into a freezing river, where she stayed for three days, and then a burning oven, and was transfigured into a bird, and at her own funeral levitated from her coffin and perched in the eaves of the church, castigating the congregation! But the point is—you are right— they had these shared narratives about spiritual practices then. Now, if today we had something like that, which wasn't seen as a set of "disorders" to be treated—around some idea of a normal body with normal desires—I think we would be in much better shape. There is much to be learned from the religious past around the relationship to the body.

RK: But that is the past. What is to be done now? Today, here and now, in New York City, 2013.

SC: I am sure you could meet a dozen Astonishing Christinas on Fourteenth Street.

RK: And what would you say to them?

SC: To Christina, right now? Well, the whole thing has so utterly changed, transformed into all kinds of other things. Look at the dizzying success of *Fifty Shades of Grey*. It's symptomatic of a yearning for something, though I don't think you'll find it in *that* book. I think we are in a very bad place, actually, because there is no real way in which to think about these things. I'm preparing a course on mysticism at the moment and have been trying to put together a number of texts to approach these things. As well as the female mystics, we'll look at the Pseudo-Dionysius, Cusanus, Eckhart, and some more modern figures like Bataille and Amy Hollywood. I find the whole challenge fascinating.

RK: So, in light of all this, would you call yourself a mystical anarchist after all?

SC: No, I'd call myself someone who would *like* to be a mystical anarchist.

RK: You seem attracted to it in several recent essays and books.

SC: Yes, I am "strongly" attracted to it. It's a thoroughly powerful seduction. And what interested me most in writing about it in *Faith of the Faithless* was the experience of disaffection of a lot of the undergraduate students I have at The New School. In the years leading up to the Occupy movement, I witnessed groups like The Invisible Committee trying to put together a history of resistance. I understand why one wants to secede from the world and sabotage the TGV networks. I get that. You can't just denounce this resistance; you have to try to understand it.

RK: What about the disaffection of the marathon day bombers in Boston? Dzhokhar Tsarnaev was not Marguerite Porete, after all.

SC: No, but we have to think about this. We witness a desperate attempt to make these people "Other" in order to give ourselves the narrative where we can feel good about being American. You wrote about this in your piece on the bombing for the *Irish Times*. I think it's difficult. I'm not sure anything can or should be done, once the usual hand-wringing around the events is over—if only there had been better surveillance, etcetera. But what went on with these brothers makes sense to me. I would not take the step of making bombs! But we have to try to understand.

RK: Spinoza once said, when terrible things happen, do not complain, do not cry out; try to understand.

sc: Yes. And we desperately do not want to understand such desperation. There will always be people dressing in long black trench coats and feeling disaffected and listening to depressing music and wanting to kill all their classmates—that strikes me as completely normal. So what to do? Try to understand, then limit access to guns, making it more difficult for these youths to act out their natural fantasies of mass murder. What we never want to do is to accept our part in something—even our responsibility and culpability—where we appear to be "victims."

At the moment, I am working on the first Greek tragedy, Aeschylus's *The Persians*. Lots of interesting stuff in this play, which takes place in the court of the Persian Empire, in Susa. We see women rehearsing the defeat of the Athenians at the Battle of Salamis—which took place just seven years before the first production of the play, in 480 BC. And then we have the main scene, in which the ghost of the Persian king, Darius, appears and admonishes his son, Xerxes, for desecrating the holy altars of the Greeks, before then going on to admonish the Greeks, saying, If you think you are different from this, and if you end up doing what my son did, you will end up in the same situation.

Or, to take another example, Euripides's *The Trojan Women*: it takes place just after the destruction of Troy—the "rape of Troy," as it was called—and a cluster of women gather with Cassandra to lament their fate. Cassandra is given an amazing speech, where she prophesies that they will be sold off as house slaves and used as concubines, and she says that in this lies their legacy and history—to be people who *remember* Troy because of what the Greeks did to us. They are the barbarians, not us. So this is the greatest thing that could have happened—to be able to remember. In this way, the Greeks used their art to celebrate who they were and, at the same time, critically reflect on their own culpability, on their self-implication in their own historical narratives.

RK: Are you suggesting that we have lost this capacity for critical self-reflection?

sc: Yes. We are so desperate to prove how innocent we are. We find another to blame. But political situations are much more complicated and we have to recognize possibilities of tragic ambiguity.

RK: At the end of one of your chapters in *Faith of the Faithless*, you quote Pascal's phrase that "love is without reasons." So my last question to you on this. We agree on so much, yet there are differences. We've seen this already in the different intellectual inflections between what could be called our more "catholic" or "protestant" dispositions (I use lowercase, and *disposition* rather than *position*). Even if these dispositions do not require explicit allegiance to respective ecclesiastical institutions, they do inform our distinct take on things when it comes to the crunch.

I am with you on the Pascalian notion of "love without reasons"—a variation on Angelus Silesius's mystical musing on the "rose blooming without why." Yes. But I would not go as far as you and Derrida—or Agamben or Caputo, for that matter—in embracing a "messianicity without messianism"—that is, a faith devoid of specific hermeneutic traditions, transmissions, narratives, and practices which entail a belonging to history. Not just in the past—a past history of mystics—but history now, today. I think such a sense of belonging complements the equally crucial need for critical distance and provides some communal sharing of meaning and value, some common or quasi-common narration about what can and should be done. Shared stories make for shared actions. And I don't see either in the deconstructive atheism of Derrida or Agamben, for example (though they are both fascinated by messianic mysticism). Their "messianicity" is that of the solitary, single one, the lonely mystic. The atheistic knight of faith alone on Mount Moriah, as Derrida once confessed. He also admitted to me that Kierkegaard was the single most important influence on his thinking. I was surprised; but when one thinks about it, it makes sense. Every time I read *Fear and Trembling* I see, I hear, Jacques Derrida, alone on the mountain, assailed by undecidable voices at the impossible moment of decision. To me, that is just too isolated and isolationist a philosophy—a stance essentially evacuated of any *practicable* ethics or politics, devoid of hermeneutic guidelines as to how we might discern between spirits and act together towards shared goals. Do you know what I mean?

SC: I do. Two lines from Pascal: "The heart has its reasons, which reason does not understand" and "Two excesses—to exclude reason; to admit nothing but reason." So one problem with

questions of love is that we could end up with a kind or irrationalism where we completely separate love (whatever that means)
from life (governed by law and rationality). I think in Agamben you find that kind of radically anomic or antinomian view.
Whereas, in Pascal, the night of fire, the moment of conversion,
is not rationally explicable, but one has to rationally account for
it after, through reading, study, contemplation, interpretation—
which allow things to become clearer and more powerful.

I also think of Paul here, because one way in which the resurgence of
interest is his work goes is to read him in terms of a radical separation of
love and law, of unreason and reason. You find that in Agamben's and
Badiou's reading of Paul—even in Heidegger's. Now, in Paul, love and
faith are always announced in relation to the new, which is the resurrected Christ. But that does not mean that the new is totally divorced
from the old. Paul explicitly describes himself as a "Hebrew born of
Hebrews, under the law blameless." Right? So, I can see the properly
Christian message as always having this relationship between love and
law, reason and unreason. And that's why, if it becomes a matter of
faith and faith alone, there is a real danger. The danger of fanaticism,
in a word. Now there probably has to be some element of "enthusiasm"
to save us from pallid rationalism. There is the need to be transported
by some things that are not yet rationally accountable. But that doesn't
mean we can simply throw off the traditions of the past. It means that the
past must be radically *rethought*.

> RK: That, as I understand it, is the ana- of anatheism. The thinking
> "again, after, back, in order to move forward." We have both just
> written books about mystical things, while presupposing a cer-
> tain rationale, reasonableness, rationality in our own discourse
> and in the understanding of our readers. No?
>
> SC: Yes.
>
> RK: But let me ask this: If you pray a prayer of faith—albeit of the
> faithless—who do you pray to? What do you pray to? What
> words come when you call or respond to the "cry in the street"?
>
> SC: I suppose I see prayer as the most fundamental aspect of lan-
> guage. Prayer as the dimension of promise, of trust.
>
> RK: Of the call?

SC: Yes. Though the content of that can be various. It can be "Here I am. I respond." Or it can be "No, I don't want to do that. I don't want to respond to the call. I protest, dissent, secede, remain silent." I think that prayer, for me, is similar to what it is for Levinas when he writes of "saying" within the very structure of the said, or what it is for Derrida and de Man when they speak of the "promissory" dimension of language.

RK: But that is all very ontological. What I am asking is whether there can be a practical or even liturgical expression of the faith of the faithless today? Or is that question, that search for a contemporary mystical life, something you feel is gone forever? I have suggested the twelve-step AA movement as a possible model, but I would also cite many more public examples, like the work of Jean Vanier with the disabled or the Berrigan brothers and Dorothy Day seeking justice.

SC: Well, the AA meeting as you described it would be one version. That would be the dream. My book begins with Oscar Wilde in his prison cell dreaming of a confraternity of the faithless.

RK: But, as the book develops, you don't come back to that or what that might mean in *real* terms, in terms of social or communal movements, in terms of some kind of everyday, lived *ecclesia*. Throughout the writing I feel there is an implicit aspiration towards a "politics" of such a faith. Something more than an incarcerated poet's cry de profundis—a lonely cry from prison or the desert. Can you flesh it out a bit?

SC: OK. I remember my friend and thesis advisor Robert Bernasconi introduced me to the idea of "church," not as a noun but as a verb. Church was not something that existed as a piece of architecture but something you could have or not have, something you "do." As in, I am going to do church, or have church— "Boy did we have church today!" So, for me, there are certain special moments in which one could say one is having church, and where that is an open question. After all, you can be in a physical space called a church and not *have* church. I would love to be able to imagine having church in a church one day. But at that stage my interests become too "aestheticized."

RK: Are such moments to be found for you in certain works of art or poetry, or in things like the Occupy movement or a certain inspiring seminar with students on mystical anarchism, when something special happens? Is that what you mean?

SC: Yes. That is church. That can be church. One of the highest pleasures in my life is when one is able to set something up—a meeting when a couple of people who don't know each other come into contact with each other and it *works*. You know, an evening when something unexpectedly interesting happens—sometimes over coffee or dinner. And church was originally that—congregating around a table, eating and drinking. That, I agree, can be sacred.

I don't want to go off into whimsy here, but I have always believed that the world is a violent, disappointing place; and I've always been surprised that people are not worse than they are. I think this is because there are certain places and practices available where genuine goodwill and common feeling can emerge. That is when we are at our best. But the problem is that we are not often allowed to be like this, because of the ideological structures we inhabit. And when the Occupy movement gets taken over by the media and individualized and scandalized it becomes a mudslinging match. If one *can* separate all that out and allow human beings to interact in some way which isn't inhibited, then something can happen. I do believe in a basic goodwill that human beings can have towards each other, and that for me is sacred—that is faith.

RK: I call that the anatheist wager of hospitality: the moment when a host meets a stranger and the *hostis*-enemy becomes the *hostis*-guest. (We have the same word for both in Latin, as in all Indo-European languages.) Such moments of impossible, surprising, unexpected welcome are sacred. In *Anatheism* I divide the wager of hospitality/hostility into three moments: protest, prophecy, and sacrament. For me, your *Faith of the Faithless* is full of protest and prophecy (as in Levinas), but it often seems to lack the sacramental. The Catholic moment accompanying the Protestant. For you, it is at the table where one has faith in the goodwill and well-being of one's fellows, right?

SC: Yes. But I'm not sure *Faith of the Faithless* has fully got to the sacramental yet. That is work to be done. Another day's work.

8

The Death of the Death of God

Dialogue with Jean-Luc Marion

Jean-Luc Marion is arguably the most original and creative living French philosopher in the phenomenological tradition. He is also the foremost proponent of the theological turn in phenomenology, who has argued consistently that phenomenology is open to transcendence and thus, by implication, that a phenomenology of religion is a legitimate philosophical task. In his essays collected as *Le visible et le révélé* (2005), Marion shows how revelation can register in phenomenology as "donation" through "saturated phenomena."

The idea of "donation" builds on Husserl's and Heidegger's solution to the Cartesian segregation of the mind from the external world and the resulting problem of subjectivism: there is no gap between mind and world because phenomena reveal themselves in their true character to consciousness. We do not construct objects of perception subjectively; rather, they are "given" or "donated." Marion then asks how divine revelation, which by definition has to be completely free to dictate its own categories of appearance, can appear truthfully, when the perceptive grid of our minds is shaped, as Heidegger rightly argued, by our cultural and linguistic horizons.

Marion's answer to this problem is "saturated phenomena," which are given in such intense fullness that they overrun and exceed our intentions and compel us, as it were, to abandon our preconceived, a priori perceptive grid in responding to their call. Such phenomena, in fact, shape us, rather than we them. Examples of such phenomena are historical events, passive bodily feeling such as suffering, or the moral imperative radiating from the face of another. Yet, for Marion, the strongest saturated phenomenon that overwhelms human intentionality is epiphany or revelation. For Christians, Marion argues, this supersaturation of revelation goes back to the impossible event of Christ himself and explains the subversive, iconoclastic nature of Christianity that overturns our own idolatrous conceptions of belief.

What, then, is the difference between theology and phenomenology? The difference is that phenomenology only clears away dogmatic restrictions about what phenomena are legitimate or possible. The possibility of God's revelation is not yet the affirmation of its actuality. This affirmation requires faith, and only with faith does phenomenology become theology.

Marion's recovery of legitimate religious phenomena connects with Kearney's anatheism just at this point. Like Marion, Kearney affirms the God who *may* be. The anatheist moment hovers between negation and affirmation before the actuality of faith, in order to freely choose—and to imagine God otherwise.

The conversation between Marion and Kearney took place in Marion's library in Paris, in January 2012.

JEAN-LUC MARION (J-L M): I find the notion of anatheism extremely pertinent for thinking about God today. It is a very powerful way of describing the state in which we find ourselves in the midst of the modern period of nihilism—after the death of God. Or, more accurately put, the period of the death of the death of God. The death of God itself has a history.

RICHARD KEARNEY (RK): Can you say something more about what this history entails, for you?

J-L M: In the first instance, the death of God is dissimulated by atheism. By this I mean that when Nietzsche announced the death of God it was received in the context of the debate concerning the existence or nonexistence of God. More precisely, it was received in terms of the disappearance of God. But this remained superficial because it ignored the question of the "essence" of God. The inability to speak of the *existence* of God is also a matter of being unable to define the *essence* of God. This is what Nietzsche called an "idol." And he was right.

So I would say that, in an anatheistic perspective, the disappearance of God has less to do with the death of God as such than with our idolatrous conceptions of God. In other words, we are entering now into a clearer understanding of the fact that what is at issue with the death of God is not God but our understanding of God. So that what is really at stake is not the question of atheism versus theism as such. The difference between those who say they believe or those who say they don't believe has become minimal, even insignificant. No, the whole polemic about the different representations of God is now outdated. So that today we can say that the death of God implies the death of the death of God. We enter into the critical relation between idols and icons.

RK: Could you explain what exactly you mean by this distinction, in relation to the anatheist debate, specifically?

J-L M: Whereas idols come from our way of regarding God, icons are ways of being regarded by God (*des prises en vue par le regard de Dieu*). They are opposites. The latter implies a complex and sophisticated phenomenological experience of being regarded by the irregardable.

RK: So we look at idols but icons look at us. Is this related to your inner reversal of Husserlian phenomenology, to what you call "inverted intentionality"?

J-L M: It is a question of realizing the idolatrous character of the classic formulas regarding propositional beliefs about the existence or nonexistence of God. What interests me is how anatheism may help us define the current situation of passing from the death of God to the death of the death of God. We are no longer in an atheist society but a post-atheist one. And here we can talk of the double sense of the ana- of anatheism. Namely, as both a non-theism and as a return to something beyond atheism and theism. I would speak of "*la remontée à l'anatheisme.*"

What is problematic here is the very term *theism*, which is itself a notion tied to metaphysics. This is why I very much endorse your term *anatheism*, for putting a second prefix *a* after the first *a*. A double prefix, in other words, meaning a primary passing beyond theism (atheism) and a second passing beyond that passing to a third way, the hyperbolic way of mystical theology. One then moves into a new theological register which offers a better description.

> RK: How would you connect this to the deconstructive move inaugurated by Heidegger après Nietzsche? How does it supplement or supplant it?
>
> J-L M: We can relate the anatheist situation here to two main terms. We can talk of the "destruction" of metaphysics in the sense of Heidegger's *Abbau* and ask how the deconstruction of the death of God relates to the deconstruction of metaphysics. This is the main thrust of Jean-Luc Nancy's recent thinking about the "deconstruction of Christianity." But I think what remains questionable and unsteady here is the notion of "Christianity" (*Christianisme*). As Nancy points out, Christianity is not a normal religion but the religion of the exit from religion (borrowing from Weber's and Gauchet's formula, *la sortie de la religion*). The truth of Christianity is, therefore, not to serve as one religion among others—superior for some, equal or inferior for others—but to make religion disappear as idolatry, idolatry being understood here as the human attempt to construct and conceptualize God from our human point of view, from below (*d'en bas*). That is why the first Christians were often persecuted and condemned for being atheists.
>
> RK: And later, several Christian mystics like Eckhart and others. Even Teresa of Avila and John of the Cross had their brushes with the Inquisition.
>
> J-L M: Yes. And why? Because they refused to equate God with a cult of unity and identity—that is, with a nation, tribe, or society. They resisted the "identitarian" temptation (*la tentation identitaire*). Christianity, from its inception, is a radical commitment to a universalism beyond religious or sectarian distinctions between Christian and Jew, etcetera, in favor of a vertical realization

of the person before the Father. And this realization destroys the religious relation and replaces it with something else.

So we should not confuse Christianity with religion, even to say that Christianity is the religion of the exit from religions. Nancy is correct to speak, at one level, of the deconstruction of Christianity, if he also asks the prior question: Where does this deconstruction come from? Namely, from Christ himself. The deconstructive power of Christianity originates in Christ; something totally different emerges: the extraordinary event that a man claims to be God, dies and rises again, and that certain people believe him. That is the unbelievable event (*l'événement invraisemblable*). Is this a religion? Debatable. Does it imply a representation of God? Also debatable. Does it occur in the world or beyond the world? That is still more debatable. The characterization of this event, and the repetition of the event in the practice of faith, is not based on a "religious" phenomenon as such. And I think this is really essential. What you describe as anatheism is true, I think, of the final moment of the story of the visible discrepancy between the Christian event and any religion. During a long time, the Christian event was said, proclaimed, professed "as if" it was one more religion amongst others—pagan, Jewish, Islamic—tied to a nation or group of nations, to a territory or state. This was the classical position of political religion.

> RK: And it has not completely disappeared. One finds it still existing in modern national or state religions in the West—England or the Nordic countries, for example, where the monarch is obliged to be of the national Protestant religion—as well as in certain non-Western theocracies.
>
> J-L M: This political idolatry often went hand in hand with conceptual idolatry—namely, the reductive identification of the event of Christianity with the highest form of knowledge (the system of Christian metaphysics). So we witnessed a double idolatry, which served to cover over the radical Christian resistance to all forms of idolatry. And, in a way, the death of God is the end of such historical betrayals of Christianity. After the death of God we find ourselves in a moment where the event of Christ cannot and should not be taken anymore as a new item of religion.

And this fact is very well captured in the term *anatheism*, in the sense of indicating something *more* than religion, which refuses all kinds of identifications of God with nondivine bodies—political, moral, social, metaphysical, ideological, etcetera. So we might say that, with anatheism, the question of the "meaning" of the death of Christianity is, in a way, opened up for the first time.

RK: But why today? Why, in your view, does the anatheist moment arrive now, in the wake of Nietzsche and Heidegger and the fall-out of the death of God? Why does it have to be part of an his-torical or philosophical genealogy rather than simply occurring in the original event of Christ? Wasn't anatheism already there in the Christ event itself? And in the inaugural movement of the desert fathers and the first mystical theologians, like Dionysius or Nyssa?

J-L M: It was. Yes. The moment of anatheism is as old as the Gospel itself. But as we all know, from the very beginning, from the first instant of Christ's life on earth, there arose deep resistance. This is at the core of the difference between Christ and the Pharisees. The Gospels are very clear. The Pharisiacal movement was very committed to the bond between God and Israel, as a people, as a nation, as a state. So conflict and contradiction were inevitable from the beginning.

RK: But couldn't one say that anatheism was already there—not only with Christ and as Christ but *before* Christ? After all, Jesus declares, "Before Abraham was, I am." And this is why I locate the anatheist turn already in the Abrahamic movement away from idolatry in Genesis, in Jacob's wrestle with the angel, in the Mosaic exodus and the prophets' annunciation of a messianic era of justice to come. Would you not agree that these are already movements of anatheistic deconstruction—or, at the very least, proto-deconstruction?

J-L M: Of course. You are right. Anatheism is already there as soon as one recognizes that God is an event with no name, as soon as one realizes that any names or images or representations we attribute to God are already speaking "as if" God were this or that. Exodus 3:14 makes this clear: God refuses to be captured or caught in a proper name. There has always been a pregnant and irreducible tension between the election of Israel as a unique people and the original vocation to universal election. The whole sacred history of old Israel shows many critical signs of this tension.

RK: So you would say that the friction between freeing oneself from idols and the temptation to identify God with a particular territory, land, or people was always there?

J-L M: Yes. And it manifested itself in the double meaning of Jerusalem as both a real city and an eschatological city. This was true for both Judaism and Christianity. It was clear to Christians from the very beginning, though often lost sight of later on. And I see this as central to the anatheist awakening. The event of Christ inaugurated a new community, one which was spreading its seed into a new civilization—or indeed, different civilizations—which meant experiencing all kinds of possible opportunities to embody this tension of double belonging to both an historical and eschatological city. The history of Christianity is the history of the various attempts to embrace or evade the anatheist vocation. So, alongside genuine anatheist Christianity, we witness a long litany of evasions, running from the Holy Roman Empire and Byzantium to medieval Christendom and subsequent Christian kingdoms, nations, states—and, later again, secularized Christian states, multireligious and secular states, blending part of Christian tradition with other sacred and secular traditions. And at the end of all that history we have the death of God, which marks the end of any further possibilities of compromise between the event of Christ and sociopolitical entities.

RK: Do you consider that the story of the death of God, variously enunciated by Nietzsche and Heidegger, develops into more radical deconstructive announcements in Derrida or yourself (in works like *L'idole et la distance*), not to mention fellow travelers like Nancy, Chrétien, Caputo, or Vattimo? How do we situate the post-Nietzschean, post-Heideggerian moment of deconstruction in terms of our Western intellectual history?

J-L M: Well, I think we have to trust Nietzsche when he says that we are now in a situation of nihilism, which starts roughly in the second half of the nineteenth century and lasts for two hundred years. "I will tell you the story of the two coming centuries,"

Nietzsche proclaims. And we are in the middle of it! And what we now realize is that the decision about the event of Christ is not just about religious idolatry, as such, but about any form of idolatry. The whole question of our representations of the event of Christ, as I mentioned at the outset, no longer relates to the old question of the existence or nonexistence of Christ, because we no longer claim to have any knowledge of the "essence" of God. The decisive border no longer runs between two different kinds of representation. We are all anatheists now, to the extent that we all share a common experience of no longer having a representation of God. When I discuss this with my nonbelieving colleagues, we all agree on this. So, when people say that after the end of the representation of God there is no God, they remain within metaphysics, which presupposes that there could be something that gives itself as representation. They miss the point.

RK: But what does it really mean to say that there is no "essence" of God? Why is this such a crucial point for you?

J-L M: Let me refer here to the Kantian critique of the ontological proof for the existence of God. It is in fact, I dare say, a very weak argument. Kant argues: "to be" is to be able to be thought (*gedacht, denken*) and, in addition, to be established outside of thought, a matter of "position" (*gesetzt*). But what does it mean to say there is no possible "position" for the existence of God? Does it mean there is no access to the existence of God? But you could just admit that this definition of Being does not apply to God, and that this is exactly part of what should be admitted for something to deserve the very strange title of "God." After all, if something called God does not appear as an exception to the usual rule, it should not deserve to be named God.

And then we have Kant's additional argument, by absurdity—namely, if the ontological proof succeeded, there would be "more" in the real world than in my mind, against the traditional definition of truth as *adaequatio rei et intellectus*; for if the same thing which has the perfection of God's essence in my mind does, in addition, have its existence outside of my mind, then there would be no adequation between the essence existing in my mind and the same thing now existing outside of my mind, because the real thing would be greater than my mental representation. And this argument by absurdity proves itself to be absurd.

More, Kant's objection retrieves precisely the core expression of Saint Anselm's so-called ontological argument, according to which what we could ever call "God" should be greater than any representation or thought we can have of him. So the argument by Kant *against* the existence of God is exactly the same as the argument by Anselm *for* the existence of God. We should not resist revisiting Anselm's argument rather than Kant's, for, if we could ever think something as "God," we should be able to think of something greater than what we can think. This is a paradox—a paradox only true in the case of God. Only such a paradox is true of God as God. If it were not such a paradox, then we would not be thinking of God at all but of an idol (a metaphysical one).

So, when Jean-Luc Nancy and others engage in the intellectual attempt to deconstruct the empty place of God, they sometimes ignore or overlook the fact that the real legacy of "Christianity" for human thought lies precisely in that the place of God *is* empty—and should be empty. My question to Nancy is: What does it mean to say the place of God is empty? If it is not empty, it would remain a part of the world which is not for God, because God admits no other place than itself (everything remains *within* God, and God, *nowhere than in itself*). So I conclude that we must take very seriously the fact that if God is God, this must be an *exception*.

RK: But what do you mean by an exception? An exception to what?

J-L M: An exception to spontaneous representations and conceptualizations, which are doomed by finitude. We can surely agree on this. So the recognition of the unavoidable finitude of any possible representation of God, the acknowledgment of this "contradiction," is itself perhaps a portal to God, if we fully assume it. But it is important to cross the contradiction rather than see it as a final step or full stop in the quest for God.

RK: The contradiction is not just a cessation or privation.

J-L M: Precisely. It is the game of this language, in the sense of Wittgenstein's "language games."

RK: I agree with you about the need to go beyond representations of God in the sense of political and metaphysical idolatries, but in *Anatheism* I do insist on the indispensable role of narrative imagination and testimony. I am wary of leaving empty spaces too empty, so I endorse a sacred poetics of epiphany in the works of Joyce, Proust, and Woolf—Stephen's definition of God as a "cry in the street," Proust's *"petits miracles,"* Woolf's "daily miracles," etcetera. There is a claim here for the deployment of a certain poetic license in our language games about God, an acknowledgment of the crucial role of metaphor, symbol, image, and story in our approach to God. And all of this I call, at one point, a "hermeneutics of sacramental imagination," resisting both theistic-metaphysical idolatry and pure atheistic negation. I want to attend to anatheist traversals of the contradictions and crossings in the imagining and reimagining of the sacred. And I propose that these poetic testimonies may, in turn, be supplemented and complemented by ethical testimonies of sacramental action in the lives of exemplary anatheists like Dorothy Day, Etty Hillesum, or Jean Vanier, to take some contemporary figures— lives which embody and incarnate the sacred. This signals a *kataphasis* of imagination and witness, which serves as indispensable counterpoint to the apophasis of pure deconstruction,

J-L M: I agree that this shift to narrative—whether of fiction or of historical destiny—involves a crucial hermeneutics. I fully concur that we cannot experience anything without interpreting it in a narrative of some kind, public or private. And when we say "narrative," we say "history," with its repetitions and innovations, both performative and creative, backwards and forwards, *Zukunft und Ankunft.* In such a hermeneutics of identity—in both your work and Ricoeur's, for example—what is at stake, once again, is the "event." And the event, in my particular toolbox, as in yours, ultimately and inevitably confronts us with the same paradox: something impossible happened de facto—and happened, furthermore, without compromise. The narrator is ready to witness this fact to the death, but this does not imply that he himself, or an actor of history, can explain how the event was so enacted. Narratives can testify to this very strange situation vis à vis our regular sense of belonging and identity. For the paradox is that the impossible becomes possible without becoming understandable. The event of the impossible becoming possible remains unintelligible and unconceptualizable. And yet this very paradoxical event produces the very strange effect, effectivity, reality that reopens a whole new field of possibilities.

RK: So God becomes the impossible possible, the possible beyond the impossible, the impossibility of impossibility.

J-L M: Yes. And when we realize how this effective event opens a new range of possibles, we experience our situation as a history, destiny, and future. And this very destiny is the contradiction of the concept, which is exactly what I call the event of Christ—the very paradigm of the strange situation. For me, there is no difficulty, consequently, in accepting what you say in *Anatheism* about sacramental imagination and narrative testimony. For this work is necessary to describe exactly where we find ourselves here and now, living in the field of the "impossible made real." Like the recent birth of my grandchild. The impossible made actual! No one can understand or explain what happens in such an event.

RK: "*Un petit miracle.*"

J-L M: Exactly. And it is the same for death as for birth. We think death is a terrible trial and tribulation. But what do we know? The fact is that we do not know anything about it. We simply don't. We project in it all our fears, anxieties, anticipations, but we simply do not know.

RK: So, would you say that the event of Christ is the paradigm for all these other key events of birth and death—indeed, for all events *tout court*?

J-L M: Yes. To be Christian means to say that the Christ event is the paradigm of all events.

RK: Which reminds me of the poet Gerald Manley Hopkins, who—following Duns Scotus and Ignatius—wrote of the omnipresence of Christ in all persons and things. And von Balthasar, who has so influenced your own thought, develops this in his theological commentary on G. M. Hopkins's Christian poetics. In the introduction to *Anatheism*, I quote Hopkins as a key anatheist poet—returning to God after the disappearance of God during the dark night of the soul, as witnessed so powerfully in his dark sonnets.

J-L M: Let me repeat: what separates the Christian from a non-Christian does not lie in a matter of different ways of representing God but in experiencing (or not) the paradox of the Christ event as it unfolds in the nonmetaphysical relation between the possible and the impossible. In normal life we start with what is possible—feasible, practicable, realizable, thinkable—and work from there. But with the event, we start with the impossible and work from the opposite. From that moment on, you have the opportunity to explore new possibilities "after" the impossible that would have been utterly unthinkable according to the range of effective possibilities "before" the event.

RK: But if you say that both Christians and non-Christians share the basic realization that our "ideas" and "representations" of God are now defunct, would you also claim that the "impossible after the possible" is available to non-Christians (even anti-Christians)? Or is it the exclusive prerogative of Christians?

J-L M: I would say that anyone who experiences the event and understands what they are experiencing is already a Christian—"*anima naturaliter Christiana*," as Tertullian rightly said.

RK: Fair enough. But where does that leave non-Christians or non-believers who claim to experience the event of the impossible becoming possible (for example, Derrida, who says he is an atheist, claims this)? Or think of AA, which invokes a "higher power, however one chooses to define it" as the grace which makes the impossible possible (namely, the cure from addiction). It remains very open and ecumenical—all atheists and agnostics are eligible. Or would you be closer to someone like Karl Rahner who speaks of "anonymous Christians"? This would amount to saying that those who experience the impossible becoming possible are already partaking of the Christ event, even if they do not know it.

J-L M: I wonder if the idea of the "anonymous Christian" in other religions or nonreligions is not an abstract thesis. I am not aware of any other culture where people think that way without referring to the only moment in history where the contradiction of the event is taken as core—namely, the Christ event. As if there was some kind of "pure nature" which preexisted the event. We find such an abstract hypothesis in Spanish late Scholasticism, where one posited the idea of a pristine form of existence before creation, or original sin, a pure innocence, exemplified perhaps by the Indians of the New World. But they, too, have their stories and histories. And they are different.

RK: So you agree with Lévi-Strauss when he says the there is no nature independent of culture?

J-L M: Of course. For me, the idea of an anonymous Christian remains very abstract. There is a huge difference between being a Confucian and a Christian. And the idea that there is some prior "pure nature" makes no sense.

RK: But can one experience the Christ event without ever having been party to the historical narrative of Christian revelation?

J-L M: My question is: Is there *any* place in the world today where one is not to some extent aware of the Christ event? My answer is no. It is too late.

RK: Too late for innocence or ignorance? Too late for a space free from revelation?

J-L M: Yes. Just as it is too late for any place in the world to remain free from technology. Even in the heart of the Sahara it is too late. There is the ubiquitous cell phone. It is everywhere. We have to take history seriously.

RK: But if it is too late now, was it ever too early? What about a pre-Christian revelation of the event? What about Abraham?

J-L M: Yes, the case of the Old Testament is puzzling. Abraham and his descendants are constantly open to non-Jews beyond the elected nation. The priest Melchizedek came from elsewhere, as did Job and Jonah. The more election is focused on the Jewish people, the stronger the insistence on the non-Jews, who seek out universal election and salvation precisely from the revelation to the Jews. From the earliest genealogies of the Old Testament— and again in the genealogy leading up to Christ, recounted in Matthew and Luke—we find several non-Jews in the line of David—for instance, Ruth the Moabite, before David, and Uriah's Hittite wife, Bathsheba, who married David and there-fore was an ancestor of Christ. So one can say that Christ was both a Jew and a non-Jew. What I am saying is that it is not pos-sible to draw an absolute line between those who are party to the event and those who are not. This opening to the universal is not just in Christianity; it was already there before.

RK: So what prevents you from going all the way and saying this involves some kind of natural theology and that, by our very nature, we are all somehow predisposed or exposed to the Christ event?

J-L M: I see what you mean. But why stick to the idea of natural and nonnatural? This difference is blurred from the beginning. The distinction natural–supernatural, pagan–elect is blurred from the very start.

RK: So the anatheist notion of a radical exposure to the stranger, the other, the alien is, you would agree, there ab initio?

J-L M: Yes. Anatheism is the true situation. The wrong situation was to imagine that the Christ event is just one among others and that we could range the various events into some kind of comparative or sequential system.

RK: Supersessionism . . . apologetics . . . comparative phenomenology of religions?

J-L M: Yes, reducing the Christ event to a history of religions. Why not? But it misses the point.

RK: "Before Abraham was, I am." So, in a word, to come back to our starting point, how do you understand anatheism *now*—that is, in view of our current philosophical and cultural situation in history?

J-L M: In anatheism one does not need to talk about precedence or consequence. One does not need to return to "theism" as something that came before, or to "atheism" as something that came after. That is a matter of history and metaphysics, perhaps even the history of metaphysics. The question for us today is not the decision about what is the most adequate or satisfactory concept of the "essence" of God. The decision is more of an "ethical" question, in Levinas's sense. God is a matter of decision and response, not thought and proposition. Of event rather than of being and essence.

RK: I can see how you are aligning yourself here with Levinas's ethical relation to the event of the Other outside of history or hermeneutics. One might even invoke a sort of Kierkegaardian wager, though that is not your style. But my question to you would be, Why is this not decisionism? Or fideism? Or, indeed, the Derridean notion that we can only "read in the dark"? That our decisions do not come from us but from some Other in us? Without knowledge? *Sans voir, sans avoir, sans savoir.* I myself explore a number of parallels between anatheism and deconstruction. I want to hold open the enigma of the gift—so brilliantly explored by you and Derrida. But I would also want to hold to a certain hermeneutics of discernment, a dimension of practical wisdom (Aristotle) and reflective judgment (Kant), which guides and informs our wagers of hospitality and gift.

J-L M: I think that anatheism definitely involves an openness to the event as the impossible.

RK: And to the advent of the newly possible after, through, and beyond the impossible.

J-L M: Yes. I think we agree on that. But careful; this is already the horizon of Nietzsche when he speaks of our expectations regarding the Last Man, Dionysus, the New God, the One to Come, the Crucified, etcetera.

RK: Or the horizon of Heidegger, too, when he speaks of our waiting for the return of the Gods, the arrival of the Last God, the advent of Being. I am thinking of his famous claim, in his *Der Spiegel* interview, that "Only a God can save us now."

J-L-M: It is all a question of our disposition to the coming of the event. We can agree or disagree about the identity of the event—and this is inevitable, given that the event is precisely something which escapes our identifications! We do not identify the event. The event identifies us. It is not our decision. It is the event's.

RK: So it is not, for you, a matter of decisionism or voluntarism, but more the choice of an answer, a response to a call. Responding to a prior claim. But even in that case, do we not still have the problem of how to discern between Nietzsche's Dionysus or Heidegger's Last God or Derrida's Messianic Other? Or Christ? What makes the difference between these various responses to the event, and our various responses to these responses?

J-L M: These are important questions. But the important thing for now is that we all get out of metaphysics, because the question is

not one of "foundations," "first causes," etcetera, but of expect-
ing the future, the event. A reversal of metaphysics. I would say
that all serious philosophy today agrees on that. That's the new
situation. And it is something *real*. What the new time brings,
I cannot predict. But we must take this situation for what it is.

And this raises the question of reason. The actual leaders of the world
today—political leaders, economic leaders, and even church leaders—
seem quite unaware of this. They are still using the old roles, trying to
foresee the future, to prepare for the next crisis, the new epoch, etcetera.
But this is just a disguised form of the old nostalgia for a "first cause,"
a foundation or plan, transposed to the future. They think that we can
predict the future, as if the event were a time which could be projected
or produced by us—a time issuing from us. So the real situation we are
in, since the world wars—or rather, since what we might call, more accurately, the Thirty Years' World War [1914–1944]—is the witnessing of
the end of the Enlightenment project, a project which reduced reason to
rationality, claiming that we are masters of history, engineers of the technological age of the world, with no exposure to unpredictable events. We
are now witnessing the end of all that and realizing that we are not the
masters or owners of the future.

RK: But what do you mean when you speak of a reason after rationality? Can you give me some examples?

J-L M: I mean "rationality" here in the sense of the principle of sufficient reason (Leibniz), later enforced as the principle of efficient
rationality, what today is often referred to as technological reason. This goes back to the disjunction between Bacon's *augmen-
tis scientiarum* and the claim for wisdom. Foucault has written
about this, but one finds it in theology, as well. It refers back to
the moment when the direct connection between the increase
of exact knowledge and the education into wisdom is severed.
Nietzsche sees this, too, without going to the heart of the problem. And Spinoza appears a key figure in his claim that the more
we "know," *more geometrico,* the "wiser" we become. Bacon, Descartes, Leibniz were all aware that this connection was broken,
but Spinoza was not. (Spinoza was not a revolutionary but a

deeply conservative metaphysical thinker—the last medievalist, in a way, though without the standard religious array.) In many respects, Spinoza was the last to imagine that rationality was the same as reason. And this results in the conviction that we are the only and ultimate foundation, the alpha and omega, the beginning and the end—a conviction which, when pushed to its logical extreme, expresses itself in the whole encyclopedist project.

RK: Which is ultimately a humanist project, whether we view the foundation as individual (*res cogitans*, transcendental ego, sovereign citizen) or collective (species, humanity, society). But many would say that today we find ourselves in a post-humanist situation.

J-L M: Yes, indeed.

RK: And, to speak philosophically, doesn't this post-humanist, post-metaphysical, post-theist, post-atheist situation require that we find ourselves in an anatheist disposition of hospitality towards the stranger who is always knocking at our door? As when Gide recommends that our "*désir soit moins une attente qu'une disposition à l'accueil.*" But my question remains: If so many thinkers today share this postmetaphysical openness to the unpredictable, unrepresentable, unconceptualizable, unmasterable event, how can we distinguish—if at all—between the anatheist disposition and the deconstructionist position of Nietzsche, Heidegger, Derrida (and we might add Caputo, Nancy, Agamben, and yourself) which we have been discussing?

J-L M: We can take one more step, and perhaps we have already taken it. I think there are *vestigia* in the world. Even in the nihilistic situation. What is erased is the idea that everything is considered in terms of "value." Evaluation itself becomes alienated. The system where everything is converted into the value of stock and property, as in the stock exchange—commodities, goods, men, life itself. Everything becomes a matter of exchange, of human mastery and measurement. So the task for philosophy is not to respond to the current global financial crisis, for example, by returning to "values." That is precisely the problem—the omnipresence of calculation in terms of values! If morality is supposed to respond to this crisis of values, it cannot do so in terms of values. You cannot combat a contagion of evaluation with more evaluation.

RK: You are saying that values are the problem, not the solution.

J-L M: Exactly. It is a basic Nietzschean point, of course—the vicious circle of nihilism. So, a far better response, in my view, is to show how, in our everyday lives, we are already experiencing real things which cannot be experienced or represented as values but only as the "impossible": birth, death, Eros, God. These are events, impossibilities from the point of view of metaphysical or humanist "evaluation."

RK: These impossible events are what you call "saturated phenomena" in *Being Given*, and what I call "epiphanies" in *Anatheism*.

J-L M: Just so. They resist every possible evaluation. If anything, we could say that it is we who are evaluated by them! Events are already there before we represent them. So, what is needed is a new hermeneutic of our nihilistic world, which can pick out what is irreducible to the question of value. This is where we may encounter what you call the event of radical hospitality and what I call the gift.

RK: And you would agree that we are helped in this by a hermeneutics of narrative imagination and discernment.

J-L M: Yes, that is the only way. To tell and retell our story so that we can explain to ourselves how it may be possible to discern where there is a saturated phenomenon rather than a "value." It is a matter, to use Levinas's language, of vertical election rather than horizontal selection. And in this process, we may discover our real identity not as something we give to ourselves but as something given to us.

9

Anatheism and Radical Hermeneutics

Dialogue with John Caputo

John Caputo is an American philosopher of religion with particular expertise in phenomenology, hermeneutics, and deconstruction. He is widely known for developing Derrida's deconstruction into "radical hermeneutics," a philosophy that subverts any essentialist claims and resists arresting the play of interpretation.[1] This radical hermeneutics is closely aligned with Caputo's interest in theopoetics, a term that is variously defined by practitioners but that entails the notion that both God and life are best described poetically rather than rationalistically. Theopoetics, at least in Caputo's radical hermeneutics, and also in Kearney's anatheism, has connotations of *poiein*, of making or remaking God through our imagination.

This imagining God "otherwise" is at the heart of both Kearney's anatheism project and Caputo's more recent extensions of radical hermeneutics to theology. In his book *The Weakness of God* (2006), Caputo pursues a "poetics of the impossible," an evocative rather than a normative or logical discourse on religion. The poetics of the impossible evokes the disruptive force of God as an event that subverts our expectations at every turn and thus opens us to the "life-transforming force" of God's kingdom.

In the following dialogue, Caputo asks for clarification on three elements of Kearney's anatheism: First, does Kearney, together with Ricoeur and Gadamer, succumb to a crypto-Hegelianism by seeking to reconcile opposing views in a "third way"? Second, is Kearney's understanding of divine kenosis closer to classical theology or to Caputo's own, more radical understanding of the term? And third, what kind of truth do anatheists assume to be at work in interreligious dialogue? Are our truth convictions absolute truths or historically determined ones?

This conversation between Caputo and Kearney took place at Harvard University, in March 2012, and is followed by questions from the audience, addressed to both speakers.[2]

JOHN (JACK) CAPUTO (JC): Richard Kearney has written a clear, imaginative, fascinating, and robust account of the life of faith in the postmodern world, a world marked by cultural plurality and religious strife, the astonishing transformations brought on by the new information technologies, as well as a strident materialistic critique of religion. The title *Anatheism* is a function of the prefix *ana-*, which is here used in the sense of "back" or "again," so that it is a theism that comes after theism, that returns to theism once having passed through a certain non-theism or atheism, which Kearney ably identifies in various postmodern movements.

Richard is defending a recovery, rediscovery, or retrieval of faith in the midst of a world marked by militant faiths and militant attacks on faith. This return to faith after doubt is described in his subtitle, *Returning to God After God*. The movement here described is from theism "through" atheism or non-theism and back again, repeating *forward*. The project is inspired, I would say, by Paul Ricoeur (discussed in chapter 3 of *Anatheism*), with whom Kearney studied in Paris, who used to speak of faith in terms of a "second innocence," to which one returns after one's first and naive innocence has been disturbed by critique and suspicion. Ricoeur also described this as a "hermeneutics of affirmation" that follows upon a "hermeneutics of suspicion." One passes through atheism/suspicion in order to come back to an affirmation/faith now more tested, more mature and complex than in its initial and more innocent form. Following Ricoeur, Kearney thus argues for a more critical theism relieved of an earlier dogmatism, a theism that itself stands in need of constant renewal or repetition. So, to be very precise, he is "after God," as in a search for God, but also after God, as in "after atheism" or "after doubt" or "after the death of God."

Kearney finds this paradigm applicable to a wide range of phenomena in philosophy, religion, politics, and art. Indeed, Kearney's ability to move among these several domains and to encompass a vast amount of literature in pursuit of his thesis is very impressive, to say the least—a tour de force, really. The paradigm is basic to mystical and negative theology, where our understanding of God must pass through the abyss or dark night of non-knowing. It is also found in the theology of the Incarnation, where the transcendence of God passes through the flesh of a man; in the structure of hospitality, where the consolidation of the home is interrupted by the visit of the stranger, which elicits either resistance or embrace. Such hospitality, Kearney holds, is the very structure of biblical religions, emblematically represented by the visits of the three angels to Abraham and Sarah, of Gabriel both to Mary in the famous annunciation scene and to Muhammad in his cave. Hospitality, it would seem, is first among the virtues for Kearney—meaning both the hospitality that religion is and the hospitality to be shown among the religions. The book is everything we have come to expect from Richard Kearney.

Richard and I have been in a deep and fertile conversation over the years, and I want to take this occasion to say that one of the great blessings of my professional life has been the coming of the Irish stranger from Dublin to the "New World." Richard and I enjoy a productive proximity and difference. We occupy the same space between philosophy and theology, philosophy and religion, philosophy and literature, although Richard knows a great deal more about literature than I do. Despite coming from different countries, we have the same questions, the same concerns, and we share many background practices and assumptions. We converge again and again.

The distance lies in the background figures that inspire the two of us. My guess—and I don't think it's a wild guess; I think Richard would say this—is that the contemporary philosophical figure that matters the most for him is Paul Ricoeur. Perhaps Richard could comment on that later. The figure who is most behind my work is Jacques Derrida. So, we have this massive overlap: we both know the medieval scholastic tradition, have traditional preparations in philosophy, and share a common

Catholic heritage. I think we are both playing hermeneutic tunes—but we do so in different keys. His is a more dialectical hermeneutics, mine a more deconstructive or, as I like to call it, radical hermeneutics. You can see this difference in Richard's focus on a hermeneutics or a poetics of the possible and my focus on a hermeneutics or poetics of the impossible.

When I think of my dialogue with Richard, I think of the construction of the transcontinental railroad in the United States—one party starting on the East Coast, the other on the West, hoping to join rails in the middle. If there is a middle for us, it is "the possibility of the impossible." On a more grandiose scale, one might also think of the ceiling of the Sistine Chapel, of the *Creation of Adam*, of God and Adam trying to touch fingertips.

> RICHARD KEARNEY (RK): Which one of us is Adam?
>
> JC: I am certainly Adam.
>
> RK: No, I'm Adam!
>
> JC: Here, in Boston, surrounded by all these Irishmen, I would not dream of aspiring to any higher station than that of Adam. In Boston, it is you, Richard, who must assume the mantle of omnipotence!

So, the pivotal figure that we are both always meditating, the point where the fingertips of our work touch, what we are both always talking about in one way or the other, is this figure of the possibility of the impossible, the poetics of the possible, of the im-possible. The hyphen in the im-possible—that is the proximity of our distance, the distance in our proximity. Allow me now to raise three questions about this important book.

First, one of the things that I have always been wary of in the hermeneutics of both Ricoeur and Gadamer is a lingering residual presence of a certain Hegel. That is, both Gadamer and Ricoeur conceive hermeneutics in a way that fuses horizons or moves through a moment of suspicion and then returns to a higher unity, to a more robust beginning, a more robust faith or affirmation. Richard knows this, and he takes precautions to avoid allowing it too free a hand. He explicitly cautions us about treating anatheism as a form of Hegelianism. Of course, I am speaking only of a certain Hegel. I do not mean a strong Hegelianism, with the absolute

Spirit and the *Begriff* and the teleology, but a certain Hegelian "moment," what I called in *Radical Hermeneutics*, speaking of Gadamer, a "closet" Hegelianism. By this I mean the moment of reconciliation, the deeper, richer, more mature concretion of two moments that, taken by themselves, are one-sided and abstract. I hear that in anatheism—the schema of theism–atheism–anatheism; faith–doubt–second faith; position, opposition, composition. So, while I know that Richard is trying to avoid making anatheism into a too simple schema of reconciliation, I still worry that Hegel is in his closet.

Let me put it another way. When I think of theism and atheism, instead of some movement past, beyond, after them, I think of displacement. I think the reason these two things are pitted against each other is that there is something wrong with both of them.

Now, we must be careful here, because so far that is just a good Hegelian point. The postmodernists are always warning us that Hegel is almost inescapable. If you argue "against" Hegel, you end up being his opposition, his very own opposition, and you are swallowed whole as a negative moment in the Hegelian machine! Hegel would say these positions are both "abstract," and yet to be reconciled by passing through them, letting their momentum unfold into a higher unity. But I do not want to let their momentum unfold. I want to stop them in their tracks, undermine them before they get rolling.

What's wrong with theism and atheism for me is they both are, from the start, what we call "positions," whereas what I would like to do is displace the positions themselves before the opposition in these positions arises. I seek not a higher composition but to decompose, deconstruct each one in its place. I want to drop the discussion of the two and see that there is a more fundamental undecidability that besets both of them—not "after" them but "before" them, not "above" them but "beneath" them, with the priority of an undecidability that is not transcendental but quasi transcendental.

RK: *Beneath* theism and atheism? I go along with that.

JC: Beneath them, yes; an undecidability prior to both. I do not think that our lives are contained by taking up a stand in one of these positions. What marks our lives, what makes us who we are, is dealing with their undecidability, with the undecidable fluctuation in which opposing "positions" like this are caught up. In a very real sense, for me, they never get off the ground, never acquire the momentum or the positivity of a position. I want to relativize these positions before they get underway, not to come along "after" either one of them. As Richard says, instead of anatheism, we could speak of "ana-atheism." You say that in the book?

RK: Yes.

JC: This deserves attention, because that helps me relativize these positions, helps me say that there's some deeper "affirmation" beneath them, something that is more affirmative than positions are "positive," something which runs beneath both theism and atheism, which prompts us to drop the discussion, to displace the distinction between theism and atheism. So I would relativize those positions not in the name of some arbitrary caprice or relativism but in the name of a prior affirmation, or a deeper sense of confession, of genuinely confessing that we're "lost." This being "lost" is not removed or resolved or gotten on top of by any positing or position, even if you call it "anatheistic," but is co-constitutive of a more deep-set desire or affirmation.

Second, Richard and I share a common critique of the classical theory of omnipotence, of God as sovereign. Both of us are interested in the notion of kenosis, and in the kenotic figure of Jesus. History has recorded numerous divine and heroic figures who were born of woman but fathered by a god, in antiquity. What makes Jesus unique, however, is that he is not the classical Greek god or typical pagan hero who smites his enemies, who manifests his divine provenance by the power with which he slays his adversaries. What is distinctive of the divinity of Jesus is that this divine being is a victim—crucified, humiliated—even as his teaching is not one of divine retribution but of uncompromising forgiveness.

Now, Paul says that Jesus is the icon of the living God. If we are to take that seriously, then the icon of God is weakness, a kind of weak force, weak strength, like the weak force of forgiveness. We remember the story of the Grand Inquisitor. When Jesus is recognized in the crowd by the lord cardinal, he is arrested and submitted to a long soliloquy in which the Grand Inquisitor warns Jesus about how much power the cardinal has over him, who tells him that he plans to have Jesus executed in the morning, just as he has done to many others who have dared defy him in the past. Why have you come back to interfere with the work of the Church? the cardinal asks. Jesus listens quietly to this soliloquy and then, when it is over, Jesus goes up to the lord cardinal and kisses him. This powerful man, the lord cardinal Grand Inquisitor, is disarmed—by a kiss. The kiss is the weak force, like forgiveness; if it is a power at all, it is the power of weakness.

Now, there are two ways to think about kenosis, this self-emptying of God. The first is the classical doctrine of kenosis, which goes back to Paul's famous saying in Philippians 2:6–8, in which Paul says that Jesus, "though he was in the form of God did not think equality with God something to be exploited, but emptied himself, taking the form of a slave." According to the classical account, God in Christ voluntarily withholds his power and empties himself into someone who, "being born in human likeness, and being found in human form, humbled himself and became obedient to the point of death, even death on a cross." Christ does not think it necessary or even seemly to make a show of his divine power, but freely takes on the likeness of human beings.

In this case, the kenotic action, the self-emptying of divinity, is freely undertaken. But that, I would say, is the mark not of the abdication of sovereign power but of an even more supremely sovereign power. What greater power than the power to withhold the exercise of power which one still retains, which shows who is *really* powerful? Such a kenosis, I would say, far from divesting oneself of power, is really an exercise of *ultra* power, of *ultra* sovereignty.

That's the classical account, which I reject for just that reason. The other way to read kenosis, the one that I defend, is not so classical and not at all orthodox. This other account first emerges in German idealists, who repeat a saying of Meister Eckhart in a radical way: that God needs us as much as we need God. God is not a supremely powerful agent or hyperbeing but a potency that has to come into the world in order to acquire actuality. God as such, in his pure "*an sich sein*," is abstract being, a concept that has to acquire reality in the world and become divine in and through humanity, so that God really and truly is not God until we come along. The divine life is incarnated in us, and we are the ones who do all the heavy lifting, because God as God is a kind of abstract, one-sided concept that lacks independent reality. It's in *us* that God becomes God.

That's really the first version of the death of God. God really does die on the cross—and then what you have after that is the Spirit; that is to say, the human community in or of the Spirit. God as a supreme power is gone. Of course, even that position is too "strong" for me—by which I mean too metaphysical. My own view on the "weakness" of God is less metaphysical but also more radical than that, describing the weakness of the event that is harbored in the name of God. That goes further than the German idealists, who have transcribed and relocated a good deal of classical metaphysical theology from transcendence to the plane of imma-nence. But elaborating that would take us off in a different direction. My point is that there is another tradition in which God and the divine omnipotence are more radically emptied into the world.

So what I want to know is, how far does Richard's critique of omnipo-tence and of the sovereignty of God go? Is this a classical notion of keno-sis? Is it something like the Hegelian or German idealist account of the emptying of divine sovereignty? I think we need some clarification about exactly what this notion of the emptying of divine sovereignty means and how it is related to the classical theory.

Finally, I am curious to learn more of your notion of "religious truth," a question that I think is raised by the work you have been doing on interfaith dialogue and hospitality to the stranger. One might certainly describe the question of the relationship among the faiths and "religious" traditions around the world—what we in the West call, in Christian Latin, "religions"—as a question of hospitality. But what I want to know is what happens to "truth" under the impact of this hospitality; what sort of truth obtains in these different and differing religious traditions?

Allow me to illustrate what I mean. Richard and I are sometimes invited to speak at Christian colleges, which are often conservative evan-gelical institutions. The students and faculty there have a very firm idea of religious truth, which goes something like this: "Jesus is the son of God. That assertion is either true or not true. That point is the bottom line, and you're either with us or you're against us on that point." These people might be very polite with other people, perhaps even grant that others get a lot of things right and have traditions that are otherwise valuable, but on a few central points like this they have to say, If others deny this, they are either wrong or in ignorance. Even if these people say that, as a political matter, they agree with the idea of religious tolerance, with a democratic freedom of religion, and do not advocate a state-established religion, they reserve the right to say that, in matters of religious truth, the others are "wrong"; they are free, but in this case, they are free to be wrong. That's one version of religious truth, and it is not uncommon.

The other one goes something like this. I recently spent a week in the Sultanate of Oman, which is a very prosperous, tolerant, and Western-looking Islamic state. Islam is the established religion, but their laws provide for freedom of religion to non-Muslims. There are churches and synagogues. Women are treated well, encouraged to go to school and to go to university, and hold high-ranking posts in the sultan's council.

I was talking to a professor of philosophy there, and he said to me, "Look, the reason I am a Muslim is that I was born in Oman, as were my parents. Practically everybody I know is Islamic. I was born a Muslim in an Islamic country. And the reason you are a Christian is that you were born in a Christian world." I don't think he was denying that we need to examine and interiorize the things we inherit, but we all know what he is talking about.

So, there is another theory of religious truth. There are many different religions, and the one we belong to is to a great extent an accident of birth. One would not want to say that any one of them is true at the cost of the truth of the others, the way these more conservative Christians do, no more than one would say that one language is true. There are multiple religious traditions, each of which is true in its own way, and with a truth that does not subtract from the truth of others.

In the first case, we have a more absolutist sense of truth, and in the second case, a more contextual one. So what conception of religious truth is implied in your work on hermeneutics, hospitality, and religious pluralism?

RK: Thank you, Jack. They are great questions. On your first point about Gadamer/Ricoeur versus Derrida, I think you're right. All I would add is that, if I certainly owe a great debt to Ricoeur, one of the reasons is because, as he says at the end of *Time and Narrative*, volume three, "I renounce Hegel." You may say, "Well, that implies that there's a temptation." And it is true. But the renouncing of Hegel is absolutely capital. And here I would consider Levinas as important as Ricoeur, in terms of the break with any kind of "totality"—understood by Levinas as a totalizing "sameness" of being, a system of inevitable progress towards the completion of all the bits and pieces of history, an elimination of singularity. I share Levinas's ethical critique of such totality, as I do Ricoeur's repeated insistence on an irreducible "conflict of interpretations"—a "radical pluralism," which is the very opposite of Hegel's Absolute Spirit and the absolutism of fundamentalist religions. Not that Hegel and fundamentalism can be equated, except that, in their very different ways, they both embrace the notion of truth as ultimately "the same." Gadamer, by contrast, is closer to Hegel at times. His "fusion of horizons" misses the radical "conflict of interpretations" that we find in Ricoeur's hermeneutics, which has that moment of critical suspicion and diacritical discernment that upsets the goal of speculative idealism. Gadamer is, deep down, Hegelian. Ricoeur is post-Hegelian—or, as he liked to say, a "post-Hegelian Kantian."

Then, the question of reconciliation. Coming back to my reading of *perichoresis*, I think I agree with much of what you are saying. You talk about that space before the dichotomy into theism and atheism. That is where I think anatheism is also initially located. The question of whether there is something after that space, undecidability in terms of deciding between theism and atheism--and I am for such decision—that may be a difference between us. I claim that the repositioning that follows the initial dis-positioning of anatheism may be either atheistic or theistic in new kinds of ways. And these new theistic or atheistic "repositions" once again need to be dispositioned, superseded, and aftered by a new anatheistic moment—and so on indefinitely. Anatheism never ends. It is before the beginning and after the end, so to speak.

And that, for me, is what is interesting about the figure of the perichoresis: the movement of seeming communing and presencing, where all is recapitulated, is itself accompanied by a countermovement of radical distanciation and displacement. There are two steps in the same dance. Nearing and withdrawing. Placing and displacing. Converging and diverging. The ceding and seceding of one person to another. *Circum-in-cessio* as both *cedere* and *sedere*. It's not like one ever arrives at a final faith or "position"—some absolute confession called anatheism—having traversed theism and atheism. And it's not even a matter of going from first faith to a second faith, as you say Ricoeur recommends. There is a third and fourth and fifth faith. It's faith after faith after faith, ad infinitum.

I recall here Fanny Howe's wonderful line, "the guest must leave the host in order to remain a guest." For if the guest stays in the house too long, having been welcomed in by the host, she eventually replaces the host or becomes one with the house master. The doors shut and there is no longer really any host or guest as distinct others, separate selves who receive and give. That's not hospitality. That's fusion. Or in terms of inter-religious dialogue, it is false ecumenism—"you-come-in-ism," as a former Irish cardinal once put it. So, the guest must be able to leave the host in order to remain a guest, in order to remain a stranger.

And here—and I would say it in terms of position and disposition—I would like to invoke André Gide's wonderful line about desire: "I pray your desire be less an expectation than a disposition to welcome" (*Que ton désir soit moins une attente qu'une disposition à l'accueil*). Hospitality is about keeping desire alive between host and guest—and, as the perichoresis shows, between the human and the divine within the theoerotic dance. If desire goes out of God, if there's no gap or space and displacement in God—the *diastema* between each of the persons and the *chora* around which they all move—God stops dead.

These images and terms are, of course, all figures of our imagination, signs and symbols, which fortunately shift, change, and mutate throughout history. "Supreme fictions," as Wallace Stevens puts it, which does not, for me, mean false or illusory. They may well be the closest we can get to truth. Every religion worth its salt is a battleground of images, of tropes, narratives, metaphors, and metonymies—but always aiming and illustrating something, some moment of "truth." (I will come back to your question about this shortly.) So I would say that the choral space of Eros, which must be retained within this anatheist image of perichoresis, is disposition as *disponibilité*, an openness or availability to the stranger, to the ever-returning and arriving other. Eros as the impossibility of closure.

For me, in short, perichoresis is the opposite of an omnipotent God. It is far removed from the idea of God as a metaphysical power that decides to condescend to us mortals by emptying into a world made flesh: Christ. I think what Paul means in Philippians, when he speaks of the "weakness" of God (something you know better than anyone, Jack), is not that God was all-powerful and then chose to be weak, but that God, as Christ, resisted the temptation of omnipotence—just as he resisted the temptations of Satan in the desert (for three kinds of power, as Dostoyevsky so brilliantly reminds us in "The Grand Inquisitor": mystery, authority, and miracle). What Christ refused—though what Christendom all too often idolized—is the *eidolon* of omnipotence, the illusion of sovereign power, which is basically then the great temptation of every religion, the addictive lure of Totality, constantly to be fought against. So I see Christ's identification with the stranger as the resistance of that temptation. And, as Paul confesses, "Jesus was subject to every temptation." He knew every darkness. And there is nothing darker than the allure of total power.

As the Gospel scene of the temptation in the desert reminds us, Jesus constantly has to struggle with himself—"Get thee behind me, Satan!"—as Jacob did with his inner angel, in order to return to the anatheist moment of weakness, vulnerability, love—the naked destitute face, the widow, the orphan, the stranger. That's the real radicality of Matthew 25, isn't it? Christ's identification with the stranger as the very "least of these" (*elachistos*). If you give to the least of these—not the *greatest* of these—you give to me. Christianity is the trumping of power with powerlessness. That's pretty revolutionary!

And so I now come to your question about "truth." When Christ says, "I am the way and the truth and the life. No one comes to the Father except through me" (John 14:6), that sounds pretty exclusivist, doesn't it? It sure does. Unless you read the "except through me" as the exception of exception—that is, as the exclusion of exclusion. In other words, it all depends here on who "me" is! Who is the Christ who speaks here? And that's why I insist we read John 14 anatheistically through Matthew 25. For what he is actually saying is that you can find the Messiah only in the least of beings. The infinite is the infinitesimal. God is the guest we meet every day and can accept or refuse, feed or reject, love or hate, care for or kill. Christ is nothing other than the *hospes* we so often ignore or pass by. So when, in Matthew, Jesus identifies himself four times with the stranger who goes unrecognized by those in search of the great, omnipotent Alpha God, he means there is no one excluded from the divine. The divine is in every stranger we meet, and we meet them on every street—and even in our dearest ones, even in ourselves.

I'm not talking here about Karl Rahner's idea of the "anonymous Christian." You know the claim: We are all encountering Christ, only most people don't know it. Everyone is Christ and Christianity governs the world. You are all Christ incognito (whether you like it or not). There can be something quasi-imperalistic about that kind of inclusivism. By contrast, I am talking about the stranger in *every* religion, not just Christian religion, eponymously or anonymously. You don't need to be baptized or cleansed in the blood of the lamb to see the stranger. In Judaism and Islam, as I indicate in *Anatheism*, there are also narratives of sacred hospitality. And in Buddhism and Hinduism and other religions, too, as I tried to show elsewhere (*Hosting the Stranger: Between Religions* and *Traversing the Heart: Journeys of the Inter-Religious Imagination*).

So the "truth" of radical hospitality is to be found in each of these religions, albeit in very distinct ways. It's different in each case. And I think to be true to this ethic in one's own religion—if you assume one, as I do my Christianity—is to travel through others; the traversal of other faiths, other religions, strange beliefs, strange gods. I actually believe that this is essential to the truth of religion—understood as radical openness to the stranger, as radical pluralism rather than totalizing inclusivism. So when Rahner (the great Jesuit theologian) went to Kyoto and greeted the Buddhist monks as "anonymous Christians," they were right to greet him back as an "anonymous Buddhist"! And I think, in fairness, Rahner took the point well.

So, in terms of truth, I would say it is a kenotic emptying towards the other in the hopes that the gesture of radical hospitality can eventually lead to a promise of peace. I would see truth as a troth—namely, a promise, pledge, commitment—to greater peace, greater love, greater justice, as when a Shakespearean character says, "By my troth." That is possible within all the religions, but always speaking in very different voices. That is to say, I'm for Babel, for remembering that we all live "after" Babel. Translation is key here. It fosters polysemic pluralism and resists the great temptation of monolingualism—the fantasy of one pure, perfect, original language. The triumph of one *Logos*, one totalizing, subsuming, consuming Word, would be the end of true religion. So truth, I would say, is the realization that we can never reach absolute truth absolutely. But it's the troth, the trust, the hope that peace between selves and others, between hosts and strangers, may be possible through the radical openness and receptivity of hospitality.

QUESTION AND ANSWER WITH THE AUDIENCE

QUESTIONER 1: This is a question for Professor Kearney. I appreciate your last point about religious truth, but I was immediately struck by the image of—if you'll forgive the absurdity of it—Karl Rahner going to a convention of, say, axe murderers. Would he then say, "I consider you all anonymous Christians"? Is there not something about the way in which the Buddhist faith was embodied there in Kyoto? In other words, isn't the religious truth question still a live question? It wasn't just anyone that was identified as an anonymous Christian. So what was Karl Rahner's criterion for truth, and what is yours? I mean it's not just anybody. . . .

RK: Well, actually—it's a great question—I would say it *is* potentially anybody and everybody. Why? Because no matter how awful and appalling people can be, there is always the possibility that anatheistically they may retrieve—like Etty Hillesum witnessed in the concentration camps—a moment, and it might just be a moment, where there's a leap of openness to an insight or gesture of love or justice.

So, within each person—no matter how hostile—there is the possibility that something may happen, that hostility may flip into hospitality. It may not. But it may. And that is why the anatheist stranger is not just the good Buddhist in Kyoto. Right? Or the starving beggar in the street with a benign face. It's also the person with the gun. Absolutely. And if one doesn't hold out the hand to the person with the gun—if Gandhi didn't hold his hand out to the British officer who was beating him over the head, if John Hume didn't open his hand to Gerry Adams and the IRA gunmen (for which he was denounced as a traitor by the political establishment), if Mandela didn't shake hands with his apartheid oppressors . . . if they hadn't made those unthinkably hospitable gestures, there would never have been peace in India, in Northern Ireland, in South Africa, anywhere. Without those impossible handshakes nothing would have happened. If you don't shake hands with the devil, the divine can never come.

Hosting the stranger, in the most radical sense, means being prepared to talk with the enemy. The *hostis* (as the original double sense of the term says) is the enemy as well as the potential friend. And that's the real risk, because you are quite right: if you just go around saying to nice Buddhists, nice Hindus, and nice atheists, "You're like us," then that's easy. But when faced with the stranger—like Abraham in the desert, Mary in her chamber, Christ on the cross—one's initial response is fear, terror, and confusion. And, often, if there isn't that first moment of not knowing, then it's not genuine or truthful hospitality. Hosting the stranger is a risk and a wager, a daring leap, an adventure. In all these cases, fear precedes love and forgiveness.

Let me give another, more contemporary example. Dorothy Day, who set up hospitality houses in several downtown slums in American cities, has a wonderful reflection in one of her journals, of a night, where she describes a stranger knocking at the door at three o'clock in the morning—drunk, filthy, speaking foul language. What do you do? If you believe, as she did, that Christ is in everybody, do you let them in, given their terrifying appearance and potentially destructive conduct? Do you trust—trust as troth and truth, if you like—that maybe there's something in them that, if you open the door and let them in, if they cross the threshold, might bring about a change of heart? It is very risky because, as she put it, she has a house with battered women, homeless girls, vulnerable young men and children, and letting in this person could put them at further risk. "How do I know if it's Jack the Ripper or Jesus Christ?" she asks.

That's the real moment of anatheistic wagering, and if there isn't the choice between two possibilities, then it's not an act of radical hospitality. It's a fait accompli, a forgone conclusion. There must be responsible hermeneutic discernment as to whether this is the right thing to do. But there has to be the moment of not knowing, the moment of negative capability, while you "ponder" (*dialogizomai*—like Mary) in fear and trembling, before you respond. You're troubled as you ponder. And pondering is the moment of hermeneutic discernment—between spirits, between faces, between bodies, minds, and souls. There is nothing more difficult, dangerous, and daring than the move from war to peace, from hostility to hospitality.

JC: Then, are you saying that the underlying truth, the sort of deep truth of religion, is hospitality, a kind of ethico-religious hospitality, and that all the great religious traditions have their own figures and their own narratives in which they express this, but the core of religious truth is hospitality to the stranger?

RK: Correct. But it's always partnered with the possibility of hostility, within every religion. So, religion is not necessarily good.

JC: Yes. I'm not going there now. That's another argument we have! But let me make my question more specific. What about something like the annunciation? What's the "truth status" of the annunciation? It's a figure of something, right? First of all, nobody was there to record that conversation. Secondly, half the people in the New Testament never heard that story. I dare say Mary never heard that story. Take the lectern in the background of Botticelli's painting, that you pointed out. The chances that Miriam of Nazareth, a peasant teenage girl in a dusty little village in first-century Galilee, was able to read would be a greater miracle than the annunciation!

So, there's a truth of hospitality, and then there are these religious "figures." These religious figures do not represent a fact of the matter. They're *stories*, and different religions have different stories, and the stories one knows are an accident of birth. But that does not mean they do not have truth of another sort, and it is that sort of truth that I am trying to get at.

RK: Biology is not destiny. Birth is not fate.

JC: I agree. I did not mean to imply otherwise.

RK: And yes, of course they are special, exemplary stories, sacred stories. They're called sacred because they belong to a canon that a number of people say are holy to them. They're not facts; they are narratives, translatable back into actions by virtue of how people "refigure" or reenact these narratives. People *do* extend the hand of friendship. They do the sacred thing and thus make the impossible possible again—just like it says in the sacred stories. The sacred stories of scripture thus give rise to new historical actions (in our own time, people like Gandhi, Martin Luther King, Etty Hillesum, John Hume, Mandela), which in turn form new existential testimonies, inscribing themselves into an ongoing narrative of sacred hospitality. (This comprises a sort of holy history, if you like, of what in the old days would have been called "the communion of saints.") It's all about the movement between praxis and *poiesis*, between action and narration.

Let me give one of my own favorite stories of such a breakthrough story in Irish history. In the sixteenth century, after the Anglo-Norman invasion, there was a bitter war between the Butlers and the Fitzgeralds. They were slaughtering each other in an endless cycle of revenge, not unlike the tit-for-tat carnage witnessed in Northern Ireland in the nineteen seventies and eighties. It was going back and forth, just endless hostility, until at one point Gerald Fitzgerald, Earl of Kildare, said, "This is ridiculous." So he went up to the Butlers, who were besieged in Dublin cathedral, and he said, "Let me in." He knocked at the door, a stranger appealing to his archenemies. "Let me in." And the Butlers replied, "No, we won't. We don't trust you." And Fitzgerald said, "Look, I come as a friend, not an enemy" (*hostis* can mean "friend" or "enemy," as mentioned), and to prove it, he asked them to make a hole in the big wooden entrance door (the hole is still there!) so he could put his arm through. And they did, and he took off his armor and extended his bare arm through the hole. And at that point his Butler enemies trusted him, because he had exposed himself radically; he was utterly vulnerable. "He chanced his arm," as the phrase still goes in Ireland to this day. He wagered and won. The Butlers had the choice to cut off his hand or to shake it. They shook it, and the war was over.

I think Levinas's point is similar about the naked face: it disarms you. Gandhi's face disarmed the British government. It has happened again and again. Martin Luther King brought about basic rights for blacks in this country. It works, however provisionally. Step by step. Bit by bit. Stories effect actions, which in turn produce new stories of those actions. Or, to put it in the more technical terms of Ricoeur's hermeneutic circle of narrative action, we move from action (prefiguration) to text (configuration) to action again (refiguration). It is an ongoing dialectic between story and history, testimonies and events—one which can bring about the impossible, as it did in remarkable ways, at least for a while, in India, Ireland, and South Africa.

QUESTIONER 2: Just a quick question about faith and the atheistic moment that precedes faith. When Mary hovers in an atheistic moment of fear and trembling and then says "Yes," is that atheistic hesitation swallowed up into faith? Dissolved into faith? Or does the atheistic moment remain as a kind of accompaniment of faith—in which case, you could say that the faith was flawed?

RK: Well, a quick answer: I would describe Mary's "pondering" as anatheistic and would claim that this moment does remain within the act of faith. I would not see this remainder as flawed but rather as truthful and faithful to the deeply human nature of Mary's wager. If anatheistic pondering disappeared altogether, faith would congeal into certainty. And I think *that* would be flawed faith, dogmatic faith. Mary, like anyone, is constantly being re-called to renew her faith—from Jesus's disappearing into the temple as a child right up to the cross and Resurrection. The pietà must have been full of anatheist pondering and wagering. There is no leap of faith, once and for all—not for Abraham, not for Mary, not for Jesus, not for anyone. When it comes to faith, we are all anatheists in one way or another.

QUESTIONER 3 (Q3): I wonder if you could expand briefly upon something that you talked about in passing, the mystical Eros. Often, such Eros refers to something outside of discourse, to a powerful mood or emotion which triggers a collapse of alterity, of otherness. How does such mystical experience play into the anatheistic encounter?

RK: In the Song of Songs—which Rashi called the holiest book in the Bible, although it was anathematized and censored for centuries by certain Jewish and Christian authorities—we find a song of desire for somebody who comes out of nowhere. The sentinels try to contain the Shulamite lover, but she eventually frees herself for love. And then it's reversible, because the lover who's coming towards her is also unnamable, and at times you don't know who's speaking—Solomon, the shepherd, or the Lord himself? The lover or the beloved? And that indeterminacy, that interanimation of both lovers, is an endless play of mystical Eros, because they remain estranged to each other even in the most intimate moments.

And this prefigures or serves as a kind of paradigm for similar isomorphic moments in all the great mystics, who generally speak—from Dionysius the Areopagite through Teresa of Avila and John of the Cross to Beguines and Marguerite Porete—a language of Eros, of theoerotic passion. It's not a language of agape—not that the two are incompatible. As Dionysius says, "You cannot oppose agape and Eros." They are interconvertible. But in mystical encounter it is generally Eros which sings louder.

So I would say there is an anatheistic moment of desire that is always for something or someone you do not know. And Teresa says that in *The Interior Castle*: you go deeper and deeper into the heart, through the different circles and chambers, until you reach the most intimate, interior room of the heart—where you encounter the lover. But it's in the moment of not knowing that you find this encounter with the stranger—the Other who resides at the deepest point within you. It is a moment of profound trust. In that sense, desire is the catalyst of a mystical dynamism towards the God who is always coming but never fully arrives.

Q3: So there's no complete union?

RK: There's a moment of mystical exchange, but it is only recognized *after* (ana-) the event. And as Teresa of Avila says, the event may only last a second. You've got that wonderful Bernini portrait of the beautiful angel's spear going into Teresa's heart, her womb, her entrails actually, and it's a very erotic-ecstatic moment. But it's not a moment that can endure. It immediately disappears, and after the event you're left wondering what exactly it is. So it's constantly got to be desired again (ana-). It is never a final consummation, where you've reached mystical union once and for all.

QUESTIONER 4 (Q4): This is a question for Professor Caputo. Basically I was wondering if you could explicate the particulars that separate the theological undecidability from merely inquisitive agnosticism, or suspicious agnosticism.

JC: Undecidability is the condition of possibility of a deeper affirmation, which is not a matter of being merely inquisitive or suspicious and would be very poorly described as agnostic, even if it is deeply structured by a kind of non-knowing. What I'm interested in is the structure of affirmation that underlies the positions that we take. We say, "Hermeneutics goes all the way down." In a matter like religion, that means that the things we think, the thoughts we have, the stories we tell, the narratives we recite are all contingent and inherited. They're local materials and they're deeply tied up with the language that we inherited. They are accidents of birth. That is fine. I don't think that undermines their value, by any means. I think that exactly the same thing is true of literature: the literature we learn to read and learn to love, to cite and recite, is the literature we inherit in our native language. That's an accident of birth, too. And so those differences cannot count in the long run.

What does count is the underlying affirmations that are enacted or deployed in the several traditions. Agnosticism is just as narrow or uninteresting as are theism or atheism for me. Agnosticism is just more jockeying, positioning, more positionality—in this case, trying to strike a pose of positional equilibrium or equidistance. The notion of agnosticism was first proposed by Thomas Huxley as a rival position to atheism. It's the kind of thing that comes up in the context of a debate about a monotheistic god, and it is a function of that discourse. It's a position that you can play, if you want to be a player in that kind of game.

For example, sometimes people make dramatic, famous conversions from one position to the other—atheists become theists, and theists become atheists. So what? There's no underlying impact on the grid, no significance for the underlying depth dimension of the "affirmation" I am speaking about. Different people are stationed at different points on the grid, and even the same person might move from one point to the other, might at one point in his life be deeply theistic and at another point deeply atheistic and then finally end up being agnostic. That is a journey taken by an individual who was perhaps affirming or seeking some unobjectifiable and unrepresentable affirmation that runs throughout all these positions, each of which is an attempt to present something ultimately unpresentable. It is this deeper structure of the self and of being under way, underlying all of those various positions, that interests me. I want to emphasize the distinction between a presentable position and an unpresentable affirmation, and affirmation is the sort of thing that people from very different worlds can talk about, even though they belong to different worlds and have different desires.

Q4: This is for Richard Kearney. I had a question about how far you want to push this idea of uncertainty in the moment of risk and wager. All the examples you give are about being in a moment of uncertainty where hospitality is extended. But does one always have to be uncertain, pondering, guessing, wagering before acting as a host towards a guest? Might not uncertainty also express itself as fear?

RK: That's a good question. I think, probably, if you were to do a statistical inventory of this, most human experiences of radical uncertainty are experienced as fear. And a very common expression of fear, if it goes deep enough, is phobia and violence. It's a retraction of the self and it's a scapegoating of the other, very often as enemy. So, in the moment of uncertainty, it can go either way. And maybe the instants of hospitality are the "impossible" moments that come rarely. There's no sure way of predicting that. And maybe they come much more frequently, provisionally, momentarily, and then are swallowed up into fear again, into a closure to others. There's no guarantee.

The examples I've given, I acknowledge, are decisive inaugural moments of hospitality. But there are countless counterexamples of uncertainty leading to closure—to fundamentalist clinging to false certainties, wars with enemies (including the most vicious kinds of religious wars). Uncertainty so often triggers fear of the other, which in turn leads one to close oneself in dogmatism. But, in spite of statistics, one still lives in hope that the impossible can become possible, and that is why it is important to keep on recalling and recounting exemplary cases of that—stories, histories, memories, myths, parables, testimonies.

QUESTIONER 5 (Q5): It seems that you're trying to show the value and merit of the anatheistic moment as a moment of indecision and undecidability, and yet it is precisely then that we have to choose either hospitality or hostility. But couldn't undecidability be a choosing not to choose? A choosing of the undecidable itself?

RK: That's a wonderful question. But let me say, straight off, that anatheist decision is not decisionism. It's informed, I would say, by narrative memories, traditions, and inheritances—like Mary reading from the lectern (even if, as Jack implies, she may not have been able to read). Even if we are illiterate, we are still hermeneutically informed by other stories; our choice and actions don't come out of nowhere. So if there is a wagering on hospitality over hostility, it's because other people have been there before you, done that, and come out the other side better people, altered, opened up, transformed. They made that impossible leap from hostility and fear into surprise and grace.

So we're hermeneutically informed by those stories from the beginning. And here Jack and I are at one. As Aristotle says, if you want to teach a virtue, tell a story. If you want to teach somebody patience, don't define patience as an abstract virtue; tell the story of Penelope. Courage: tell the story of Achilles. Wisdom: tell the story of Tiresias. So you tell the story and then people are hermeneutically formed and informed by that. Hospitality does not arise from nothing. It is a story with a history, and we are all part of that history—or should I say, "histories," for there are many different wisdom traditions, mythologies, and literatures where hospitality wins out over hostility. In the Western religious tradition from which I and Jack both hail, the sacred stories of Abraham and Mary are exemplary, but by no means exclusive. There are many others.

Q5: But why choose to act hospitably over remaining in undecidability itself?

RK: Because there comes a point when you've got to act. Somebody's drowning; I'm uncertain whether I should risk it. But you act. You jump in and try to save them. As Kierkegaard said, "God is a deed." Or Augustine: "You do the truth" (*facere veritatem*). There comes a point when pondering ends and action begins. But even then, the not knowing never disappears. Even after you've jumped, you might say, "Oh my God, why did I jump into the river? The person has disappeared under the water. I'm freezing to death, and I'm probably going to die. Maybe I shouldn't have done that." Now that's carnal: your body thinks that. You don't have time to reflect on it like Descartes or Kant. There are no a prioris when it comes to acting hospitably. You're never sure.

You're never absolutely certain. If you were, then I don't think you'd be hospitable. You know what I mean? You'd be a preprogrammed holy person for the rest of your life. And I don't think even the gods were that holy.

JC: Allow me to add a little postscript. I object to describing undecidability as "choosing not to choose." Undecidability is the condition of possibility of a choice; otherwise, the choice is rule-governed and it's easy to know what to do, there's no problem. The opposite of undecidability, which is a technical term in axiomatic theory, is not a decision but programmability, which means that a choice is dictated by a program or a rule. Then it's not much of a choice. Choices get to be choices, they have teeth in them, precisely when you don't know what to do, when you're faced with a radical undecidability, even as the urgency of the action imposes itself on you.

So, don't think about undecidability—or at least don't associate that with me or with Derrida or, I would think, with Richard—as "choosing not to choose." That's a phrase from *Either/Or*, in which Kierkegaard is describing the aesthete. That's certainly not undecidability, which goes beyond any aestheticism. Undecidability is *Fear and Trembling*; the situation Abraham faced, stationed between Isaac and God; the conflict of not knowing what to do in the face of two equally impossible options. Unless you don't know what to do, you're not going to do anything that will really have teeth in it. Unless you're paralyzed, you won't be able to move. Unless it's impossible, a true decision is not possible. That's undecidability.

QUESTIONER 6 (Q6): What's the difference, then? Just as agnosticism wouldn't exist without atheism, theism, and so on, surely undecidability has a relation to decidability?

JC: Undecidability is related to decision as its underlying condition. Decidability is its opposite; it means that there's a formula, a formal rule, that guides the decision. The difference between decidability and undecidability is the difference between the formalizable and the unformalizable. But undecidability is not the opposite of a decision; on the contrary, undecidability is the condition of possibility of deciding.

Now, what does that have to with affirmation? In religious matters, confessional "positions" are largely contingent on accidents of birth, like whether I am a Muslim or a Baptist. But the underlying affirmation, like hospitality, which is Richard's focus, has a deeper reach, which touches upon the level of a genuine decision and is able to show up, to be presented, in different, even opposing, "positions"—like theists and atheists equally committed to justice for the least among us, or theists and atheists equally resolved on maintaining privilege and hierarchy.

> RK: I'd like to add something on the discussion of the term *position*. As I understand it, each "position" comes from a "dis-position" and is always open to new dis-positions in turn. Taking a position means saying, "Here I stand." But the danger is that if you stay in a position for too long it becomes rigid, arrogant, a refusal to alter or change. "Here I stand/Here we stand" can then become Paisleyism, Thatcherism, or worse. "What we have, we hold." "No surrender." "We don't go anywhere from here." Then you get the siege or fortress mentality. On the other hand, a position constantly informed by a dialectic of dis-position and re-position is more like what Jack calls an "affirmation." A yes of action that moves freely and vigilantly in relation to a no of detachment; a wise and sensitive fragility. See what I mean?
>
> Q6: I do, but I am still unclear about the exact relationship between undecidability and position.
>
> JC: In cases like this, when Derrida was pressed on this point, he said (and Richard was commenting on this earlier on), "I rightly pass for an atheist." He doesn't say, "I am (*je suis; c'est moi*) an atheist," because that would somehow solidify his being in a position. He is saying, If you are content to locate my "position" on a map of intellectual or cultural geography, you could say it is "atheism." By the standards of the local rabbi or priest, Derrida is certainly an atheist. But that obviously doesn't cut very deeply one way or the other, and he could move felicitously between "positions" that seem now atheistic, now very Jewish. That description does not get very far with him. What he was concerned with was questions of justice, of hospitality, forgiveness, the gift, etcetera.

You're right: it's absolutely impossible for the sorts of deeper affirmations that we make not to reflect and take the form of the cultural possibilities that we inherited. We begin where we are; we speak the language that we inherit. We make choices within the framework within which we find ourselves. But we try to exercise a certain vigilance about that, maintain a certain ironic distance from the cultural positions we inherit, in order to burn through to the deeper affirmations. But we'll never succeed in doing that; otherwise, we would claim to be able to engage in pure transcendental reflection, which every phenomenologist after Husserl rejected. That would require extricating ourselves from our language and our culture and looking back down upon ourselves from above, which we're never going to do.

QUESTIONER 7 (Q7): Is there a bad sense of ana- as well as a good one? Is there such a thing as ana-genocide? Can ana- be regressive?

RK: The distinction I would make is something like this: ana- is an affirmation; it's a "yes" to the stranger that comes. So you could not have an ana-genocide, as I define ana-. Genocide abolishes strangers. There are certainly bad forms of repetition, reactionary returns to violence in revenge cycles that can lead to genocide. Violence is a recurring addiction: Kosovo, Northern Ireland, the Middle East. One gets paralyzed and addicted to violence and, in that instance, it's a repetition compulsion in Freud's sense—an addictive closure that becomes powerless to break out of itself, repeating itself backwards. Whereas ana- is the repetition forwards, as Kierkegaard understands it.

Q7: I would like to come back to the wager of hospitality. Can it ever go the other way? Can God ever be a host? There's something beautiful and compelling about the weak God, but can a weak God host you?

RK: It is a great question. I think there's a reversibility of hosting. You find it in the Gospel, just to take the Christian example. "Knock on the door and it shall be opened." Here, God is host and we are guests. But in the book of Revelation it is God knocking at the door wanting to be received as a guest, with us as hosts. God plays both host and guest. And if the host can't also become a guest, we are in trouble, it seems to me. It's got to go both ways for the vulnerable, fragile, powerless God—which both Jack and I espouse—to prevail. It's a provisional home. God does not have one mansion but many mansions. And guests have to enter all of them in different ways in order to keep God hospitable. And vice versa. Humanity also has many mansions (churches, temples, synagogues, mosques, mangers, huts!), and we've got to be open to the stranger as the guest to keep ourselves hospitable, whether that stranger is human or divine. And that is a question we need to address at some point: Where is the border between one kind of stranger and another? Is there a border? Is there a difference? That is a fundamental issue.

Sometimes there is only the thinnest of differences between the *hostis* as host or guest, friend or enemy, human or divine. How to tell the difference? And why call the stranger who invites us to impossible love and justice "God" at all? Why call it "holy"? Why call it "sacred"? It is the question of the limits of humanism. I myself think it is important to recall the radical role of the stranger in great religious texts, and I think this can actually help humanism be more humanistic. The dialogical relationship between humanist atheism and anatheism is for me a crucial, ongoing question.

10

Theism, Atheism, Anatheism

A Panel Discussion with David Tracy,

Merold Westphal, and Jens Zimmermann

In the following conversation, Richard Kearney's book *Anatheism* is engaged by one theologian and two theologically inclined philosophers. David Tracy is a well-known Roman Catholic theologian at the University of Chicago Divinity School, who has written important works on hermeneutics and theology (*The Analogical Imagination: Christian Theology and the Culture of Pluralism* and *On Naming the Present: Reflections on God, Hermeneutics, and Church*) and has contributed immensely to interfaith dialogue. In much of his work, Tracy argues for a hermeneutic faith and recovers the incomprehensible God of the mystics, a God who reveals himself in weakness and suffering. Tracy shares this emphasis on the incomprehensible God with Kearney's anatheism, but he also asks critically whether Kearney's appeal to the radical apophatic tradition pays enough attention to another apophatic strand: the classical Christian mysticisms of the Word, Trinitarian mysticism, and love mysticism. For these mysticisms affirm apophasis but also know of a postapophatic, affirmative dimension without which, Tracy fears, anatheism may not be able to develop its full potential in engaging other religious traditions.

Kearney's second interlocutor, Merold Westphal, is an internationally renowned authority on continental philosophy, phenomenology, and existentialism, and on Kierkegaard in particular. Westphal is also a philosophical theologian especially well acquainted with the Reformed Christian tradition. Like Kearney, Westphal is committed to a hermeneutical conception of truth, but he worries that anatheism too easily gives up on traditional Christian notions of God and theology. He singles out the biblical concepts of God's sovereignty and sacrifice to voice his suspicion that Kearney risks caricaturing these concepts in his appeal to an anatheistic alternative.

The final response to Kearney's *Anatheism* comes from Jens Zimmermann, a German-Canadian philosophical theologian and holder of the Canada Research Chair in Interpretation, Religion and Culture, in Vancouver, Canada. In his own work, Zimmermann draws from philosophical hermeneutics and existential phenomenology (Heidegger, Levinas, and Gadamer) to argue for a religiously based humanism as common ground between secular and religious thought. Like the previous two interlocutors, he affirms the importance of Kearney's work but raises questions of clarification, regarding anatheistic interpretations of the Trinity and of Bonhoeffer's theology. Zimmermann wonders whether Kearney's anatheism does full justice to the Incarnation and its hermeneutic implications.

With characteristic verve and insight, Kearney addresses each of the respondents' concerns and concludes the conversation by restating the intentions of his work in light of the interactions with his interlocutors in this volume. This colloquium on Kearney's work took place at Boston College on April 21, 2010, and was chaired by theologian Catherine Cornille.

DAVID TRACY

I have followed Richard Kearney's remarkable career for many years. I have learned so many important ideas from his philosophy that I can list only some of them here. First, his notion of a poetics beyond dialectic and rhetoric in his first work, *Poétique du possible*. Second, in that same early work, one finds Kearney's first development of what became the very important category of "the possible"—a category that will find its most important articulation years later, in his rethinking and retrieval of Nicholas of Cusa's concept of *"possest"* into Kearney's own notion of the possible God beyond the now more familiar notion of the impossible—from Silesius, Kierkegaard, Derrida, Caputo, Marion, and others—that is, Kearney's "possible God beyond the impossible" or, in the title of that path-breaking book before *Anatheism*, *The God Who May Be*.

Third, Kearney has consistently maintained, in continuity with his major mentor, Paul Ricoeur, a very subtle philosophy that insists on the hermeneutical character of all thinking, including the thinking of any phenomenology that considers itself, through the *epoché*, free from hermeneutics as well as from any theology that claims to be nonhermeneutical. As Kearney argues in *Anatheism*, " 'In the beginning was the Word' also means 'In the beginning was hermeneutics.' " Indeed, hermeneutics all the way down.

Fourth, Kearney's hermeneutics has also yielded an advanced notion of the hermeneutics of narrative—even beyond that of Ricoeur, I believe—along with the fact that he actually writes narratives, two stunning novels. It is, after all, unusual to find an accomplished philosopher who also writes good novels or plays in the modern period: Gabriel Marcel, Jean-Paul Sartre, Simone de Beauvoir, Georges Bataille, Iris Murdoch, and Richard Kearney. It is just as unusual to find a novelist who can also work out a theory of the novel. Here, Dostoyevsky in a way needed Bakhtin, just as Proust needed Kristeva, and the Joyce of *Finnegans Wake* needed Derrida, while the Joyce of *Ulysses*, as you know from this book, needed Kearney.

Fifth, Kearney's hermeneutics opens up to ready dialogue and argument with Derrida's often officially antihermeneutical arguments against Gadamer (especially the famous dispute in Paris in 1981) and to John Caputo's claims to a post-hermeneutical philosophy beyond Gadamer, Ricoeur, and Levinas alike. Kearney's dialogical and pluralistic hermeneutics is a singular one—that is, one built upon the major hermeneutical traditions of the Heidegger of *Being and Time* and the complex post-Gadamer hermeneutics of Paul Ricoeur, while still able, in his own way, to dialogue with, argue with, and learn from the deconstructive positions of Derrida and Caputo. Richard Kearney has a right to claim, if he so chose, that over the years he has in fact cumulatively articulated, as I read him, what could be called the "new hermeneutics," analogous to, and indeed often in dialogical argument with, Jean-Luc Marion, Jean-Louis Chrétien, Jean-Yves Lacoste, and others who claimed to have developed a "new phenomenology." I hope Richard Kearney one day does develop further what I read him as having developed over these many years, not only new hermeneutical categories that may help us—like his categories "strangers" and "monsters," the *possest* God, the God who may be, and the hermeneutical wager, in this book, as a wager of anatheism—but also a rethinking philosophically how a new hermeneutics might be formulated today in dialogical relationship to both the new phenomenology and to deconstruction, which, in fact, he's doing.

Pierre Hadot—who died three days ago, I regret to say—in his magisterial works on ancient philosophy, has reminded us all that the philosophy of the ancients did not only describe a theoretical vision of reality but also outlined a way of life with attendant "daily spiritual exercises" reciprocally related to that vision or theory of reality. In my judgment, one of the major tasks in contemporary theology and philosophy is to reunite a vision or theory of reality with a way of life, as you can see in several such attempts, like Wittgenstein's or the late Foucault's or Lonergan's.

Several modern philosophers have bravely attempted to heal the fatal separations enforced by classical Enlightenment modernity. First, the separation of thought and feeling; hence, Kearney's novels and his frequent philosophical recoveries of the Irish literary and philosophical traditions, traditions particularly rich in passionate and thoughtful philosophies and literature, from John Eriugena through Seamus Heaney. Second, the separation of form and content; hence, Kearney's hermeneutics as a narrative hermeneutics. Third, the separation of theory from praxis (or practice), including theory from a way of life. *Anatheism* is a way of life, as I read it, a wager for a way of life related to the vision or theory of the God who may be. Hence, Kearney's insistence in part three of *Anatheism* that an anatheistic wager become an intellectual and spiritual way of life for the philosopher, by embracing the "fertile tension between theism and atheism in our day" and thus recovering, through that tension, the radically apophatic-mystical thinkers in all traditions—for example, in the Christian tradition of Meister Eckhart or Marguerite Porete. For precisely through their dark nights and their experiences of nothingness, the apophatic mystical traditions of contemplation yield a shock, as Breton says—a shock of nothingness that returns one to ordinary life, to the beauty of poetry itself in nature (as in John of the Cross and Gerard Manley Hopkins and Teresa of Avila), and to the struggles for an impossible justice and love to come, in our radically unjust societies and a global situation that is often defined by massive global suffering (as in Walter Benjamin, Simone Weil, Derrida, Gutiérrez, Breton, Gandhi, Dorothy Day, and Jean Vanier).

Kearney's book *The God Who May Be* defines, I believe, his major contribution to date to the contemporary discussion on God (or, anatheistically stated, the God after the death of a certain God). Kearney's contribution to the theory side of that debate is clear: a recovery of the incomparable Nicholas of Cusa's notion of God as *possest* (*posse* and *esse* together), in a contemporary theory of God as possibility beyond the impossible. This notion is particularly important because one of the great puzzles of Western intellectual thought is why Nicholas of Cusa's work—the first significant synthesis after the problems of nominalism in the fourteenth century—was not followed through in the fifteenth century. Now it is.

Anatheism describes a way of life, as Kearney understands it, that is intrinsically related to his own theory of a Cusan apophatic, mystical, philosophical God who may be (*possest*). This new book uses certain fragments (more exactly, fragments of different traditions), so that the fragments have become, in Kearney's work, what I myself would call "frag-events"—that is to say, in the very shattering of the fragments, a disclosure of the infinite possible God who may be and a spiritual way of life attendant to devotion to that God; namely, in this book, hospitality to the stranger, work for the downtrodden and oppressed, by means of the new wager of love working through justice after the experience of the dark night of the death of a certain God. Hence, one lives in an open space where one can learn to listen again to all the voices of the traditions, especially the voices of the oppressed and the fragmentary memories of the sufferings of the oppressed, in the words of Walter Benjamin or Johann Baptist Metz, and with new hope in a messianic justice to come, in the words of Derrida.

Kearney's hermeneutical anatheistic wager should be read, therefore, not as a new theoretical "ism" to replace other isms such as theism, atheism, gnosticism, pantheism, or panentheism, but as a way of life directly related to the theory/vision of the "God who may be" of his previous work. The book *Anatheism* is a plausible and often moving account of one great option of our troubled and promising time. The book seems sometimes tempted to declare this radically apophatic, anatheistic way to be the only way to speak responsibly and philosophically of God today. I admit that I only trust "onlys" when they are necessary at the moment for the speaker, like Martin Luther, when he said, "Here I stand," or

Richard Kearney's creative and courageous "Here I stand" in *Anatheism*. But such onlys can also eventually lead to—even with Luther, if the Finnish school is right—a more pluralistic stand, as in Kearney's case, the pluralistic stand in the rest of *Anatheism*.

There ought always to be apophatic moments in any serious effort to try to "think God," or what a Jew, Christian, or Muslim—the radical monotheist—means by God, as one sees clearly in Thomas Aquinas. However, in the radically apophatic Christian mystical tradition to which Kearney principally appeals, the apophatic can serve as a moment—but not the final moment (in my reading; he doesn't emphasize this)—in a more encompassing mystical thought, as in the influential Dionysius the Areopagite, whose final word is neither the cataphatic God of the good or the apophatic nothingness, but the liturgically transformed mystical knowing of his final work, *Mystical Theology*.

I hope, therefore, that in his future work Richard Kearney may relate his new apophatic, anatheistic way to the other three great forms of Christian mysticism (he's also working out his spirituality here): the mysticism of the Word, Trinitarian mysticism, and love mysticism. These other three classical mystical wagers all possess apophatic moments, although rarely as radical an apophaticism as those of Eckhart or John of the Cross or Vladimir Lossky or the anatheism of Richard Kearney. But, without further attention to these other three ways, the anatheistic way might be tempted to close its doors too soon to certain postapophatic (not nonapophatic) options of religious life, in the monotheisms and in all the great religious traditions, including Taoism, Bhakti Hinduism, and Bodhisattva Buddhism, and the communal-cosmic and nature-oriented character of most indigenous religions, like Native American religions. But this is a call simply to construe the anatheistic way as not the only way to think responsibly about God today, even after the death of a certain God. The anatheistic way is, however, surely a central and important way for all of us to try to rethink God after the death of God.

I will conclude these brief reflections with a call for clarifications on three categories in *Anatheism*: power, kenosis, and messianism. Even if my suggestions on these categories are accepted by him, they would not, in fact, challenge the central anatheist paradigm of his remarkable book. I present them simply in the hope that alternative readings—on power, kenosis, and messianism—may help to strengthen certain arguments of his book, or at least they may prove to be three further flying buttresses to secure the anatheistic cathedral.

First question: Is Kearney's expression "God's powerless power" (analogous to John Caputo's *The Weakness of God*, in his book of that name) really so clear a concept to serve, without further clarifications, as the preferred way for understanding the kenotic, vulnerable suffering and, at the limit, the crucified God? I personally think not—at least not without the further clarification of the interrelated categories of power and kenosis as they are employed in *Anatheism*.

Logically, "power" is a relational term. Power requires more than one term for a complete statement. And if more than one of the terms is a person, then power will also be a social term, a social relation (as David Hume and Friedrich Nietzsche argued).[1] The relationships of power, moreover, form a spectrum of domination and coercion, on one extreme of the spectrum, to influence, persuasion, love on the other extreme, with authority in the middle of the spectrum (that is, authority as in "a classic text is authoritative," not authoritarian, as in authoritarian political systems).[2] But it is a spectrum. My claim is that talk of the weakness and strength of God is often too dependent upon a sense of power as *only* domination.

The monotheistic God of both the Bible and the Koran is portrayed, in different passages of both the Bible and the Koran, in all three of the alternatives. God's power is, to be sure, often displayed in terms of domination or coercion—most prominently in the book of Job, in the vision of God as pure power—as it is in other texts and other traditions, like the disclosure of Krishna as pure power in the Bhagavad Gita, or as in the god Dionysus of Euripides's *Bacchae*, or theologically in the strict Calvinist notion of double predestination. All these are notions of God's power as domination.

God's power is also portrayed, however, in the Bible and the Koran, as influence, persuasion—and especially the exceptionally persuasive and, indeed, transformative power of God's love, justice, and mercy in the three monotheisms (as in Alfred North Whitehead).[3] Prophetic Judaism, after all, emphasizes that—as Derrida insists, and Kearney does, too—God's messianic justice is to come. In Judaism, moreover, Franz Rosenzweig emphasizes the Song of Songs as the key text to the Hebrew Bible, and thereby erotic love as the key category for understanding God. Christianity usually emphasizes love, especially in the most important Christian metaphor in 1 John, "God is love." Islam emphasizes, in every text of the

Koran, the ever-benevolent and merciful power of Allah, as in the constant refrain to Allah "the ever-benevolent and merciful."

Thus, in all three traditions, a major ethical, political, and philosophical-theological task is to try to work out the proper relationships between the two divine powers: justice and love. Sometimes justice and love, as powers, are related dialectically, as in Reinhold Niebuhr's reformed theological ethic, where love functions, for Niebuhr, as a dialectically impossible ideal geared to try to ensure humane justice. Sometimes justice and love are related analogically, as in Thomas Aquinas's paradigm, where grace (in this case, divine love) does not destroy but perfects nature (in this case, philosophical justice).

Now, in the crucified God of the cross (not only in Moltmann; Augustine also speaks of the crucified God), it is of course theologically accurate to speak of the powerless God of the Crucifixion (and if you're Balthasarian, in the descent into hell). In my judgment, however, the crucified God, however real, is not an entirely accurate phrase for God's other kenotic actions in creation, covenant, and incarnation, leading up to the cross, which in turn leads up to the Resurrection, Pentecost and, in the eschatological future, the Second Coming, in the Christian symbol system. Thus, it makes more biblical and theological sense to speak of God's power either as self-limiting (the covenant)—as in many covenantal theologies, such as Calvin's (or even before Calvin, the nominalists)—or, as I prefer, as kenotically (meaning infinitely loving and thereby infinitely powerful through infinite love) a vulnerable and suffering God and, at the limit, the powerless, crucified God at the cross. But only in the very infinity of God's love is it fully appropriate, I believe, to speak of God as powerless. Otherwise, kenosis (through creation, covenant, incarnation, and then on to the Resurrection) is erroneously described, if one thinks of power only as domination. God's power is the very great power of pure, unbounded love, as in Wesley's famous hymn, and love is not power as domination. Love is power as an empowerment and persuasion to new cooperative, noncompetitive life with God.

Related to this notion of divine power as infinite love, the Christian theological category of kenosis, from Paul's hymn in Philippians, is a much-contested category in the history of philosophy and theology, especially in the modern period since Hegel. As profound and still widely influential as Hegel's kenotic, philosophical theology—or rather more accurately theological philosophy—is, Hegel has not helped, in my judgment, to understand the heart of a Christian theological notion of God's power as kenosis. Sergei Bulgakov's Russian Orthodox theological transformation of Hegel's notion of kenosis, united to his theological transformation of the late Schelling's philosophy of mythology and revelation, is a far more reliable guide, in my judgment, to a proper use of kenosis in modern theology.

In my own understanding, kenosis is the self-emptying, divine love, expressing God's love as love throughout the whole symbol system: creation, covenant, incarnation, cross, Resurrection, and second messianic coming—the "not yet." If divine power is considered as only dominative and coercive, and you have too-ready speech about the "weak" God (as in Caputo), then God's loving relationship to us—which, after all, for the Christian is grounded in the intra-Trinitarian relationships of love as the condition of the possibility of kenosis—would be construed as a competitive relationship between God and humans, between a strong God (that is, as in the old, metaphysically omnipotent, ontotheological, doubly predestinating God) and a weak human being (that is, an unfree and coerced one). Now, clearly, Kearney's entire position is against the strict Calvinist position I just cited. Therefore, it seems to me a clarification of the categories "power" and "kenosis" might help to strengthen his intention.[4]

One further clarification: New Testament eschatology includes a "not yet," which can be well described as the Messianic justice to come—for Christians, in the Second Coming of the Messiah; for Jews, in the coming of the Messiah; for Shia Muslims, in traditions on the future coming of the Hidden Imam. But New Testament eschatology is, in fact, a fertile tension of an "already" and a "not yet," in terms of temporality. New Testament eschatology does include, I repeat, the Messianic Christ to come and the Second Coming, which must involve a "not yet." Many good theologians—Johan Baptist Metz and Jürgen Moltmann, for instance—have tried to recover the power of the Second Coming and not just hand over the Second Coming to fundamentalists, which is what most liberal theologians, I admit, do. I did so for years; Rahner did it; Bultmann did it. Nevertheless, Christ will come in the future for the Christian (already; not yet). Christ will come because he has already come for the Christian, because he continues to come as his continuing presence among us, in Word, sacrament, and driving the struggle for justice and love for all—

especially the widows, orphans, and strangers, as in Kearney's wonderful work. And Christ will come again.

But my questions are just three minor questions for clarification on kenosis, power, messianism, and eschatology. More importantly, Richard Kearney's amazing intellectual and spiritual journey should prove, once again, for his readers an occasion for celebration. All serious thinkers who are alert to the difficulty of thinking (adequately and responsibly) God may be freed to think anew in the rich and emancipating context of the anatheistic and epiphanic thoughts of Richard Kearney.

MEROLD WESTPHAL

I'm grateful for the invitation to be a part of this event and to enter into conversation with Richard Kearney and other friends. I think his book describes three possible journeys: perhaps a biographical journey that is his journey in some way; a cultural journey that maps out what is sometimes signified by the term *return of religion*—and both of those would be mostly descriptive. But I think the most useful way to read the book is as a prescription, as the account of a journey that he recommends that all of us should take: a journey away from certain gods into a desert of disorientation, in order to be reoriented in a better way. And it is in that sense that I shall speak about it.

There is a great deal about the book that I like. Richard is not just a charming fellow, but he writes charmingly, which means gracefully, clearly, and with a great deal of water behind the dam. Among the things I especially like about this book are its hermeneutical character and the repetitive use of the notion of "wager" in that connection that he has taken over from his teacher Paul Ricoeur and used so effectively. I love the way he uses the stranger motif, building on what he did in *Strangers, Gods and Monsters*. The nice thing about the stranger metaphor is that he uses it both with reference to God and with reference to the neighbor—the widow, the stranger, and the orphan. I like the notion that reorientation presupposes disorientation, and that when God is a stranger who keeps coming to us as a stranger, we should expect to be disoriented in order to be reoriented. I like that the book has as its culmination the meditations on Dorothy Day, Jean Vanier, and Mahatma Gandhi, which in a way, I think, makes the book a commentary on Galatians 5:6: the only thing that matters is "faith working as love."

But I'm a little worried about the faith. I take it that I was invited here not simply for a love-in—though I love Richard dearly—but to raise, in the gracious way that David Tracy put it, some questions for clarification. How could one say it more gently than that?

The first indication that clarifications are needed is what seem to me to be a series of false antitheses that occur with some regularity throughout the book: an omnipotent causality or a self-emptying service, as if that was an either/or, or a zero-sum game—God as a sovereign or as a stranger. Why not a sovereign stranger? Sovereignty or hospitality. Why couldn't the king throw a feast? Service or sacrificial bloodletting, the worker-priest or metaphysics. And so I want to pick up a couple of the themes in which those kinds of what seem to me to be unnecessary alternatives work out. From having talked to Jens beforehand, and from having heard what David Tracy said, I get the impression that in a certain sense it will look as if we have ganged up on anatheism, because we're asking some very similar questions.

When I said I was worried about the faith, another way to say that would be that on this journey, from faith through some desert, through some darkness, through some doubts, through some disorientation, there is no single, clear way in which the path back to anatheism is mapped out. Kearney wants us to travel lightly, and it seems to me that perhaps he wants us to travel too lightly. And the first thing it seems to me he wants us unnecessarily to give up is the sovereignty of God.

Here I want to appeal to what I call the "Naas fallacy." Michael Naas has written a wonderful book about Derrida in which he offers a Derridean deconstruction of the three sovereignties: the sovereign self, the sovereign state, and the sovereign God. He offers something that looks a like a deconstruction of the sovereign self and the sovereign state, but the first time I read the book I couldn't find a deconstruction of the sovereign God. So I read it again, and I still couldn't find it. All I could find was filiation—that was the key word.

What's wrong with the sovereign God is that the sovereign state has usurped to itself the prerogatives that were traditionally assigned to a sovereign God. Being "human, all too human," when the sovereign state deifies itself and treats itself as sovereign, as above any law except the laws it gives to itself, all hell breaks loose—quite literally. I said to Michael Nass, "That's the only thing I can find. That looks like a complaint about the state, not about God. That's not a reason why God shouldn't be sovereign; it's a reason why states shouldn't claim to be sovereign and deify themselves." And his answer was, "Yes, well, I guess you're probably right. I think you probably could give a Derridean deconstruction of God, but I guess I didn't do it in the book."

You see, the logic of the Naas fallacy is something like this: There's a police department that has certain legitimate authority, and it has a certain power that it has been given to exercise this authority. But some criminal gang has been dressing itself up in stolen police uniforms and going around committing crimes under the cover of being the police, or in the name of the police. These are violent crimes of murder and rape and so forth. So the solution should be to reduce the authority of the police department and to lessen their power to carry out whatever authority they have.

That doesn't make a lot of sense to me. When you have the problem of people who do not legitimately have an authority usurping it for themselves, and doing wicked things with that authority that they would not do without that authority, the solution is to attack the usurpation, not to attack the legitimate authority that has been usurped. And it seems to me that our good friend Jack Caputo, talking about the weakness of God, and on occasion, Richard, in *Anatheism*, commit what I call the Naas fallacy. He clearly wants us to abandon a sovereign God, and he talks about religion too often assuming the power of sovereignty, resulting in theocracy. He talks about a sovereign power being too easily transferred to human agencies. And who could dispute that? History is full of instances of that kind. But it seems to me that the solution to that problem is not to abandon the sovereignty of God but to complain about human entities that deify themselves and do wicked things in the name of God.

A second argument that we're offered for the abandoning the sovereignty of God is the kenosis argument—the appeal to that beautiful hymn in Philippians 2, which speaks of Jesus having "emptied himself" (that's what the Greek word *kenosis* is about). There's a double emptying in that text. First, the Son empties himself in becoming human. He empties himself of divine power and prerogative. And then, having become human, he empties himself in becoming "obedient unto death, even death on a cross." So you have a picture of Jesus as a weak and emptied person.

There are two reasons why it doesn't seem to me that this provides any evidence at all for a "weakness of God" thesis or for an abandonment of the sovereignty of God. The first has to do with the Trinitarian context in which it occurs. Neither in the epistle to the Philippians nor in any of Paul's other writings is there any suggestion that God the Father or God the Holy Spirit has been emptied of their divine authority and their divine power. The Son has done this willingly in relationship to the Father, but the Father is not emptied. It's only Hegel and, following Hegel, Vattimo and Altizer who interpret the Incarnation as the death of God the Father and the bringing of the deity completely to earth. And then the death of Jesus is the death of any particular deity on earth. In other words, the Resurrection is simply the discovery that the earthly divinity is the human community and not to be equated with any human individual, such as Jesus. That's an essentially Hegelian doctrine of the Trinity that both Vattimo and Altizer have sought to—if you'll pardon the term—resurrect. But that certainly is not Paul, and one cannot appeal to Pauline kenosis for a notion of God as having emptied Godself of divinity and its power and its authority.

The second reason is simply textual. If you go to Philippians 2 and just read to the end of that hymn—much less the rest of the epistle, to the rest the Pauline corpus, and to the parables of Jesus—just to the end of that hymn, it concludes that "God has highly exalted him and given him a name that is above every name, that at the name of Jesus every knee will bow . . . and every tongue confess that Jesus Christ is Lord, to the glory of God the Father." That's a picture of a sovereign God. The kenosis is not the kenosis of the entire Trinity, and even for the Son it is only temporary kenosis. At the end of the story, as envisaged in this very hymn, Jesus is the one to whom every knee is bowing and every tongue confessing that Jesus Christ is Lord, to the glory of God the Father.

Now, the word *Lord* in this context is doubly loaded. If there were Jewish readers or listeners in the Philippian church, they would have recognized that "Lord" is, in the Jewish translation of Hebrew Scriptures—the Septuagint—the translation for YHWH. Most of the Philippian believers were gentiles, and the word *Lord* would have connoted for them one of the titles that Caesar attributed to himself. So, if Jesus is Lord, the claim there is that on the one hand, Jesus is as fully lord and sovereign of the universe as the God of Israel is; and, on the other hand, it is Jesus and not Caesar who is lord of the world. That is not a hymn to the weakness of God. That is a hymn to the sovereignty of God.

I know *Anatheism* does not purport to be a work of theology; it is a work of philosophy. Therefore, one is entitled to pick texts from Homer, Shakespeare, anywhere you want to, and put them to work doing your phenomenological, hermeneutical project. You don't have to have the constraints upon you that you would have if you were a theologian. But when you pick and choose the parts of biblical texts you like and leave out the parts you don't like, the danger is that the text that results will be, as Marion points out so powerfully in *God Without Being*, a mirror of the author or the community out of which the author speaks, and the result will be a God created in our image, whoever we happen to be. Philosophy has a name for that. Philosophy calls it "ideology," when our theories are reflections of who we are, that do us the service of justifying who we are, in return. And I'm suggesting a moment of suspicion in relationship to this, appealing to Richard's teacher, Paul Ricoeur.

The other theme that I want to say something about is sacrifice. In biblical theism, sacrifice plays a significant role. It's a central theme in both the Hebrew Scriptures and in the New Testament. Richard is worried about it. He talks about periodic bloodletting to satisfy a divine bloodlust. He talks about scapegoating strangers and repetitive human bloodlust. He associates these with the notions of sacrifice and suggests that we should come back to a God who is, if I've understood him correctly, no longer associated with the notion of sacrifice. I want to say something about the biblical notion of sacrifice as I understand it, which suggests that there is no reason we should unload it from our luggage in order to travel lightly on our way back to God.

First of all, right from the creation story in Genesis, in the biblical perspective sin is a capital offense in the eyes of God. Now, that notion may be offensive to us. It certainly doesn't correspond to our anxieties about capital punishment as practiced by the state. It makes us uncomfortable in several ways. But let me just throw in this hint: if God does keep coming to us as a stranger, as Richard insists, then one of the ways in which God might be a stranger to us is as the God for whom sin is a capital offense in which those who have abused the gift of life have forfeited it.

In the second step, I quote two scriptures, one from the Hebrew Scriptures and one from the New Testament. Ezekiel says, "As I live, says the Lord God, I have no pleasure in the death of the wicked, but that the wicked turn from their ways and live. Turn back, turn back from your evil ways, for why should you die?" And then, in 2 Peter, God is portrayed in "not wanting any to perish, but all to come to repentance." We do not have a picture of a bloodlusty God here. We have the picture of a loving parent who doesn't want to bring the law down on those who have become guilty.

So what does God do? God provides substitutes twice over. In the Hebrew Scripture, he provides animal sacrifices. There's one particular sacrifice that is not a sacrifice; the scapegoat, in the narrowest sense, is one that is sent off into the wilderness. But in the larger context of the sacrificial system, I think all of the atoning sacrifices, which do involve the slaying of the sacrificial animal, are scapegoatings. They are placing upon the scapegoat the sins of the people, so the judgment of God can be enacted without having to violate the God of Ezekiel and the God of 2 Peter, who takes no delight in the sinner as such but wants to leave open the option of repentance. In the new covenant, one gets the only human sacrifice that the biblical God is interested in. It's not the sacrifice of Abraham's son by Abraham. That got stopped. It's the sacrifice of God's son by God, with the consent of the son. Jesus, as the Lamb of God who takes away the sin of the world, is the scapegoat. Jesus is the one on whom the sins of the world have been laid so that the wrath of God can fall on that one scapegoat and not have to fall on anyone else.

Now, that's all theological; it seems to me fairly straightforward Christianity. My point is this: there's nothing in that biblical narrative about God providing substitutionary sacrifices to atone for our sins that suggests that we should go out and offer anyone else in some periodic bloodletting. And I just give you this example. The Nazis participated in an enormous bloodletting, but I haven't read anywhere that they understood what they were doing was sacrificing Jews in atonement for their Aryan sins. That whole idea is just incomprehensible. It seems to me that, if one wants to get away from religious justifications of violence, as I think we all do, one doesn't have to abandon the biblical notion of sacrifice, because there's nothing in the biblical notion of sacrifice that suggests or is even compatible with the notion that one human group has the right, "in the name of God," to kill other human groups and to consider it, somehow or another, as an atoning sacrifice for their own sins.

JENS ZIMMERMANN

Along with my colleagues, I am grateful for being able to participate in this anatheist discussion, one of many occasions on which Richard Kearney practices the very hospitality he preaches in his recent book *Anatheism*. At heart, anatheism is profoundly a hermeneutic project that seeks to mediate between various religious and nonreligious conceptions of transcendence in order to speak again about God after the death of the God of metaphysicians and philosophers. This effort involves the drawing of anatheist elements from all religious traditions, for the sake of dialogue.

Hermeneutics, as Gadamer taught us, always involves translating one language or thought world into another. Such translation requires a double effort of reflection: to make conscious, as far as possible, the interpreter's guiding questions and the traditions that guide them, and also to render another's position or argument as strongly as possible. Only then can the transformative event occur that Gadamer called "fusion of horizons," in which the interpreter's horizon merges with another's in a way that enlarges his own perspective on a subject matter. Especially Richard's teacher Ricoeur insisted on keeping otherness alive in interpretation, so that the friction of difference remains and effects a transformation of one's own interpretive framework. Hermeneutics is never assimilation but transformative dialogue that allows us to see things *again*, but with new eyes.

If I have understood Richard correctly, this hermeneutic process of translating in order to speak again of God is at the heart of anatheism. Now, like my two colleagues, I greatly admire how Richard's concept of anatheism captures the urgent need of our time for dialogue and ways to recover talk about God. Yet, at the same time, I wonder whether anatheism is hermeneutical enough—that is, whether it has enough patience to endure the double demand of understanding one's own tradition and to endure the tension of difference by making another's view as strong as possible. It seems to me that sometimes the anatheist host is too eager to shape the character of his guests in his own image rather than allow them to present themselves. (Ironically, it is perhaps some of the guests from his own Christian tradition that suffer from assimilation at the hands of anatheism.)

Richard seems to sense this himself when responding to theological criticisms of his work. The more he takes philosophy into the boundary regions of theology, the more frequent become his appeals to poetic or, as he puts it, "heretical license," on the grounds that he's doing philosophy rather than theology. The funny thing about theology, however, is that as soon as one engages theology in detail and reads biblical texts, one is actually doing theology nolens volens. Whenever one reflects on the meaning of biblical texts or reasons about God, one is, in fact, doing theology. My question is, How accurately does the anatheist engage Christian traditions and "translate" existent theological concepts?

Very briefly, I want to look at the anatheistic treatment of two central Christian doctrines, the Incarnation and the Trinity, to illustrate my concern about anatheism's ability to translate religious concepts faithfully. Merold already alluded to the problematic opposition of kenosis to divine sovereignty. For Kearney, God's "self-emptying" in the Incarnation is anatheist shorthand for God's involvement in the world; for the unity of secular and sacred; for a religion of humility and service rather than one of institutionalized power, political dominion, triumphalism, and nationalist aspirations.[5] Yet, these laudable prospects are bought at the price of erecting a series of seemingly dogmatic binary oppositions. Anatheist Christianity opposes the God of kenosis to the sovereign God, the God of becoming to the God of absolute being, the God of compassion to the God of judgment; it opposes the God of the actual to the God of the possible, the ineffable God to the God of dogma. Do not these binary oppositions indicate a God that is too small, too much domesticated by the imagination of continental philosophy, and too little shaped by the actual biblical texts and their interpretive traditions?

Traditional Christology has avoided this facile opposition and embraced the essential paradoxical nature of Christianity, expressed in a series of "both/ands": both God and man; both transcendent and immanent; both self-sufficient, sovereign deity and kenotic, suffering servant. The Catholic theologian Henri de Lubac rightly insisted that the great attraction of Christianity and its inherent potential for self-criticism, self-renewal, and constant self-adaptation—in short, its anatheistic qualities—depend on maintaining rather than resolving paradox.[6] Viewed through the eyes of the greater Christian tradition, Richard Kearney's God talk is shot through with unnecessary binary oppositions.

It is a puzzling inconsistency that anatheism celebrates the Incarnation by finding God in the sacramental presence and poetic refigurations of the stranger while at the same time deriving so much polemic mileage from opposing immanence to transcendence, divine presence to absence, divine being from becoming. One of anatheism's own patron saints, Dietrich Bonhoeffer, shows us that casting down the God of metaphysics requires no such antinomies. Bonhoeffer's notion of "religionless Christianity" does indeed mean that we should not define presence in the world in spatial or metaphysical terms; the great mystery of God's becoming human and dying on the cross while remaining the sustaining center of reality undermines any such spatial pretentions. God's solidarity with humanity to the point of utter powerlessness in death defines Bonhoeffer's nonreligious interpretation of Christianity. Religious interpretations worship a God of power, a God who defeats enemies, the tribal God. Christianity, by contrast, speaks of the God who dies for the sake of all human beings. Nonreligious Christianity is participation in God's being as expressed in Jesus: the freedom to be for others.[7]

Now, all of this sounds, indeed, very anatheistic, except that Bonhoeffer nowhere opposes faith to dogma, presence to eschatology, immanence to transcendence, or God' s being to his becoming. God is still omniscient, omnipotent, and sovereign. Bonhoeffer avoids anatheistic antinomies because of his high Christology. In his *Ethics*, he argues that all of reality is oriented toward and governed by the Christ in whom all things have their being. Bonhoeffer believed reality to be one "Christ-reality" (*Christuswirklichkeit*). This one Christ-reality is the basis for a theological engagement of the world that is deeply hermeneutical, without advocating the kind of opposition between divine kenosis and sovereignty Kearney seems to cherish. Bonhoeffer argued that, just as God revealed himself to us by becoming human, so all revelation comes to us through human mediation—through language, history, tradition, and living out our faith in concrete life situations. The sacred, as Bonhoeffer liked to put it, is found only in the profane, and the revelational only in the rational. For him, theology is by definition hermeneutical, while God remains sovereign. Divine sovereignty and hermeneutics are not, then, mutually exclusive.

Moreover, according to Bonhoeffer, the Incarnation ensures that divine sovereignty is the very basis for Christian humanism, for a life in the service of charity and human flourishing. God's sovereign rule over reality had to be interpreted Christologically, and the divine attributes had to be interpreted in light of the God who became human for the sake of the world, who shares our suffering and historicity, and in whom we are thus *ontologically* linked with every human being as brother or sister: "Inasmuch as we participate in Christ, the incarnate one, we also have a part in all of humanity, which is borne by him. Since we know ourselves to be accepted and borne within the humanity of Jesus, our new humanity now also consists in bearing the troubles and the sins of all others. The incarnate one transforms his disciples into brothers and sisters of all human beings."[8] Divine power and weakness are thus not opposed, but omnipotence expresses itself as love to the point of death for the sake of human solidarity.

The same incarnational dynamic also informs Bonhoeffer's view of the church, which retains, contrary to Critchley's assertions, a central role for the mediation of God's presence in Bonhoeffer. Yet Bonhoeffer defines the church, anatheistically, so to speak, as "Christ existing in community," whose members are shaped into Christ's own philanthropic likeness as people who "exist for others"—and Bonhoeffer means *all* others. Bonhoeffer's incarnational anatheism is, therefore, at heart also a humanism, providing a link Kearney is explicitly reaching for.

Bonhoeffer may well be the most profitable theological voice for anatheism, because, like Kearney, he was deeply disenchanted with the theological establishment. And yet his deeply Chalcedonian Christology prevented him from opposing anatheistic language to traditional Christian teachings about God's freedom and sovereignty. Anatheism would greatly benefit from a better acquaintance with Bonhoeffer and other theological thinkers, such as Eberhard Jüngel, who have shown that God's being and becoming are not antinomies.[9]

My second example of a possible anatheist misreading of the Christian tradition is Kearney's translation of the Trinity with the help of postmodern philosophy. Once again, Kearney sets out to revise an impersonal, faceless concept of postmodern transcendence, the Derridean *khora*, in personal terms. Derrida appropriates this Platonic idea of an impersonal, neutral container of the forms as an image for the nonobjectifiable, impersonal, unnamable other of deconstruction. Richard rightly wonders about this arbitrary choice but, rather than oppose khora to God, integrates this concept into the Christian Trinity.[10] Yet this integration, once again, produces an unorthodox hybrid of the patristic *perichoresis*, rather than allowing traditional and arguably more biblical descriptions of God to emerge.[11]

In Richard Kearney's version, "different persons move endlessly around an empty center (khora), always deferring one to the other, the familiar to the foreign, the resident to the alien. Without the *gap* in the middle there could be no leap, no love, no faith."[12] Richard, of course, does not have to worry that the Christian tradition knows of no such *empty* space or gap in the Trinity, since he offers a "weak" or "anatheistic" reading of the Trinity to offset triumphalistic interpretations of full Trinitarian presence. Yet the absence of a gap in traditional Christian Trinitarian doctrine has its reason. Richard rightly identifies Trinitarian communion as the highest intimacy and trust without surrendering individuality. This theological ideal for interpersonal communion, however, falls apart when an impersonal, empty center of the Trinity places something at the heart of divine communion that is nonpersonal and alien to God. To use creedal language, Kearney introduces another substance into the communion of persons of *homoousia*. There is, of course, something other in the Trinitarian circumincession, but it is not impersonal or an "empty space," but rather God's humanity in Christ.[13]

Contrary to Kearney's speculations, Andrei Rublev's icon of the Trinity does not depict three angels seated around an *empty* chalice. Kearney interprets this "empty" container, conveniently, as "the gap in our time and space where the radically other may arrive."[14] The problem is that the chalice is not empty but contains the very sacrificial offering that makes hospitality essential to the Christian faith. With the Incarnation, the radically other has already arrived as God, who has become one of us. Rublev's icon stands within a long iconographic tradition that interpreted Genesis 18—Abraham's hosting of three divine visitors—in Christological terms. The loaves and the calf offered by Sarah to the guests became a type for the sacrificial offering of Christ's body on the cross, and the meal therefore a type of the Eucharist meal. The iconic tradition later reduced the meal image to a single chalice containing a calf's head, representing Christ's sacrifice, the ultimate act of divine generosity and hospitality. Rublev's icon has followed this tradition. Far from representing a "gap," Rublev's chalice depicts the eucharistic *presence* of Christ. The chalice does not indicate empty space but "the self-offering of the Son," who reveals the Father's glory and makes possible humanity's communion with the divine through the Spirit, the ultimate heavenly hospitality.[15]

As might be expected, poetry, rather than philosophy or theology, offers us the best depiction of how not khora but the humanity of God within the Trinity places hospitality at the very heart of what it means to be human. Dante offers perhaps the finest poetic expression of the Trinity's power to induce the love that marks divine hospitality. Dante's beatific vision of the Trinity also includes a strange intrusion within the three divine persons, but in his case this is not an empty gap but "our human effigy."[16] Seeking an interpretation of this oddity, from God, the poet does not receive an answer but is drawn into the Trinitarian dance and brings himself to move in the rhythm of divine agape, pulsing with the rhythm of its love for humanity. This interpretation is also borne out by the many icons of the Trinity in which the three persons of the Godhead are grouped not around an empty center but around the sacrificial Eucharist cup, the symbol of divine love for humanity.

Anatheism's call to hospitality in order to recover God after the death of God is a vital initiative for our current cultural and political climate. It is important, however, that the guests invited into the anatheistic tent of hospitality are allowed to retain their true character. As I have tried to show from Christian examples, my worry is that when anatheism sends out the invitation cards to dialogue, some guests might not recognize their name and thus might neglect or even refuse to enter this vital conversation Richard has initiated with so much courage and energy.

Epilogue: In Guise
of a Response

RICHARD KEARNEY

Thank you for these questions. Rather than respond to each individually, let me try grouping the main points under a few recurring headings: the challenge of the new hermeneutics, power and sovereignty, the key questions of *perichoresis* and kenosis.

I

I will start with a few words on hermeneutics—or what David Tracy calls the "new hermeneutics." I begin *Anatheism* with a question that Paul Ricoeur asked me when I first attended his seminar in Paris, in 1977. He went around the room and asked each new student, "D'où parlez-vous?" Where do you speak from? Where do you come from? This is, of course, the first hermeneutic question: What is your story? What is your situation? Or, more particularly, what are the particular perspectives that serve as filters for your way of sensing the world, understanding society, interpreting yourself and others? What, in short, are your presuppositions, prejudices, preconceptions?

I was very persuaded by that inaugural lesson in hermeneutic exchange. We do filter things when we speak and read. The term *hermeneutics*, as you know, comes from the Greek *hermeneuein*, to interpret secret, hidden messages. These were originally messages from the Gods, as the eponymous Hermes (messenger of the Gods) reminds us. But hermeneutics is not just about theology or hierophany. In the late Middle Ages it became a method applied in law (adjudicating between competing versions of evidence) and philology (interpreting different genealogical layers of words); and later, with Schleiermacher, Dilthey, and Heidegger, it was extended to philosophical and historical–cultural understanding generally. But even at the most basic, ordinary level, the way we try to read between lines is always according to a certain kind of selection, through a particular grid or filter. That doesn't mean à la carte relativism. And it certainly shouldn't mean imposing ideological agenda on persons, texts, or things (though such deformation and distortion can occur). At best, hermeneutics is just being responsible for "where we're speaking from" and, when it comes to religion (the topic of our discussion today), recognizing that we all have a particular cut on God, informed by our respective traditions and cultures.

So we find ourselves in a hermeneutic circle. Heidegger, Gadamer, and Ricoeur all agree on this. We are born into an historical conversation that precedes us, and we interpret our lives accordingly, being as responsible and free as we can by turning our heritage into a project. By giving a future to our past. The question of existence—Who am I? Who are you? Who are we?—invariably implies the question of interpretation, what Ricoeur calls the "grafting" of hermeneutics onto phenomenology. So, when it comes to the question of religion, I do not see God as a "thing" out there that we can describe phenomenologically in some essentialist way. I believe that God is a call, cry, summons that invites us to different interpretations by asking us—to cite the Christian version of the question—"Who do you say that I am?" That, to me, is an invitation to hermeneutics, and I'll come back to this in a moment. It's an invitation to constant questioning.

But, to begin from a more intimate perspective, where do I "speak from" personally? Well, at the most trivial, anecdotal level, I speak as a man from Cork, in his middle ages, who loves fishing, philosophy, dogs, and God—though not necessarily in that order. The reason I mention philosophy and God is because that's what *Anatheism* is about. The reason I mention fishing and dogs is because they are actually two of the things I love most in the world, after philosophy and God (and my wife!). These are primary filterings for me, since I spend three months of my time fishing every summer—and I do most of my thinking there. As they say in Cork, if you are ever anguished, confused, or tormented, just "be philosophical about it and don't give it another thought." Well, when I'm out fishing, I'm not philosophizing in that sense. I'm just trying to give things another thought, as I am trying to do again, here, today.

This is anecdotal, but in a way, if hermeneutics goes all the way down, then if you spend a lot of time on the sea fishing, and if you spend a lot of time walking your dog, when you come to read sacred texts you're going to filter it in certain ways. You read it as a Catholic or a Protestant, as an Irishman or a Frenchman, or in terms of certain very simple identifications. When I was reading recently the paschal and postpaschal passages, I was struck that, when the risen Jesus appears to the disciples, he asks them not for declarations of faith or fidelity but for *fish*: "Have you got any fish here?" And then, when he appears to them on the shore at Galilee, he says, "Come and have breakfast." And guess what is for breakfast? Fish! Twice in a day. He's a Galilean fisherman, for God's sake!

Now, somebody brought up on a sheep farm might go for Jesus the shepherd, somebody who gardens a lot might go for Jesus the gardener (appearing to Mary Magdalene), while somebody from a medical background might emphasize Jesus the healer, and so on. All I am saying is that these little existential inflections, marked by our lived experience, inform our way of reading and seeing, from top to bottom, from head to toe. Hermeneutics goes all the way down! And it's not just about projections—it's not a matter of relativism—because, of course, Jesus *was* a shepherd and a gardener and a fisherman and a healer. Where we come from, no matter how humble our origins, affects the way we think.

Now, I never quite got to dogs, but let me simply add that Argos— Odysseus's hound—is my favorite character in the *Odyssey* because he's the one who has the hermeneutic flair to recognize Odysseus when he comes home. We need hermeneutic flair when we are interpreting texts, too, even sacred texts—perhaps especially sacred texts.

So the answer to the question "*D'où parlez-vous?*" involves extending circles of influence and importance, from past to present. In the preface to *Anatheism* I try to acknowledge how my cultural and intellectual background affects my reading of God, as anybody's hermeneutic framework does. In addition to the biographical points mentioned, let me just mention one more historical factor that informed my thinking about the question of suffering: war.

I was born less than a decade after the Second World War and grew up in an Ireland divided by religious violence. My fathers and uncles were in World War II, and their stories affected me greatly. Obviously, a post-holocaust Europe was a Europe where the question of theodicy had to be taken seriously. Did God die in the hangman's rope at Auschwitz, as Elie Wiesel said? Why did God not intercede on behalf of his suffering people? Or was Etty Hillesum right to say that since "God could do nothing," it was up to humans to "help God be God"? I'll come back to this when I address the sovereignty of God. Suffice it to say, for now, that if God could intervene and didn't, if God held back and allowed innocents be slaughtered, then we are talking about a "sacrificial" God in the bad sense—not a sacrificial God in the good sense of loving self-giving.

We need to discriminate hermeneutically between two kinds of sacrifice. On the one hand, the God of sacrificial bloodletting, which sees the oblation of victims as part of a periodic expiatory ritual—something repeated down through history in perverse "imitation of Christ," and which I witnessed in Northern Ireland, where the God of sacrificial purgation was invoked by both sides to fortify their cause and justify violence. This is an ideological misrepresentation of the true sacrifice of Christ, which involved a laying down of life for one's friends, in the service of others. Truly the Crucifixion is read through the hermeneutic filters of the washing of the feet at the Last Supper and the postpaschal scenes at Emmaus, and other moments of sharing food and drink, echoing the radical eschatological eucharistics of Matthew 25.

So, when Jens and Merold accuse me of jettisoning the notion of Christian sacrifice, this is not true at all. I simply wish to critically distinguish between two different interpretations/practices of sacrifice: one, periodic bloodletting and scapegoating as propitiatory ransom to a bloodthirsty God (which I believe, with René Girard and Ricoeur, is a betrayal of genuine Christianity); and two, sacrifice as a laying down of one's life for love of one's friends, which is what I believe Christ did.

But hermeneutic formation is intellectual as well as historical—as the references to Girard and Ricoeur suggest. So, in my own case, the formative experience of growing up in Ireland and Europe after the Second World War, and witnessing a thirty-year civil war going in the northern part of my country, was accompanied by my philosophical training. This involved a very narrow form of scholastic philosophy in University College Dublin in the early seventies, before being liberated by teachers like Patrick Masterson and Denys Turner into new forms of philosophy (including transcendental Thomism and existentialism), and then going on to do graduate research with Charles Taylor in Montreal and to complete my doctoral studies in Paris, where I embraced the hermeneutical thinking of Ricoeur, the ethical thinking of Levinas, the deconstructive thinking of Derrida, and the mystical thinking of Stanislas Breton. All of these became further intellectual and spiritual filterings for me, frameworks from which to read the great, inherited texts.

So, in a basic way, hermeneutics for me has always been an ana-hermeneutics—going back to read *again* (ana-). And in my anatheist rereadings I am influenced not just by contemporary philosophers but by key figures from the Christian mystical tradition—David Tracy has mentioned some of the great mystics; for example, Dionysius, Cusanus, Eckhart, Teresa of Avila, and John of the Cross. Those constant scholarly retrievals are an integral part of where I was coming from and where I am going. And this ongoing process of hermeneutic back-and-forth deeply informs my readings of the Scriptures themselves. A primary example here is my reading of God as the one who "may be," in light of Cusanus's notion of divine *posse*—God as possibility who calls to humans to be realized, embodied, made flesh. This is a typical example of a back-and-forth between philosophical and scriptural notions, to which I will return in a moment.

So these are some very basic hermeneutic legacies from which I speak, and which I readily profess, lest I give the erroneous impression that anatheism is something new or original. Anatheism, as I present it, is a hermeneutic interpretation issuing from a particular set of inherited narratives, life experiences, philosophies, whereby I attempt to make some sense of scriptures in the Abrahamic tradition from which I derive, and in other religions, to the extent that I believe that anatheism is an openness to interreligious dialogue, and that other religions have much to teach me.

II

But let me repeat, I am not a professional theologian. Many of the theological points cited in *Anatheism* are made by people who are much better versed than me in that whole discipline. I feel like a guest or visitor to theology. Desmond Connell, the cardinal of Ireland, when he read my first book, *Poétique du possible*, pulled me aside and said, "Richard, I want to say to you what Yahweh said to Adam after the Fall: 'Where are you?'" That was thirty-five years ago and I still don't know where I am. I am still searching, and anatheism is a way of continuing that search.

I suppose that "not knowing" for sure and going off the path, which is another definition of heresy, is a way of trying to find one's way back. That's what I'd like to think anatheism is doing. It takes an interdisciplinary approach, mixing philosophy with art, religion, literature. In its approach to God it has been described as a philosophical theology—a philosophical questioning of religious issues, of faith issues, of theological issues, but from a philosophical perspective. I hope this is a fertile interanimation, as I hope the journeys through poetics and politics in the different chapters of the book are likewise.

This "new hermeneutics," as David Tracy calls it—which is also an old hermeneutics, an ana-hermeneutics, because there's nothing new under the sun in anatheism—this anatheist hermeneutics is a retrieval of stories, narratives, revelations that are already there, albeit in a "re-newed" way. And if there is anything re-newing about it, it is certainly not in the sense of some teleological synthesis or supersession. It is about opening a space—an anatheistic space—which is *before* theism and atheism, and *after* them. That is the double sense of ana-: back and forward at the same time. It's an "opening" (to borrow a term from Rilke and Nancy) where we do not "know" for certain any longer what is divine and what is not, where we have no absolute answers about the absolute.

This is not the first time this has been said. It has been said by many philosophers, and indeed many negative theologians, in the past. It was what Socrates meant when he said that, before you ask philosophical questions, you need to confess that you don't know any answers. It was what Cusanus said about the *docta ignorantia*, the mystical way of not knowing. It was the apophasis of the mystics that David Tracy just spoke about—namely, that we do not know what God is, and only by not knowing what God is can we return to another, deeper kind of questioning. It is the "negative capability" of John Keats, which I invoke when I'm trying to read certain texts, the condition of being in the midst of mystery, uncertainty, and doubt without the "irritable reaching after fact and reason." This negative capability—which, for Keats, is the origin of all poetic sensibilities, attunements, and attentions to the world—is another form of anatheistic not knowing, a radical opening to what is infinitely strange, what is utterly beyond or beneath us.

Anatheism is a dis-position vis-à-vis different positions. Theism is a position. Atheism is a position. And they are both legitimate. Anatheism is a dis-position, which invites new re-positionings by trying philosophically to retrieve certain key inaugural moments—moments which all of us face sometime in life, when we no longer know for sure what it all means, when we open ourselves again to radical questioning, to extreme attention towards being—what is being done, said, called—towards what is and what might be. At those instants, we're back with Socrates, we're back with Cusanus, we are even back with Descartes's moment of doubt, Hume's tabula rasa, Husserl's *epoché*, where suddenly we let go of all fixed certainties in order to occupy a space where we are disposed to listen and attend. Anatheism is, above all, a listening—a listening followed by a "speaking again." And this prior listening is not just to your own tradition, which you can anatheistically and ana-hermeneutically retrieve, but to *other* traditions.

So, to return to David's and Jens' question, I would say anatheism is not the only way. On the contrary, it's a way open to many ways; it's a disposition that invites you to reposition yourself again and again by engaging with others' positions. It is the very opposite of ideology. It is not a new religion but a way of living religion in new ways.

In this regard, let me say another word about the hermeneutic approach of Paul Ricoeur. I see it as a sort of mediating between Gadamer's hermeneutics of dialogue with tradition (you go back) and Habermas's critical hermeneutics of the "ideal speech situation" (you go forward). What I'm trying to develop in *Anatheism* and other writings is a third position, closer to Ricoeur, which I call diacritical hermeneutics, that brings these two positions together. The term *diacritical* means a careful, vigilant reading between the lines, between positions and oppositions. In the technical, linguistic sense, a diacritical sign is an accented mark—diaeresis, circumflex, acute accent—which can give different meanings to otherwise identically spelled words. The tiniest inflection of a letter can make for a very different sense—for example, *ou* or *où* in French, meaning "or" or "where." But you have to be hyperattentive, you have to see and hear acutely, you have to really attend to the letters and what lies between them.

Likewise, at the broader level of reading whole texts, or human dialogues, or even human faces, we have, I argue, real need of a diacritical acoustic and diagnosis. The medical term is important here. *Diakrisis/ diakrinein* was originally a Greek term for how we discriminate and discern between signs of the body, how we read skin and flesh and fever diacritically, in a kind of carnal hermeneutics. It was a matter of attending carefully to somatic signs, changes in temperature, tactility, or complexion which were symptomatic of underlying disease or healing. And, so doing, you diagnosed what is going on within the body.

So I like to think of ana-hermeneutics as this kind of diacritical, vigilant, attentive reading of texts as well as bodies. And that doesn't mean just new texts; it also means, very importantly, old texts, the oldest stories in the book. In the case of *Anatheism*, for example, I try to read Joyce and Proust diacritically alongside Homer and the Gospels. And, in this kind of ana-hermeneutic gesture, I take my cue from thinkers like Ricoeur, Gadamer, and Heidegger—the great modern hermeneutic thinkers— who agreed you cannot think anew without thinking back. Which means going back to go forward, or what Kierkegaard famously called "repeating forwards." Ana- means hermeneutic repetition in this sense—anamnesis (remembering forward), which is also anagoge (reading ultimate spiritual meanings in given literal ones). In all cases, it is about reading diacritically between, beneath, and beyond the lines.

III

But let me leave hermeneutics aside for a moment and move onto the question of power and sovereignty, raised by all three of my interlocutors today, David, Merold, and Jens. The God of power and might. There is power and there is power. There is the power of the powerful, *imperium*, and there is the power of the powerless, the power of the possible—what I call *posse* (after Cusanus). Sometimes the former goes by the Latin term *potestas* and the latter by *potentia*—two different ways of translating the Greek δυναμός.

Power as *potestas* is sovereignty understood as "one and indivisible," from Plato to Rousseau and Hobbes. The Platonic form is one and indivisible. It is outside of time, it is outside of movement, it is outside of desire. When applied to the divine, it excludes the human, and this God of Platonism, of Western metaphysics, of ontotheology, as it is called after Heidegger, becomes a God of sovereign plenitude and totality, a unity without division, difference, change, possibility—or humanity. This becomes God as pure act, or *causa sui*, in the more reductive forms of Scholasticism: *Deus est purus actus non habens aliquid de potentialitate.*

That is, of course, just one interpretation of scholastic metaphysics; there are others (especially Scotus, Eckhart, and Breton) that are much more liberating, in my view. But that notion of an unmoved and unmoving God, of an indivisible God, of a God who, when taken as model for worldly power becomes the one and indivisible emperor, the one and indivisible sovereign king, and then the one and indivisible sovereign state or nation-state—that imperial paradigm of sovereignty is a recipe for war. It's bad politics, and I think it's bad theology. And I'm not putting this all on the head of Plato; it wasn't Plato (certainly not Socrates) but bad Platonism.

What I am saying is that if you apply that model of sovereign Form to the biblical God or the gods of other religions, you are doing something Socrates himself would have never dreamed of doing. You are imposing a certain metaphysical category of pure actuality onto something divine, which also and crucially contains *possibility*—the divine ability to become (the *possest* or *posse-esse* of Cusanus), which expresses itself as an invitation to love and to justice in time and space. And that, as the analytic philosophers say, is a category mistake. With important consequences.

So, when Jens objects that I am embracing a metaphysical dualism or antinomy between omnipotence and impotence, between the God of power and the God of the powerless, this is not so at all. And the same applies to related distinctions—cited by Jens—between immanence and transcendence, being and becoming, sacrifice and service. Let me be quite clear: contrary to what Jens claims, I am not at all affirming such binary oppositions but destabilizing and deconstructing them, for the sake of something deeper and higher, which these binaries betray. In *Anatheism*, for example, I speak again and again of transcendence in immanence. And elsewhere I call for subtle distinctions between different kinds of service (love rather than slavery) and different kinds sacrifice (life affirming rather than death dealing). And, I might add, between different kinds of being and different kinds of becoming. Indeed, one of the main efforts of my philosophizing, from *Poétique du possible* (1984) to *The God Who May Be* (2001), has been to rethink the divine in terms of *both* ontological being *and* eschatological becoming. Hence my embrace of *onto-eschatology*, in contrast to the "God without Being" of Levinas, Derrida, and Marion.

In all these cases, it is question of *overcoming*—not endorsing—the old binary oppositions in favor of more authentic hermeneutic discernments, crossings, and retrievals. On the vexed matter of divine omnipotence, to come back to this central discussion, I am trying to distinguish between two *kinds* of power, one divine and one nondivine. The divine is precisely the power of the powerless—which is not no power but a power greater than any nondivine power.

My quarrel with the supporters of a sovereign omni-God is that they often confuse the two forms of divine and nondivine power; that is, one, the loving/power/*posse* of the powerless, and two, the fully actualized all-power of an emperor God. If "omnipotence" is interpreted to mean the divine power of the powerless, I have absolutely no problem with it. But I regret to say that the triumphalist aspects of the history of Christendom and ontotheology do not convince me that this was always so. Likewise, if "sovereign" implies genuine respect for the Lord of love and justice, I obviously have no objection to that either; au contraire! But it has not always meant that, in our Western metaphysical constructions of sovereignty.

Again, it all depends what exactly we mean when we use these terms— omnipotence, sovereignty, sacrifice. These influential concepts are part of an ongoing hermeneutic play of interpretations—a robust "conflict of interpretations," as Ricoeur says—and I am simply recognizing my part in that hermeneutic conversation; and acknowledging that anatheism encourages a plurality of readings. So one needs to be humble and discerning in declaring, for example, what a "true Christian" means. Who decides? Who knows in any absolutely dogmatic, infallible way? No one. Hence the salutary detour through a hermeneutic "negative capability" of faith and trust (faith as *fides*/fidelity; truth as troth/trust). One makes a wager based on witness and experience, as much as on theology and doctrine. For my part, as an anatheist, I support those from Jesus, Saint Francis, and Teresa of Avila up to modern reformers, liberation theologians, and new monastics, who are struggling against an imperial Church in favor of an *ecclesia* of the poor and powerless. I place my wager on the church of the widow, orphan, and stranger—and not just "out there," beyond the border of us and them, but here also, inside ourselves, where we are always, irreducibly, strangers to ourselves in important ways.

My views are, I readily admit, informed by my own Christian story. I am not alone, and what I am identifying is, it seems to me, an important wager that has been made down through the centuries—and dramatically staged by Dostoyevsky in his vivid depiction of Christ refusing the imperial temptations of the Grand Inquisitor. It is a perennial struggle. There really are two types of power in Dostoyevsky's account—the one epitomized by Christ, the other by the Inquisitor—and I fear that many historical invocations of "omnipotence" have been, all too often, on the side of the latter.

So let me try to be clear about this essential point. Anatheism proposes a notion of divine power, not as sovereign imperial *potestas* but as loving *posse*. As interpreted by Nicolas of Cusa (Cusanus), divine *posse* is the power to be able to be, the power to be all that one is capable of becoming—namely love. *Posse* is an invitation, whereas *potestas* is an imposition—*imperium*. Cusanus compares *posse* to a child's call in the street. It is a cry in the wilderness, as the Gospel says, that invites us to respond, to give *esse* to *posse* so that God can become more historically divine as *possest*, to give flesh to the Word. And if we don't say yes, if we don't make the cry incarnate, it doesn't happen. God is up to us, in the end. There is no question of sovereign power here, no *imperium* imposing itself, no force enforcing itself. The call, the cry, the claim, the plea invites us to say yes or no—to the God of desire. A sovereign being without possibility is a being without Eros or becoming. The desiring lovers in the Song of Songs (going back to David Tracy's point) signal a God who seeks out human beings, who is hungry for us, who cannot be given flesh without us.

And yet, the wondrous paradox: nothing can change the world like this power of the powerless. "Thoughts that come on dove's wings guide the world," Nietzsche said, having declared the death of the sovereign God. And, in my view, he was right. He was being a good Christian when he said that. Because that is what Christ himself said when he compared divine power to a mustard seed or a child or a voice crying in the wilderness or a hungry stranger in the street. What is God? asks Joyce. "A shout in the street." That is right. Matthew 25.

So, when I look at the politics of Northern Ireland or, far worse, of the Second World War, I see a bellicose clash of sovereignties where one sovereign nation-state infringes upon another, because if you're one and indivisible you cannot share power. If there is absolute sovereignty, there is one people—not several and many peoples. "*Una duce una voce*," as Mussolini said. "*Ein Reich über alles*," said Hitler. Even the French Revolution fell into this: "*la souveraineté est une et indivisible*." The great national social contract. Anybody who didn't conform—foreigners, *étrangers*—were exiled or executed so that the body politic could become whole and one again. Gallows and guillotines purified the many into the one.

So, what triumphal politics is saying is basically that one nation-state cannot share sovereignty with another because it's one and indivisible. So it goes all the way down from theology to politics, from Plato's *Republic* to modern republics. I think the sovereign God—and the sovereign nation-state, which simply secularized this God—has been a source of huge misinterpretation and of huge violence. Certainly, the politics of Northern Ireland, which I grew up with, was about two sovereign nations claiming the same territory. You couldn't have a United Kingdom and a United Ireland at the same time, so people were at war for almost three hundred years, until eventually somebody said, Let's go beyond sovereignty. Let's have a post-nationalist and a post-unionist Ireland. Don't mention the S-word! And suddenly, the impossible became possible. We now have what is de facto a form of "shared sovereignty," even though de jure it is a contradiction in terms. It means that, since the Good Friday Agreement (1998), citizens of Northern Ireland can be, as the simple formula says, Irish or British or both. That has meant surpassing the idea of sovereignty as one and indivisible.

In short, what I am suggesting is that the notion of a sovereign God, no less than that of a sovereign nation, is ruinous, but fortunately deconstructable, in favor of postsovereign deities and communities.

IV

When it comes to God, a one and indivisible God . . . if you stop there, you have a betrayal of the God of little things, a reversal of the God of multiplicities and pluralities, the God who appears as three angels—not one, but three—to Abraham. The God who divides into three and then multiplications thereof is repeated, of course, in the epiphany of Christianity, in the three kings, and, again, in the three persons of the Trinity. In Andrei Rublev's wonderful portrait in the Russian Orthodox religion, the three angels of Abraham are retrieved—anatheistically, ana-hermeneutically—

in order to portray the perichoresis of Father, Son, and Spirit. So, one can come back to the beginning—the three strangers appearing to Abraham at Mamre—in order to repeat forward the perichoretic scene in an ongoing hermeneutic reinterpretation.

This, at least, is my hermeneutic wager—and faith. Rublev's *Trinity* is, of course, a painting. This is poetics, not dogma. It is an imaginative interpretation of dogma, according to a divine threesome and the creative space (*chora*) between them as they move towards and away from each other in love. So the one and indivisible sovereign that knows no movement is here hermeneutically reconfigured as an endlessly mobile, loving, interstitial deity where each person is ceding place to the other as they succeed each other. This is a poetics of kenosis full of passion and compassion, of Eros and love. I will come back to this crucial question of kenosis.

But, first, my response to Jens Zimmerman on the perichoresis. He objects that I have reduced the chalice-chora at the heart of perichoresis to an "impersonal, empty space" rather than recognizing it as the presence of "God's humanity in Christ." Far from being empty, Jens protests, the chalice is full with a sacrificial offering, epitomized in tradition by a calf's head representing Christ's sacrifice. Rublev's icon, he concludes, follows this tradition.

So let me protest to Jens's protestation. I will take each point in turn. First, the chora-chalice at the heart of the Trinitarian dance is, for me, anything but impersonal. On the contrary, it is the interpersonal space par excellence. It is the place where Mary's womb—called the *chora achoraton* in tradition—serves as the hub around which the three persons move in the moment of divine–human incarnation. Its emptiness is not opposed to fullness but, in keeping with the Christian mystery of genuine sacrificial kenotic emptying, becomes the ultimate form of eschatological presence. Jens confuses Derrida's notion of impersonal chora—drawn from Plato's *Timaeus*—with mine (a confusion based on a misreading of my essay on "God or *Khora*?" in *Strangers, Gods and Monsters*).

In short, I am not denying for one moment that the chalice is brimming with food and wine—as symbol of Abrahamic hospitality towards the stranger, which I explicitly celebrate in the opening chapter of *Anatheism*. On the contrary, the chalice of nourishment is central to my entire reading of anatheist hospitality. And I also affirm that, in the Christian narrative, the chalice-chora represents "God's humanity in Christ," but understood as a gap of *posse*; that is, as a no-place, which allows for the annunciation, reception, conception, and incarnation of the incoming divine stranger, the impossible guest—first Isaac, then Jesus, both made possible by the respective responses of Sarah and Mary. Chora is the *u-topos* where the *topos* of the Messiah may constantly arrive, promise, call, take place. This notion of emptiness that is fullness is echoed in the kabbalist notion of divine creation as "withdrawing/leaving space" (*tzimtzum*) as well as in Meister Eckhart's beautiful image of the empty bowl (linked with the beghards and beguines), which fills the more it empties and empties the more it fills—a sacred paradox also echoed, interreligiously, in the ancient Buddhist Heart Sutra, "emptiness is form."

The mystery of chora as both emptiness and fullness, absence and presence, divinity and humanity, sacrifice and service, food and natality is absolutely central to the Christian symbol of perichoresis. My reading of Rublev's icon is, therefore, as I see it, entirely in keeping with a whole sacred tradition of Abrahamic hospitality—from Genesis to Dorothy Day—and offers possibilities of extending this hospitality to other, non-Abrahamic faiths as well. Far from refusing Christian guests to "retain their true character," I believe it deeply respects the truth of Christianity.

But I, unlike perhaps Jens, believe that Christian truth, like all truth, is subject to a hermeneutic polysemy of expression and interpretation, once it is embodied in the spatiotemporal world of human finitude and language. And this means, for me, that an exemplary sacred icon like Rublev's perichoretic *Trinity* invites a rich plurality of readings—chora as cup, womb, food, sacrifice, natality—an endless hermeneutic plurality which allows, among other things, for the reinsertion of a radically feminine and spatiotemporal humanity into the eschatological image of the eternal (and, often, all-too-exclusively male) kingdom. So, once again, we find that anatheism follows a logic of both/and rather than either/or. Chiasm rather than dualism. Chora as the crossing of eternity and time, of transcendence and image, of the eschatological not-yet with the carnal here and now.

V

Anatheism is all about interpretation. It is, I repeat, a hermeneutic wager, a rereading, reimagining, retrieving, in flesh and blood as well as mind and spirit. It is carnal hermeneutics *and* conceptual hermeneutics and ultimately denies the separation of the two. I begin *Anatheism* with the three strangers coming to Abraham, followed by Abraham's hermeneutic wager—namely, to interpret the strangers as enemies or friends, or both (remember, *hostis* can mean "enemy" or "friend"). From the start, anatheism is a matter of life or death, hospitality or hostility, Eros or Thanatos.

And we find a similar scene when Gabriel comes to Mary in Nazareth, and we are told, in Luke 1:29, that she is "troubled" and "ponders." Those two words are crucial. Mary is deeply troubled (*dietarãchthe*) until the angel says, "Do not be afraid." And at the same time she ponders (*dialogizomai*) whether to say yes or no. This existential pondering is hermeneutic—reading in and through the flesh. That is why, in the Western Christian tradition, Mary is almost always portrayed in poems and paintings as accompanied by both a lily and a book. She is both scenting and reading the stranger. She hails from the tradition of the Book, a hermeneutical, rabbinical tradition, and also of the body, where Jacob famously struggled with his night stranger, hip to hip, before receiving the name of God. Mary the Nazarene has heard, one imagines, about many angelic strangers who have appeared to others before her—to Abraham and Sarah, to Jacob, to Samson's parents—angels who have answered human fear, each time, with the words "Do not be afraid." Mary's response to the stranger in Nazareth refigures hermeneutically this recurring inaugural scene—she moves forward and backward in time and space, as in the wonderful Botticelli painting of the *Cestello Annunciation*, where we see Mary's body recoiling in fear as she simultaneously goes forward in love.

This is the hermeneutical wager in action, in body and soul. And remember: if Mary *had* said no, there would be no incarnation, no Christ, no Christianity. If Mary does not accept the freedom, integral to choice, as Denise Levertov says in her poem "Annunciation"—if we see in her only "meek obedience" to a Word that's going to happen anyway, if we read Mary as submitting to a Logos of imperial divinity which imposes itself upon her—then I think we have misunderstood a fundamental message of Judeo-Christianity; namely, that God is a call, a solicitation, a desire, a *posse*—a God of little things desperately trying to be heard and heeded, to become incarnate, to make a difference.

You ask, "How small is your God?" I would say it is the smallest, most infinitesimal God you could possibly imagine. Why? Because God names the power of the powerless. The mustard seed. The cry of the widow, orphan, and stranger. The call of the child in the street. The thin, small voice. It is the power of nonviolent and nonviolating solicitation to which we are totally free to say yes or no.

A last example I would like to cite of "the quiet power of the possible" is that of healing. I am thinking particularly here of the invocation of a "higher power" in twelve-step meetings. Thomas Merton described AA as one of the most important spiritual movements of the twentieth century. And I read AA here not just as Alcoholics Anonymous but as Addicts Anonymous, generally, understanding addiction in the sense of Buddhist "attachment" or the Christian sense of sinful clinging and enclosure (Kierkegaard's "incurvature of self"). We are all addicted or attached in some form or another. I think what Merton realized is that it is the person who has reached rock bottom, the very lowest rung of the ladder, and acknowledged that he or she is "powerless" before his or her addiction, who is often in fact capable of being most open and disposed towards what AA calls a higher power, "however that is to be defined."

The qualifier is important here, and deeply hermeneutic. This is very interesting to me, because the whole process of moving from being utterly powerless to a higher power (I always prefer the lowercase)—that is, to an ineffable power beyond oneself—basically signals a moment, a space, a turn, a return, where the impossible becomes possible. That is what the messenger (*angelos*) says to Mary. And before Mary, to Jacob and Sarah. Likewise, in the case of the addict, the impossible—"it is impossible to find a cure for my attachment/addiction/abandon"—can suddenly become possible, if we let go, if we allow something "more," "other," "higher" to enter our lives and bring healing.

This is a possibility beyond the impossible, as the mystic Angelus Silesius wrote. It is "without why." As such, it works all the way down. People who suffer from addictions find there can be a healing through an invocation of this power/*potentia*/*posse* beyond the limits of their own ego/me/self. Something or someone strange and transcendent says to me, "You *can* change. You are *capable* of recovery." It doesn't have to be a traditional, supersensible God; it can be heard quite simply through the voice of the AA sponsor sitting beside you, the witnesses and fellow sufferers in recovery in the room. One only has to be disposed to receive a message from beyond oneself, ready to listen to the call of healing. And this, it seems, is far easier to do when the illusion of sovereignty—the imago of the imperial "fortress ego"—has been debunked and one is radically opened up to the call of the transcendent. I think the idea of being able to be "in recovery" is very telling here. One is always "in recovery." One is never fully recovered. It is a journey, not an end. A wager, not a guarantee. An apprenticeship, not a fait accompli. In this sense, AA is very ana-hermeneutic.

VI

Let me end with a few words on kenosis, since this came up in all three speakers. Kenosis—as I interpret it with Kristeva, Vattimo, and others—means emptiness, cut, annihilation, nothingness. After this cut, this entry into emptiness, what kind of God comes—or comes back? What kind of God comes again after the death of the Alpha God? What returns—or what can we return to—after the kenotic emptying of God (uppercase) into god (lowercase)? If we want to interpret the notion of "sacrifice" not as expiatory bloodletting but as self-giving, we may read kenosis as an anatheist letting-go of God in order to open ourselves to god (understood as God after God). I am merely echoing Meister Eckhart of course—praying to God to rid us of God. And Stanislas Breton, too, when, after Eckhart, he invokes the apophatic mystical call of *nothing*, which invites us to respond by making divine nothing into *something*— something out of nothing, ongoing recreation ex nihilo, endless rebirthing and reembodying, *ensarkosis* without end. Each time we move— perichoretically and kenotically—from God to God, we witness natality trumping and succeeding mortality, a living God replacing a dying God. We are talking here of a radically fragile, vulnerable, humble, appealing, loving divinity.

I conclude with some final examples. The Abrahamic revelation of kenosis is not the only revelation, but it is the one that calls and claims me personally, hermeneutically, and to which I try to respond here.

The first story of kenosis, in the biblical tradition, is creation. It begins with a narrative of divine descent into time, history, humanity. This is the movement from monologue to dialogue, because God, as Levinas put it in a nice image, got bored with himself and wanted somebody to talk to. And having somebody to talk to meant that two was better than one. But to "empty" into that dialogue of two meant opening up to the possibility of becoming, the risk of history, the wager that divine creation may or may not be fulfilled by humanity.

So what is this creation that remains open to co-creation? The Genesis narrative tells us it is the seventh day, the day that the divine did not fill in. And by leaving that sabbatical space empty, the divine creator entered a relation with humans where the divine stranger could be radically rejected or welcomed, hated or loved. This is to interpret creation as a form of descent, a form of carnal kenosis that is a perpetual invitation for us to co-create and to co-respond with the divine call—"co-*naissance*."

Secondly, we have the revelation of kenosis as incarnation. Here we have the classic example of Christ's kenosis, invoked by Paul in Philippians 2:7, the emptying away from the illusion of sovereign self-sufficiency ("equality with the Father") into the flesh, the *sarx* of the world, the chora of open space. Here we find the image of the matrix of natality, the womb of Mary, which was described by some of the patristic authors (as I learned from John Manoussakis) as the *chora achoraton*, container of the uncontainable—Mary as carrier of the Messiah child. Mary as *Theotokos*.

So, in this Christian narrative we have a descent into empty, free space, echoing the first *creatio ex nihilo* that, in turn, brings about the possibility of new life, but only if and when Mary says yes. Then, after the annunciation and conception, we have the story of Christ's second kenosis, a second going down, this time into water, the descent into the Jordan. And, finally, we have Christ's third moment of kenosis as he descends into the abyss of the cross. Here, Christ experiences complete abandonment as the illusory omni-God bleeds away ("My God, my God, why have you forsaken me?" [Matthew 27:46]) to let the after-God of messianic promise be reborn with the risen Christ—a Christ who, having commended his life to the one who is to come ("Unto thee I commend my Spirit"), is rebirthed as a healer and nurturer of his disciples at Emmaus, of Mary Magdalene at the empty tomb, and of other apostles at the shores of Galilee, where he bids them to "come and have breakfast." Once again, the fisherman, the fisher of men, the feeder of bodies and souls. And with each of Christ's kenotic rebirths—incarnation in the womb, baptism in water, descent/ascent from three days in Hades—there is the returning promise of the Spirit. "I must go so that the Paraclete can come," says Jesus. "Do not touch me, for I have still to go to the Father," he says to Mary Magdalene.

Or again, in Matthew 25 Jesus reveals himself to be each stranger who asks to be fed and healed. In other words, Jesus is saying, "I am the one who is always coming back and is always still to come." The ana-God who is forever a stranger (*hospes*) opening up the self, home, people, earth to ever-new natality.

I have always been struck that Christ, when risen, does not appear as sovereign king but as a foreigner, again and again—as a gardener, a fisherman, a beggar man, a cook, a wanderer at the inn. Emmaus is not a house; it is not a cathedral; it is not a temple. It is a station along the way. *Deus viator–homo viator.* This is a hungry God who keeps coming and saying, "Do you have anything to eat? I was a stranger and you did not give me to eat. I was thirsty and you did not give me to drink. I was the least of these (*elachistos*) and will always be the least and last of these." That is eschatology at its most radical, not with capital letters but in the lowercase—a micro-eschatology of the god of little things.

So let me end where I began. Back in Ireland, as a schoolboy at Glenstal Abbey, one of the first things I learned about Benedictine spirituality was hospitality to the stranger. Chapter 24 of *The Rule of Saint Benedict* spells out how every stranger who comes to the monastery, regardless of who they are, where they hail from, or what faith they believe in, should be treated as Christ. This was my first lesson about the kenotic god—the very opposite of the God of theodicy.

I won't go into Auschwitz here; I won't go into the arguments of whether God could or could not intervene to save the Jews. You know the debates. I agree with Etty Hillesum, who talks about us humans being the only ones who can "enable God to be God" through acts of radical hospitality, love, and justice. I agree with Rabbi Irving Greenberg and Elie Wiesel, who declared that the idea of a sovereign God of absolute power (who could have intervened and didn't) is a cruel God who died in the hangman's rope at Dachau. After the evils of World War II and other horrors and genocides that preceded and followed it, the God of expiatory bloodletting and sacrificial scapegoating is well and truly dead. At last. How different this is from the kenotic giving of the "suffering servant" who calls out for justice to be done and injustice avoided, for love over hate, life over death. I am with the god of service over the God of Sovereignty. I have made my wager.

Artist's Note on Cover Art

SHEILA GALLAGHER

Pneuma Hostis is a flaming halo created out of gold-leafed cigarette butts. It is a maze-mandala in the form of a commercial Lasco fan, modeled on the one installed in my studio window in Boston to clear the smoke and toxic fumes from my work space. The butts and the fan blades come together in the shape of a gold host, where inhalation and exhalation, life and death, health and illness, the addict and the saint share the same space.

The cover image points to a crossing of the sacred and the profane. This is a central insight of Richard Kearney's notion of ana-theism, which informs and inflects the conversations in this volume—the idea of returning to God "after" (*ana*) God, of rediscovering the holy in happenstance, the iconic in the ordinary, the highest in the lowest. Here the sacramental mingles with the banal, and transcendence can be found in the most base or everyday things. In short, to cite Scripture, ana-thesism is a way of retrieving the sacred in the "least of these"—even in discarded smoked-out butts.

The titular *pneuma*—air, breath, spirit in Greek—converses with the subtitular *hostis*—whose Latin ambiguity gives us both host and guest, friend and enemy. We hear the age-old ambivalence of religion as both sacrificial violence and salvific healing. What are we to make of this double legacy today, when wars are still waged in the name of One True God?

And where so many still search and work for healing and peace? No work of art ever stopped a tank, as Seamus Heaney said. But he added: "The end of art is peace." Might that this little image of alchemical play be an intimation of such peace.

NOTES

INTRODUCTION

1. For the history and possibilities of Christian humanism, see Jens Zimmermann, *Humanism and Religion* (Oxford: Oxford University Press, 2012); and *Incarnational Humanism* (Downers Grove, IL: InterVarsity Press, 2012).
2. Richard Kearney and Julia Kristeva, "Mysticism and Anatheism" in *Richard Kearney's Wager: Philosophy, Poetics, Theology*, edited by Chris Doude Von Trootswijk (Leiden: Brill, 2016).
3. Luc Ferry, *Man Made God: The Meaning of Life* (Chicago: University of Chicago Press, 2002).

1. GOD AFTER GOD: AN ANATHEIST ATTEMPT TO REIMAGINE GOD

1. See discussion of this in Richard Kearney, *Anatheism: Returning to God After God* (New York: Columbia University Press, 2010), 11–12.
2. Paul Ricoeur acknowledged the indispensible passage through atheism (at least for us moderns) on the way toward what he called a new kind of "post-religious faith." But the drama of atheism at the very heart of anatheism is not a matter of going from primary religious faith through atheism to a second religious faith, which could be seen as some final, triumphalist summation. Anatheism is the move beyond the naïveté of first faith—one's childish certainties, facile assumptions, acquired presuppositions or dogmas—into an open space of possibility, an open space that may lead either to a choice of atheism or a theism after atheism. That is the space or time of anatheism, and

it is always open—for no atheism or theism can presume to be certain of itself without falling back into another dogmatism (of belief or antibelief).

So, whether it is a matter of what I call "anatheist atheism" or "anatheist theism"—a second theism or a second atheism—it is for us to choose: it is a wager, a hermeneutic task. The anatheist moment is to be understood, accordingly, as the moment before a choice between theism and atheism insofar as it liberates into wager, action, and commitment. And in this sense it comes "after" we have abandoned the dogmatic unfreedoms of first theism or first atheism. In moving from religion through atheism to faith, a hermeneutic moment of "suspension" is indispensable. Or, to put it in terms of Ricoeur's hermeneutic arc, unless one allows the "masters of suspicion"—Freud, Marx, Nietzsche (and I would add de Beauvoir and the feminist critique)—to unmask the inherited theological corpus, one is less likely to reach a faith worth living, intellectually speaking. Such iconoclastic atheists may be deemed allies in the process of hermeneutic suspicion, which can lead, in turn (for those who so choose), to a hermeneutic reaffirmation of the sacred. See Paul Ricoeur, *The Symbolism of Evil*, trans. E. Buchanan (Boston: Beacon Press, 1968), 347–357; and "Religion, Atheism, Faith," in *The Conflict of Interpretations*, ed. Don Ihde (Evanston: Northwestern University Press, 1974), 440–467.

3. Søren Kierkegaard, *Fear and Trembling*, trans. Alastair Hannay (New York: Penguin, 1985), 41.

4. In this sense, Christ can say, "Before Abraham was, I am" and "Remember me until I come."

5. I think that several thinkers after Kierkegaard—such as Benjamin, Derrida, and Agamben—are saying something similar when they talk of "messianic time," though I personally prefer the notion of kairological or eschatological time. This ana-time translates the sacred enigma that the Kingdom already was, is now, and is yet to come. It is always already and is always still to come.

6. There is a certain deconstructive moment here of which Emmanuel Levinas and Jacques Derrida, among others, have much to teach us. Levinas talks about atheism in *Totality and Infinity* as the greatest gift that Judaism has given humanity. What I think he means is that Judaism is a prophetic prohibition against idols and illusions; its promissory messianism signals an atheist moment of "separation" from fusion with being, including fusion with God (sacrificial paganism), and that separation gives the "I," the self, a freedom and a responsibility to respond to the other, the stranger. If there is no such "atheistic" separation, there can be no ethical encounter with the stranger, who, Levinas argues, bears the face of the wounded, the destitute, the naked—"the widow, the orphan, the stranger"—which is itself, for Levinas, the "trace of

God." Derrida, for his part, talks about a "religion without religion." And if there is a difference between Derrida and myself here, it is a difference between "without" (Derrida's *sans*) and "after" (*ana-*). I talk about religion *after* religion, where he talks about religion *without* religion. But as he himself said in his discussion of my "God of perhaps" (*peut-être*), there is but the "thinnest of differences" at times between his atheism and my anatheism. See my dialogue with Derrida, which took place at New York University in October 2001, "Terror, Religion, and the New Politics," in Richard Kearney, *Debates in Continental Philosophy: Conversations with Contemporary Thinkers* (New York: Fordham University Press, 2004), 3–15. See also my related essay, "Derrida's Messianic Atheism," in Edward Baring and Peter Gordon, eds., *The Trace of God: Derrida and Religion* (New York: Fordham University Press, 2014).

7. Read anatheistically, the cross is not some expiatory sacrifice by a bloodthirsty, patriarchal God bent on ransoming his son for our sins. It is a moment of surmounting such an injurious, "theistic" temptation in a moment of "atheistic" letting go so as to open up an "anatheistic" disposition toward the new, the surprising, the gracious, the gift—resurrected life. Yet one more radical discovery of God after God (conceived as the Alpha God of theodicy). And I say "one more" for, as Christ himself revealed, it has been going on from the beginning and will never end: "Before Abraham was, I am" and "Now I must go so that the Paraclete can come." Christ here and now is always Christ before and after: anachronic, ana-Christ. On the cross and in all his human woundedness, Christ abandons the omnipotent Father God who has abandoned him. His final, ultimate lesson is one of radical kenosis and letting go of lost illusions and attachments so as to open himself to the new, the other, the strange. "My God, my God, why have you forsaken me?" is the atheist moment of negation and negative capability, which opens the space for a release and liberation into new life beyond old life—"Unto thee I commend my spirit." In this anatheist return, Christ is entrusting himself to the "thee" of each God after God, every stranger who seeks or receives food and love, as announced in Matthew 25—his hungry disciples at Galilee ("Come and have breakfast"), Mary Magdalene at the garden tomb ("Miriam!"), his fellow travelers on the road to Emmaus. Christ keeps coming back (ana-) to his followers after (ana-) he has left them, as a *hospes* they do not recognize—until he hosts them with food and touch. Only as guests again (ana-) do they recognize the divine host.

8. Anatheistically considered, the Bible is a battleground of interpretations, a site of endless conflicts of interpretation between hostility and hospitality. One does not need to recite the long litany of hostilities that have been waged, and suffered, by the three Abrahamic religions over the centuries—something

true, I suspect, of all religions. No faith is exempt, purer than pure. There is no hospitality that is not ghosted by the dark demon of hostility. That is why anatheism is always a recurring call for renewals and retrievals of the inaugural moment of grace and good, in every potential moment. There is no hospitality once and for all. Hostility is a continuing betrayal of the first promise of hospitality—the inaugural creative moment repeated in the stories of Abraham, Jacob, Moses, Christ, and so on, and in every instant of our own everyday lives. Hostility—violence, intolerance, fear, aggression, egotism—is a constant temptation for theists and atheists alike that needs to be overcome again and again in acts of "aftering," of returning and retrieving the inaugural moment of hospitality that we witness in the great stories of breakthrough and new beginning. Civilization begins with the handshake—choosing to extend an open palm rather than reach for the sword. As Emmanuel Levinas says, the face of the stranger in its nakedness presents the trace of God: the poor one, the widow, the orphan, and the stranger. See Emmanuel Levinas, *Totality and Infinity*, trans. Alphonso Lingis (Pittsburgh: Duquesne University Press, 1969), 244.

9. Kearney, *Anatheism*, 85–101.
10. John Keats, "Letter to George and Tom Keats, December 1817," in *The Norton Anthology of English Literature,* 5th ed., vol. 2 (New York: W. W. Norton & Co., 1986), 863.
11. Samuel Taylor Coleridge, *Biographia Literaria* (Oxford: Clarendon Press, 1907).
12. James Joyce, *Ulysses* (New York: Vintage, 1990), 34.
13. Virginia Woolf, *To the Lighthouse* (London: Harcourt Brace, 1990), 92.
14. Ibid., 207.
15. See the more detailed discussion of these poets in Kearney, *Anatheism*, 23–25.
16. In Rembrandt's painting *Emmaus*, Christ is a dark silhouette illuminating the two disciples with light streaming from his invisible face. The returned messianic stranger remains unknowable, no matter how familiar to them he has been during his previous lifetime. In the breaking of bread at Emmaus, Christ is there and not there, seen and not seen, recognized and unrecognizable, familiar and foreign. There is no glorious, triumphal full stop. In this moment of what Ricoeur calls "eucharistic hospitality" there is always something more, other, transcendent, exceeding, departing. It is always a matter of ongoing translation and discernment. Not a single, saturating revelation. Not a final illumination. Not some total exposure or disclosure. The anatheist moment constantly repeats itself, within each religion and from religion to religion, because it is always something strange: there is a God after God after God after God. . . . "Aftering" never stops, and if it does, you get idolatry,

triumphalism, dogmatism, fundamentalism—war between religions and within religions. That's how close the wager gets. Hospitality and hostility are etymological twins of the term *hostis*, meaning both "enemy" and "guest": a Janus face that can look either way. Ana- signals a place and time of thresholds, limits, borders, crossings, which is why Janus is the guardian of boundaries, the patron saint of translations and transitions—along with Hermes and the Paraclete. This deep doubleness, which Émile Benveniste identifies in the Indo-European roots of both *hospes* and *hostis*, goes all the way back and all the way down. See Benveniste, *Indo-European Language and Society* (London: Faber and Faber, 1973), 71–78.

17. The anatheist moment of pondering, weighing, and wagering is also indicated in the fact that, in almost all annunciation scenes, Mary is usually reading from a lectern. This suggests that she is inscribed in a narrative tradition of the Book; she's revisiting and retrieving stories and memories of those who came before her. Maybe Abraham and the strangers at Mamre? Or Jacob meeting Rachel at the well? Or Solomon and the Shulamite woman? Who knows. But whatever texts she is immersed in are surely preparing her hermeneutically—through language, narrative, memory—for this encounter with the stranger. I say "preparing" in the sense of predisposing, not predetermining, because Mary is completely free to break from those narratives or to return to them by turning them toward a new opening.

18. Luke 1:29. *Dietarāchthe* (troubled) is the term used in the Bible for responding to impossible messengers with impossible messages. It was also used to describe Sarah, Samson's mother, the shepherds of Bethlehem, and Mary.

19. If prophets and preachers give us theology, painting lets us into Mary's body and poetry into her imagination, without the slightest hint of blasphemy. Denise Levertov's poem "Annunciation" (*Selected Poems* [New York: New Directions, 2002], 162) speaks of Mary poised between her lectern (signifying thought) and lily (signifying the senses), facing an angelic visitor who stands and hovers and whom she acknowledges as guest, a *hospes*. The relevant stanza reads:

But we are told of meek obedience. No one mentions
courage.
The engendering Spirit
did not enter her without consent.
God waited.

She was free
to accept or to refuse, choice
integral to humanness.

Such verses indicate that there is no blind dictate of divine destiny. Mary's yes is not a mere "effect" of some omnipotent cause or supernatural will that ineluctably prevails, come what may. She is not the passive prey of some Alpha God. The Nazarena could refuse or accept; she was free to say yes or no. She said yes. And if she had said no, there would have been no Christianity.

20. On this, see Mircea Eliade, *The Sacred and the Profane*, trans. Willard R. Trask (Orlando, FL: Harcourt, 1959).

21. Woolf, *To the Lighthouse*, 118.

22. Kearney, *Anatheism*, 166.

4. TRANSCENDENT HUMANISM IN A SECULAR AGE: DIALOGUE WITH CHARLES TAYLOR

1. Simone Weil, *Letter to a Priest* (London and New York: Routledge, 2013), 21.

2. Ibid., 36–37.

3. The term *Entzauberung* means, literally, "de-magicalization," usually translated as "disenchantment."

4. On Sara Grant and Abhishiktananda, see Richard Kearney and Eileen Rizo-Patron, eds., *Traversing the Heart: Journeys of the Inter-Religious Imagination* (Leiden: Brill, 2010), 23–24.

5. NEW HUMANISM AND THE NEED TO BELIEVE: DIALOGUE WITH JULIA KRISTEVA

1. Julia Kristeva, "Going Beyond the Human Through Dance," *Journal of French and Francophone Philosophy* 21, no. 1 (2013): 1–12.

2. Ibid., 3.

3. See Julia Kristeva, *Pulsions du temps* (Paris: Fayard, 2013).

4. Julia Kristeva, *Cet incroyable besoin de croire* (Paris: Bayard, 2007).

5. Mohammed Merah (1988–2012) was a Franco-Algerian Islamist terrorist who murdered seven people, including three Jewish children, in March 2012, at Toulouse and Montauban.

6. La Défense is a business district in the Paris metropolitan area.

7. Although he knew Armenian and Hebrew, Paul of Tarsus cites the Hebraic Bible in the Septuagint translation.

8. Julia Kristeva, *This Incredible Need to Believe*, trans. Beverley Bie Brahic (New York: Columbia University Press, 2009), 75–76.

9. Sigmund Freud, *Group Psychology and the Analysis of the Ego*, trans. James Strachey (New York: W. W. Norton & Company, 1989).

6. ANATHEISM, NIHILISM, AND WEAK THOUGHT: DIALOGUE WITH GIANNI VATTIMO

1. Richard Kearney, *Anatheism: Returning to God After God* (New York: Columbia University Press, 2010), 8.
2. Dietrich Bonhoeffer, *Letters and Papers from Prison* (New York: Touchstone, 1997), 360–361.
3. Gianni Vattimo and Santiago Zabala, *Hermeneutic Communism: From Heidegger to Marx* (New York: Columbia University Press, 2011).
4. Martin Heidegger, *Sein und zeit* (Tübingen: Max Niemeyer, 1993), § 44, 230.
5. *Andenken*, usually deployed as a noun, is a German word often used when remembering deceased loved ones or commemorating important occasions.
6. Santiago Zabala, *The Remains of Being: Hermeneutic Ontology After Metaphysics* (New York: Columbia University Press, 2009), 17.

7. WHAT'S GOD? "A SHOUT IN THE STREET.": DIALOGUE WITH SIMON CRITCHLEY

1. Simon Critchley, *The Faith of the Faithless* (London: Verso Books, 2012), 3.
2. John Keats, "Letter to George and Tom Keats, December 1817," in *The Norton Anthology of English Literature,* 5th ed., vol. 2 (New York: W. W. Norton & Co., 1986), 863.

9. ANATHEISM AND RADICAL HERMENEUTICS: DIALOGUE WITH JOHN CAPUTO

1. John Caputo, *More Radical Hermeneutics* (Bloomington: Indiana University Press, 2000), 3.
2. This dialogue was transcribed by William Chaddock.

10. THEISM, ATHEISM, ANATHEISM: A PANEL DISCUSSION WITH DAVID TRACY, MEROLD WESTPHAL, AND JENS ZIMMERMANN

1. See Stanley I. Benn, "Power," in *The Encyclopedia of Philosophy*, reprint, ed. Paul Edwards (New York: Macmillan, 1972), 6:424–27.
2. See Hannah Arendt, "What Is Authority?" in *Between Past and Future* (New York: Penguin, 2006), 91–141.
3. See Alfred N. Whitehead, "God and the World," in *Process and Reality: An Essay in Cosmology* (New York: Macmillan, 1929), 519–33.

4. For further clarification, see Emilio Brito, "Kenose," in *Dictionnaire critique de théologie*, ed. Jean-Yves Lacoste (Paris: PUF, 1998).

5. See Richard Kearney, *Anatheism: Returning to God After God* (New York: Columbia University Press, 2010), 133–65.

6. Henri de Lubac, *Paradoxes of Faith* (San Francisco: Ignatius, 1987), 9–16.

7. Dietrich Bonhoeffer, *Widerstand und ergebung: Briefe und aufzeichnungen aus der haft*, ed. Christian Gremmels, Eberhard Bethge, and Renate Bethge (Gütersloh: Chr. Kaiser, 1998), 534. See also 558, where he says, "Our relation to God is not a 'religious one' to what we consider highest, most powerful, supreme being—this is not genuine transcendence—but our relation to God is a new life as being-there-for-others, in participation in the being of Jesus" (our translation).

8. Dietrich Bonhoeffer, *Nachfolge*, ed. Martin Kuske and Ilse Tödt (Gütersloh: Christian Kaiser, 2002), 301. Translation slightly altered to emphasize the "becoming human." The English translation has "incarnation" and "incarnate one."

9. See Eberhard Jüngel, *God's Being Is in Becoming: The Trinitarian Being of God in the Theology of Karl Barth, a Paraphrase* (Grand Rapids, MI: W. B. Eerdmans, 2001).

10. Richard Kearney, *Strangers, Gods and Monsters* (New York: Routledge, 2002), 204–5.

11. *Perichoresis* and its Latin equivalent *circumincessio* describe the intimate relation of the three "persons" within the Godhead as mutual indwelling without confusion. John of Damascus also uses this term for the interpenetration of the human and divine in the incarnation. See "Exposition of the Orthodox Faith," in *The Nicene and Post-Nicene Fathers: Second Series* (Peabody, MA: Hendrickson, 1999), 9:91.

12. Kearney, *Anatheism*, 56.

13. Kearney, *Strangers, Gods and Monsters*, 207.

14. Kearney, *Anatheism*, 25.

15. See Gabriel Bunge, *The Rublev Trinity: The Icon of the Trinity by the Monk-Painter Andrei Rublev* (Yonkers, NY: St. Vladimir's Seminary Press, 2007), 27–28, 87, 97.

16. Dante Alighieri, *The Divine Comedy of Dante Alighieri: Paradiso*, trans. Alan Mandelbaum (New York: Bantam Classics, 1986), 303.

INDEX